Paddling Wisconsin

A Guide to the State's Best Paddling Routes

Second Edition

Kevin Revolinski

FALCONGUIDES

GUILFORD, CONN

FALCONGUIDES®

An imprint of The Rowman & Littlefield Publishing Group, Inc.
4501 Forbes Blvd., Ste. 200
Lanham, MD 20706
www.rowman.com
Falcon and FalconGuides are registered trademarks and Make Adventure Your Story is a trademark of The Rowman & Littlefield Publishing Group, Inc.

Distributed by NATIONAL BOOK NETWORK

A previous edition of this book was published by Falcon Publishing, Inc. in 2015.

Photos by Kevin Revolinski unless otherwise noted
Maps by The Rowman & Littlefield Publishing Group, Inc.

British Library Cataloguing in Publication Information available

Library of Congress Cataloging-in-Publication Data available

ISBN 978-1-4930-4107-7 (paperback)
ISBN 978-1-4930-4108-4 (e-book)

∞™ The paper used in this publication meets the minimum requirements of American National Standard for Information Sciences—Permanence of Paper for Printed Library Materials, ANSI/NISO Z39.48-1992.

Printed in the United States of America

Contents

The Paddles

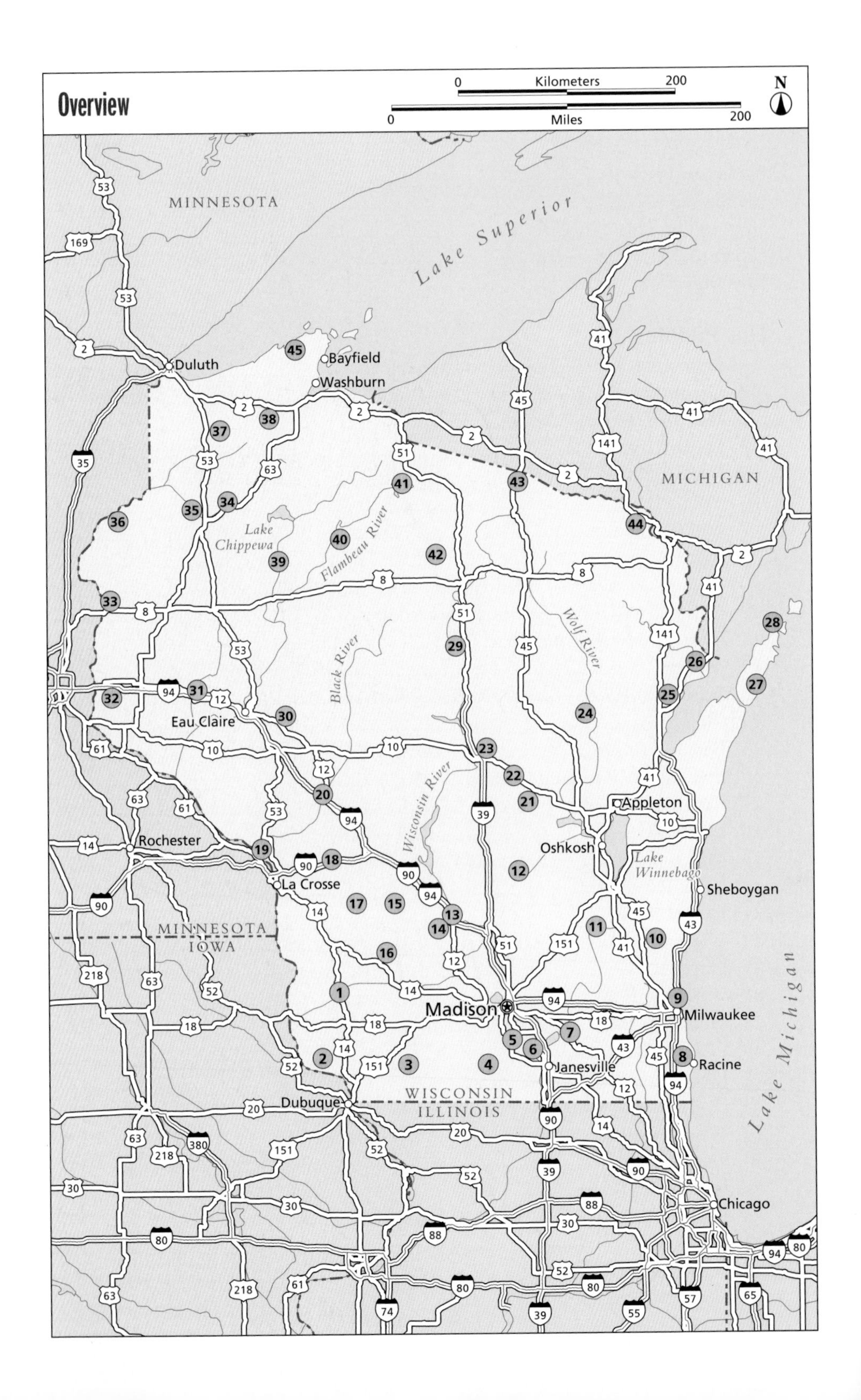
Overview
Kilometers
0
200
Miles
0
200
N
MINNESOTA
Lake Superior
MICHIGAN
Duluth
Bayfield
Washburn
Lake Chippewa
Flambeau River
Black River
Wolf River
Wisconsin River
Eau Claire
Rochester
La Crosse
Appleton
Oshkosh
Lake Winnebago
Sheboygan
Madison
Milwaukee
Janesville
Racine
MINNESOTA
IOWA
WISCONSIN
ILLINOIS
Dubuque
Chicago
Lake Michigan

Acknowledgments

I have to express my thanks to the various outfitters who helped me along the way: Scott Teuber of Wisconsin River Outings, Dave Kelly of Flambeau Sports Outfitters, Casey St. Henry of Bay Shore Outfitters, Tim Lencki of Adventure Kayak in Waupaca, Tim Conradt of Mountain Bay Outfitters, Gail Green of Living Adventure, Darren Bush of Rutabaga Paddlesports, and Jerry Dorff of Wild River Outfitters.

Also thank you to all the friends who helped me with shuttles: Kurt Revolinski (aka Dad); Jon Hamilton, the mead maker of White Winter Winery fame in Iron River; and Karla and JW of Yo Chubby Gringo Tamales.

Thanks to Todd Bucher of Delta Diner for a few backwoods tips regarding the White River; all the national and state park rangers for the same; and Traci and Rob Klepper, Jon Jarosh, and Maureen Murray—tourism people—for connecting me to the right people.

And then there are the actual paddlers who shared the canoe with me. Jim Mayer tackled the Yahara, while Dan Perreth helped me inspect sandbars in the Dells. Traveling Ted Nelson came up from Chicago just to paddle, even when the rain said "No." (Long live the Pelican!) My outdoor writing mentor, Johnny Molloy, and his then fiancée, now wife, Keri Anne, made it up from Tennessee for a paddle while passing through the area. Erica Chiarkas toughed out a rough paddle, as did Eric and Melanie Baumgart with their amazing sandboarding talents. Old friends—the best kind—Rob Schultz and Dave Sebastian were also at the paddle more than once.

As always, I need to thank my father, Kurt Revolinski, for taking me on that first canoe ride and teaching my brother and me to love the outdoors. It's in our blood now. And finally, a special thanks to my wife, Preamtip Satasuk. There isn't a better sport in the world. She did not grow up as an outdoorsy type. She had never even set foot in a canoe before this project and had deep reservations about the whole idea. She paddled in the bow on twenty-seven of these excursions and handled it like a pro. She is awesome.

Introduction

My first paddling experience was at a Cub Scout camp on Crystal Lake. And indeed, the name fit: I could see all the way to the bottom, 20 feet by my childhood reckoning. My father sat in the back of the canoe doing most of the work while my skinny arms waved a paddle around. When it came time to race the other kids, it seemed as though the canoe took on a life of its own, surging forward and leaving a wake as we glided across glass on a sunny Wisconsin summer day. The joy of being out on the water never left me. On trips to visit family up near Lake Superior, we'd cross those Northwoods riverways, tumbling whitewater through scattered boulders in forests redolent of pine. I specifically recall the Flambeau River. As I stared out the car window at the river winding away from the highway into the forest, I imagined following its trail in my own canoe. My father casually observed that a former coworker had retired up here and ran canoe trips on that river. That was it—I wanted to do exactly that.

With old childhood friends, I often ventured out onto the Wisconsin River to go camping on sandbars, paddling for days down to the Mississippi. In college, a buddy and I borrowed a dented aluminum canoe and put in on a nameless creek that intrigued me just outside town, dragging and scraping through a storm sewer just to see where it went.

Just gazing at a map of Wisconsin, I am entranced by the meandering blue lines fleeing in all directions into the Great Lakes or the Mississippi. To borrow from Norman Maclean's *A River Runs Through It*: "I am haunted by waters." I see a creek and I want to ride it into nowhere.

When I started working as a freelance writer a number of years ago, I focused on travel writing. My reply to an ad on Craigslist, of all places, landed me a contract job updating a Wisconsin camping book. Then I started writing original hiking books. One project led to another, and suddenly years had passed and I realized that a solid section of my bookshelf was dedicated to my outdoor guidebooks. But none of them involved paddling.

So it was like a dream to take on this book project. Choose the best paddling ventures in Wisconsin and chronicle them in a guidebook. Wisconsin has over 84,000 miles of rivers; and forget about trying to count all the lakes (more than 15,000). How to choose? Where to start? The Wisconsin River of course, the trail left by a mighty serpent of Native American lore, running from top to bottom and marrying the Mississippi in the end. The Great Lakes? Of course! How about a tiny trout stream like the White River? Surely one can't overlook National Scenic Riverways such as the St. Croix and its sibling Namekagon. There are some I've done many times, some I've always wanted to do, and a couple I'd never heard of. Wide slow paddles, narrow rushing ones, meadows and forests, canyons and bluffs. The trips here bear witness to the natural beauty of Wisconsin, both the glaciated wonders and the rolling texture of the Driftless Area, the pine forest up north, the oak savanna down south, and even a pleasant paddle through downtown Milwaukee.

Wildlife plays a big role in any Wisconsin outdoor experience. Of the forty-five "field work days" paddling and GPS-recording these trips, we saw at least one bald eagle on forty-two of them. Herons and kingfishers weren't even countable. A passel of joeys (baby possums) came right up to the canoe. Fish were jumping, a sturgeon raised its prehistoric head to the surface, trout gleamed in the pools. Cedar waxwings and red-winged blackbirds swooped at our heads. Beavers, minks, red squirrels, foxes, deer, muskrats, turtles, woodpeckers, ospreys, cranes, river otters, owls, hawks . . . the Wisconsin open zoo brought out nearly all the all-stars, though we didn't see any bears or wolves. Not *this* summer anyway. And what a backdrop: Wildflowers painted the banks. Fall colors, bright and burning, reflected off waters mirroring the clear blue sky. Seeps dripped out of 425-million-year-old rock.

I tried to keep this book accessible to all levels of paddlers. I spread the forty-five routes evenly throughout the state to really try to cover the incredible variety Wisconsin has to offer and to get people out of their neighborhoods and into some others. Except in extreme conditions, none of these trips is beyond an intermediate skill level; in fact, novices should be able to do most of them. We did all but three of these trips in a simple, affordable canoe (the Great Lakes required sea kayaks). On a few of them we got some help from outfitters for shuttles back to our car; for nearly half of them, I did my own bike shuttle. All the trips are day trips, though several of them come with suggestions for extensions or waterside camping. If you've been looking for an excuse to get out paddling in Wisconsin, this is it.

Weather

Wisconsin has the full four seasons, and within each of those seasons, you may experience weather from any of the other three. Many people up along Lake Superior can tell you that in their lifetimes they've seen snow in eleven of the twelve months. A storm front moving in on a hot summer day can drop the temperature 30 degrees. So be prepared. Anything involving the Great Lakes is at the whims of those minor seas. Storms come suddenly, and temperatures and winds change quickly.

The timing of the seasons can be quite different between northern and southern Wisconsin. While fall colors may start early in September along Lake Superior, there might still be autumn leaves on the trees in early November down in Madison. Winter temperatures and river/lake ice linger longer up north as well, often a month or more. Paddling season begins in spring with swollen, cold waters; throughout summer, the water levels depend on rain—except in cases of spring-fed and dam-controlled riverways, which are noted in the text. Many rivers get uncomfortably low after mid-July, though those featured here tend to remain runnable throughout the season. Paddling season extends through fall. Though many outfitters pack it up by mid-October, the rivers don't freeze over until winter really arrives, anytime in November or December.

From spring through summer to fall, thunderstorms and even tornadoes are real possibilities. Always be aware of forecasts and know where to take shelter. Springtime temperatures vary and depend on how long winter hangs on. You might have 40 degrees or less in early May, or feel the 70s in April. Generally speaking, summer is pleasant, with highs in the 70s or 80s and occasional periods of 90s. At night it is typically much cooler except in cases of heat waves. Anything close to the Great Lakes can expect noticeably cooler temperatures compared to nearby inland areas.

Flora and Fauna

Wisconsin's abundance of national, state, and county forests, plus vast tracts of farmland, wetlands, and prairies, provide space for an impressive amount of wildlife. Along the rivers you are likely to see deer, muskrats, beavers, marmots, possums, raccoons, coyotes, gray and red squirrels, and, if you are lucky, minks, river otters, pine martens, and fishers. Black bears are not unheard of, especially up north, and if you are camping on one of the rivers featured in this book, you will likely need to string up your food at night. Wisconsin has wolf packs up north, the occasional mountain lion sighting, a herd of elk, and the occasional misguided moose, but those are limited to the northern reaches of the state; encounters are quite rare and unlikely.

Bird species are extensive. Door Peninsula, the Horicon Marsh, and the Mississippi River are on bird migration routes and draw birders year-round, but especially in spring and fall. Great blue herons and kingfishers are givens. In recent years, eagles are also practically guaranteed. Hawks, sandhill cranes, owls, songbirds, woodpeckers, and a plethora of waterfowl are common. Ospreys are occasionally seen, and egrets have been spotted from time to time. Be sure to pack some waterproof binoculars.

Anglers can often expect the "usual suspects," such as northern pike, walleye, musky, panfish, and bass. But there are also great trout streams, sturgeon populations, and even salmon runs in some places.

Wildflowers grow in abundance along the banks and through the forests and prairies, depending on the season. Rare species appear in unusual environments such as special wetlands or the cool sandstone canyons around the Dells of the Wisconsin River and the Kickapoo River Valley. Do not pick anything! Hardwood forests are common and create wonderful colors in the fall. Pine forests and pine plantations fill the air with their resiny odor—and their clouds of pollen in early summer.

Wisconsin River Systems

Wisconsin rivers drain to three different places: Lake Superior, Lake Michigan, and the Mississippi River. The state doesn't break up into perfectly clear basins on a map. The Wisconsin River rises up on the border of the Upper Peninsula, for example, but manages to find the Mississippi all the way south through the state, while the Fox flows within 2 miles of the Mississippi, heading mostly north to get to Green Bay. The St. Croix and Bois Brule are similarly close, heading to the Mississippi and Lake

Superior, respectively. This created a wonderful waterway network used by Native Americans to get around, and later by European explorers to do the same. Even later the logging industry used many of these rivers to move timber, building dams to create runnable water and often to cover up dangerous rapids or waterfalls. Mills took their power from the various millponds and millruns along some of the smaller tributaries. The Wisconsin still has twenty-two dams, many of which still produce electricity.

Today many of the dams on smaller rivers—such as on the Milwaukee and Yahara Rivers—are being taken out, thus clearing out silt, creating better environments for fish and other wildlife, and restoring the rivers to their former runnable forms for paddlers.

Your Rights on the Water

Along many of these rivers and lakes, you will encounter private property. In accordance with a Wisconsin Supreme Court decision, landowners have exclusive privileges of the shore or banks for access to their land and the water. However, the public is allowed access to navigable waters in Wisconsin. You, as a public paddler, have the right to be anywhere in or on navigable water, right up to the water's edge. "Keep your feet wet" is the general rule for both river and lakes. Getting out on shore, even river bottom exposed in low water, is considered trespassing. This is a change from a law prior to 2001 that did allow the public some limited access along the banks and shores.

An exception to the rule, for *flowing waters only—not lakes*—is a "right to portage," which makes allowances for paddlers who need to use the bank to "bypass an obstruction." Obstructions may be deadfall, rocks, or debris, for example, or even shallow spots for boaters. You are obliged to take the shortest route possible and, of course, to respect the land by not leaving traces or trash or damaging anything on that land.

Note: Using the riverbank to walk downstream and scout a rapid is *not* allowed without the landowner's permission.

How to Use This Guide

This guidebook offers trips covering every corner of Wisconsin plus two of the Great Lakes and the Mississippi River along the border. The paddles are numbered 1 through 45, working their way generally from south to north. Each paddle included in this guide is featured as a day trip, although overnight camping can be done where noted. The following is a sample of the information you will find at the beginning of each paddling destination:

1 Wisconsin River—Boscobel to Woodman

This section of the Wisconsin, like the others below the final dam, is wide and steady. In medium to low flows, sandbars are abundant for stopping or even camping. But unlike areas upriver, this section is paddled less frequently; perhaps one in five paddlers choose this segment. Wooded to the banks, it shows abundant wildlife, especially birds—likely an eagle or two—and offers some narrower side channels among the islands for some more-intimate stretches. Though not far off the highways on either side, the forest of the Lower Wisconsin State Riverway keeps this section wild, and scenic bluffs are always on the horizon.

County: Grant
Start: Boscobel Boat Landing, N43 8.955' / W90 42.916'
End: Woodman Boat Landing, N43 4.573' / W90 50.651'
Length: 9.2 miles one-way
Float time: About 3 hours
Difficulty rating: Easy
Rapids: None
River type: Wide sandy and wooded pastoral river with lowlands
Current: Moderate
River gradient: 2.5 feet per mile
River gauge: USGS 05407000 Wisconsin River at Muscoda; always runnable due to minimum flow rates. Less than 3,000 cfs means lots of sandbars; greater than 20,000 cfs is dangerous and there are no sandbars for camping; 3,000–10,000 cfs is ideal for a balance between sandbars for stopping and easy channels for navigation.
Season: Spring through fall
Land status: Public boat landings, Wisconsin DNR, and some private
Fees and permits: No fees or permits required
Nearest city/town: Boscobel
Maps: USGS Boscobel, Long Hollow, Wauzeka East; *DeLorme: Wisconsin Atlas & Gazetteer*: Page 33 C5
Boats used: Canoes, kayaks, johnboats, motorized craft
Contacts: Lower Wisconsin State Riverway, Wisconsin DNR, 5808 CH C, Spring Green 53588; (608) 588-7723; dnr.wi.gov/topic/lands/lowerwisconsin
Outfitters: Wisconsin River Outings, 715 Wisconsin Ave., Boscobel 53805; (608) 375-5300; canoe-camping.com.
Local information: River to Road Triathlon—a paddle, run, and pedal race—is held in Sauk City the third Saturday of May and in Boscobel the last Saturday of September (Facebook.com/rivertoroad).

Each paddle entry begins with a short overview of the paddle trip, giving you an idea of what to expect and helping you determine whether you want to experience this waterway. This summary is followed by the river specs. (***Note:*** Not all categories will appear in every paddle.)

We can see that the paddle is in Grant County. The put-in (**Start**) is at Boscobel Boat Landing. The GPS coordinates for the put-in are given using NAD 27 datum (the base mapping collected by the US Geological Survey), which you can plug into your GPS unit for direction finding. The trip takeout (**End**) is at Woodman Boat Landing. The paddle covers 9.2 miles on the river, which I measured with a GPS during my research.

Typically, with a reasonable pace of paddling, the trip should take about 3 hours. But that doesn't take into account lingering to watch an eagle eat its lunch or stopping by a sandbar for a picnic. Use the **float time,** then, to determine just how much time you need or have to get off the river at the desired time.

The **difficulty rating** for this paddle is easy. If it were moderate or difficult, there would be some notation as to why I chose that rating, such as strong currents, frequent deadfall, or more-demanding navigation.

The river has no **rapids.** Other paddles in this book may show Class I or II, though the rating system goes as high as VI. Class I has easy waves requiring little maneuvering and few obstructions. Class II rapids may have more obstructions and require more maneuvering, plus the water may be flowing faster. Class III rapids can be difficult with numerous waves and no clear defined passage and require precise maneuvering. Classes IV to VI increase in difficulty, with Class VI being unrunnable except by the best of experts.

The **river type** classification gives some indication of the river's character, whether it is wide or narrow, and whether it flows through the woods, a marsh, or farmland. Some paddles in this guide are actually on lakes; that will be noted here as well. The **current** on this section of the Wisconsin is moderate; others may be gentle or swift.

The **river gradient** measures the rate at which the river descends during the paddle, which sometimes, but not always, gives you an idea of how fast it runs. The river gauge listed will be near the destination and will help you determine if the water levels are high enough, or too high, to paddle. Some rivers are simply not runnable when flow rates or river depths drop below a certain level. Other rivers may be dangerous when levels get too high or reach flood stage. Several rivers in this book are runnable at all times, thanks to steady springs or dam control.

Concerning the **river gauge** category, the key variable is the height of the river at a fixed point. Gauge houses, situated on most rivers, consist of a well at the river's edge with a float attached to a recording clock. The gauge reads in hundredths of feet. Rating tables are constructed for each gauge to get a cubic feet per second (cfs) reading for each level. Other gauges are measured in height, given in feet. This gauge information can be obtained quickly, often along with a gauge reading of recent rainfall at the same location. Some gauges may not be posting information at given times due to the presence of ice or even fluctuating budgets at the governmental level. USGS Real-time Water Levels for the United States can be found on the web at https://waterdata.usgs.gov/wi/nwis/rt. This in-depth website has hundreds of gauges for the entire country, updated continually, and graphs showing recent flow trends, along with historic trends for any given day of the year, available at the click of a mouse. Consult these gauges before you start your trip, but also consider calling a local outfitter. Sometimes the gauges do not tell the whole story. In the case of the Kickapoo River, for example, water levels fluctuate rapidly with rainfall, and the river valley is prone to flooding. Outfitters often have a better grasp on the moods of the river. In the case of the Kickapoo, observation of a few tributaries upstream helps guides assess whether the river is about to go much higher in a couple hours than what is showing on the gauges at present.

Season tells you the best time of year for the paddle, in this case spring through fall. **Land status** tells you how cautious you need to be in terms of trespassing rules along the riverbanks. The lands bordering the Wisconsin River are both public and private. Many paddling destinations included in this guidebook border public lands, such as state parks or national forest. (See "Your Rights on the Water" for information about your access rights on the rivers and lakes.) **Fees and permits** lets you know how much, if anything, it will cost to put in or take out your craft; none are required for the sample paddle.

Boscobel is the nearest municipality to this paddle. The **nearest city/town** listing will help you get oriented to the paddle destination area while looking at a map or looking up map information on the internet.

Though quality maps and driving directions are included with each paddle, the **maps** section lists pertinent maps you can use for more detailed information, including United States Geographical Survey (USGS) 7.5-minute quadrangle maps. These "quad maps," as they are known, cover every parcel of land in the United States. They are divided into very detailed rectangular maps. Each quad has a name, usually based on a physical feature located within the quad. In this case the paddle traverses several quad maps: Boscobel, Long Hollow, and Wauzeka East. Quad maps can be obtained online at usgs.gov. The map section also lists the page for this paddle in the *DeLorme: Wisconsin Atlas & Gazetteer*. The gazetteer is an invaluable aid in making your way through the Badger State, and I keep a battered and well-worn copy in my car at all times.

Boats used simply informs you of what other river users will be floating.

Several paddles list **organizations,** groups that take care of the particular waterway included in the paddle or, in the absence of a river-specific organization, a group with a wider area of interest in terms of Wisconsin rivers. If you are interested in learning more about the river's health and other water-quality issues, as well as simply getting involved in preserving Wisconsin's waterways, consult these groups.

Contacts are agencies that may provide more specific information on the area featured in the paddle. **Outfitters** notes if an outfitter operates on that particular segment of river. This can help with shuttles and/or rentals. Some paddles may also list **local information**—special events associated with the river or other information about the area you will be paddling in.

In addition to the information provided in the sample above, each paddle includes the following sections. **Put-in/Takeout Information** gives you turn-by-turn directions from the nearest interstate or largest community—first to the takeout, where you can leave a shuttle vehicle, then from the takeout to the put-in. Available facilities at either end are also mentioned. Several of the paddles with really nice bike shuttle options include a note to that regard.

Plan ahead: Some of the put-ins and takeouts use dirt or sand roads just before reaching the waterways or limit parking to a highway shoulder. After periods of extreme weather, such as heavy rains or long dry periods, the roads can become troublesome. If you are at all unsure about the road ahead of you, stop, get out of your vehicle, and examine the road on foot before you drive into a deep mud hole or get stuck in the sand.

The **River Overview** (or **Lake Overview**) paints a picture of the entire river, not just the section paddled. This way you can determine whether you want to paddle other sections of the river being detailed. It also gives you a better understanding of the entire watershed rather than just a section of river in space and time. Next comes the **Paddle Summary,** which is the meat and potatoes narrative, giving you detailed information about your river trip, including flora, fauna, and interesting, not-to-be-missed natural features. It also details important information required to execute the paddle, including forthcoming rapids, portages, bridges, and stops along the way, and the mileages at which you will encounter them.

Finally, most paddles have a sidebar. This is interesting information about the waterway or a nearby paddle-related site that doesn't necessarily pertain to the specific paddle but gives you some human or natural tidbit that may pique your interest to explore beyond the simple mechanics of the paddle.

Fixing to Paddle

Which Boat Do I Use?

This book covers waterways from narrow trout streams to massive muddy rivers and from still-water swamps to icy-waved Great Lakes. So with such variety, what boat do you use? There are multiple possibilities.

You have a choice of canoes and kayaks for plying the waters of Wisconsin, and one may sometimes be more appropriate than the other. When looking for a canoe, consider the type of water through which you will be paddling. Will it be through still bodies of water or moving rivers? Will you be on big lakes, mild whitewater, or sluggish streams? Canoes come in a wide array of oil-based materials and are molded for weight, performance, and durability. Don't waste your time or money on an aluminum canoe. They are extremely noisy and are more likely to hang up on underwater obstacles rather than slide over them. Consider material and design. Canoe materials can range from wood to fiberglass to composites such as Polylink 3, Royalex, Kevlar, and even graphite. Canoe design is composed of the following factors: length, width, depth, keel, and bottom curve, as well as flare, tumblehome, and rocker.

- **Length.** Canoes should be at least 16 feet, for carrying loads and better tracking. Shorter single canoes are available and are often used in ponds, small lakes, and smaller streams for shorter trips.
- **Width.** Wider canoes are more stable and can carry more loads but are slower. Go for somewhere in the middle.
- **Depth.** Deeper canoes can carry more weight and shed water, but they can get heavy. Again, go for the middle ground.
- **Keel.** A keel helps for tracking in lakes but decreases maneuverability in moving water.
- **Bottom curve.** The more curved the canoe bottom, the less stable the boat. Seek a shallowly arched boat, which is more efficient than a flat-bottom boat but not as tippy as a deeply curved boat.
- **Flare.** Flare, the outward curve of the sides of the boat, sheds water from the craft. How much flare you want depends on how much whitewater you expect to encounter.
- **Tumblehome.** Tumblehome is the inward slope of the upper body of the canoe. A more curved tumblehome allows you to get your paddle into the water easier.
- **Rocker.** Rocker, the curve of the keel line from bow to stern, is important. More rocker increases maneuverability at the expense of stability. Again, go for the middle ground.

And then there are situation-specific canoes, such as whitewater or portaging canoes. Whitewater boats will have heavy rocker and deeper flare but will be a zigzagging tub on flatwater. Portaging canoes are built with extremely light materials and will have a padded portage yoke for toting the boat on your shoulders.

Consider a multipurpose touring/tripping tandem canoe, with adequate maneuverability so that you will be able to adjust and react while paddling through rapids and boulder gardens. You want a boat that can navigate moderate whitewater, can handle loads, and can track decently through flatwater. If you are solo paddling a tandem canoe, you can weight the front with gear to make it run true. But if you have a solo boat, you can't change it to a two-person boat. Ultra-lightweight canoes, such as those built by Wenonah, are designed to be carried from lake to lake via portages.

The first consideration in choosing a kayak is deciding between a sit-on-top model, a recreational kayak, or a touring kayak. Sit-on-tops are what their name implies—paddlers sit on top of the boat—whereas a touring kayak requires you to put your body into the boat, leaving your upper half above an enclosed cockpit. The sit-on-top is less stable, as you are sitting higher than the water; the touring kayak lowers your center of gravity, as you are sitting closer to water level. To increase stability, the sit-on-top is built wider, making it also slower. Recreational kayaks are quite popular and offer a compromise. You sit inside the kayak, but your knees are exposed. This can be more comfortable than a touring kayak but can be a hassle if you ever tip and flood it. And as recreational kayaks are shorter, they often don't track well.

Ask yourself, *What types of waters am I going to paddle?* Are you going to paddle near shore on calm flat waters, or are you going to paddle bigger waters, such as Lake Superior or the shores of Door County? If paddling bigger water, you will need that cockpit and perhaps a length of 16 feet for the Great Lakes, less for calmer waters.

If you are making short day trips down a river or paddling through Turtle-Flambeau Flowage with your camping gear, that will inform your decision on how large you want to go. Something shorter is more maneuverable for rivers, while a longer craft, or even a kayak with a rudder, will track better for long distances on open water and will offer more storage for gear.

Kayak materials vary—from the traditional skin-and-wood of the Inuits to plastic and fiberglass composites like Kevlar and the waterproof cover of folding kayaks. For touring kayaks, choose a tough composite model, simply because it can withstand running up on sandbars, scratching over rocks or deadfall, or being accidentally dropped at the boat launch. For touring boats, also consider storage capacity. Gear is usually stored in waterproof compartments with hatches. Look for watertight hatches that close safely and securely. The larger the boat, the more room you will have.

Which Paddle Do I Use?

Wood is still a good choice of material for paddlers, though plastics dominate the market, especially for lower-end paddles, such as those used by outfitters. There are also ultra-light high-end paddles. You may see wooden paddles with bent shafts; some paddlers swear by them for increased paddle efficiency. This may be true if you have someplace to be in a hurry, but when it comes to maneuvering and making subtler strokes and adjustments, bent-shaft paddles don't do as well as traditional ones.

As far as the paddle blade is concerned, a rounded blade is better for precision and may leave you less tired, while the square blade offers more power. Regarding length, the shortest paddle that still allows you to reach the water is going to work best for you. The top of the blade should be right at the waterline when your other hand is at about face level. If you sit on the floor and stand the paddle on its handle right between your legs, the shoulder—where the blade meets the handle—should be at about the height of the top of your head.

Kayak paddles are double-bladed; that is, they have a blade on both sides, resulting in more efficient stroking. A lighter paddle is more desirable, but that's going to cost you. Kayak paddles typically come in two pieces that snap together in multiple positions to either line the blades up or offset them for better stroke efficiency. They also pack much better.

Whether in a canoe or a sea kayak, it's not a bad idea to bring an extra paddle. You never want to be stuck up a river should you lose one.

Paddling Accessories

Life Vest

The US Coast Guard and Wisconsin law require vessels less than 16 feet in length to be equipped with one Type I, Type II, Type III, or Type V personal flotation device (PFD) for each person on board. That includes canoes and kayaks, and Department of Natural Resources (DNR) wardens have been known to fine noncompliant paddlers. Vessels 16 feet or more in length must be equipped with one Type I, Type II, Type III, or Type V PFD for each person on board, plus at least one Type IV throwable for the boat.

Make sure your life vest is Coast Guard approved and in good, functional condition. It must be accessible at all times and not attached to the craft. Some boaters latch them up as seat covers. That isn't acceptable. Many of us don't always wear the vest, especially on hot summer days in waters we feel comfortable on, but you should always have it at the ready. Choose a vest or other PFD that is comfortable and gives you room to really move your arms.

Chair Backs

Chair backs hook onto the canoe seat to provide support for your back. Choose anything that gives you good lumbar support but doesn't interfere with your paddling. A couple hours on the river is one thing, but a couple days paddling down the Wisconsin will leave you begging for one of these. But be aware that if you are ducking under deadfall these can present a snagging problem.

Dry Bags

Waterproof dry bags are a necessity if you want to keep certain items dry at all costs. These rubber or plastic bags typically require a couple of folds at the seam and a plastic fastener and—voila!—they're waterproof. If you tip, objects remains dry and even float. A camera or matches or a change of clothes belong in one for sure. There are multiple sizes and even little flat pouches perfect for smartphones. Some paddlers like the clear bags so they can easily spot the objects they go digging for, but I've always found that condensation builds when the sun gets on them for a spell. Shoulder straps make them easier to manage and can be used to fasten them to a canoe seat so that they don't head down the river if you tip. But dry bags are not just for the unfortunate canoe tip: Waves and switching sides with your paddle all day may get gear wet just the same.

Paddlers' Checklist

- ❒ Canoe/kayak
- ❒ Paddles
- ❒ Spare paddle
- ❒ Personal flotation device
- ❒ Dry bags for gear storage
- ❒ Whistle
- ❒ Towline
- ❒ Bilge pump for kayak
- ❒ Spray skirt for kayak
- ❒ Paddle float/lanyard for kayak
- ❒ Maps
- ❒ Throw lines
- ❒ Boat sponge

Depending on your personal interests and needs, you may also want to consider some other items: fishing gear, sunglasses, trash bag, GPS unit, weather radio, camera, watch, sunscreen, lip balm, insect repellent, a good sunhat, extra batteries, binoculars, and wildlife identification books.

Traveling with Your Boat

How you load your boat depends not only on whether it is a canoe or kayak but also on what type of vehicle you have and whether you have a roof rack. Roof racks make it all a bit easier, but in the case of either craft, you can always get by with a set of kayak or canoe pads (there's a difference) and a set of good cinch straps. No matter how you carry your boat, tie it down securely, for the sake of not only your boat but also your fellow drivers, who will be endangered if your boat comes loose. After cinching your boat down, drive a short distance, then pull over and recheck your tie job. If the craft stays cinched up on your vehicle overnight, check the straps again. They may loosen up over time and with environmental changes. Flat cinch straps with buckles are recommended.

A quality aftermarket roof rack makes for a much safer way to transport boats. Invest in one of these if you paddle frequently. Roof racks can be customized to different types and numbers of boats as well. And don't skimp on tie-down straps either; this is what holds the boat to the rack.

Be careful to tie up the loose strap ends. I wish I didn't know first-hand what happens when you run over your own cinch strap with front-wheel drive.

Parking

I've never had a problem leaving my car parked for an extended time here in Wisconsin, but don't chance it. Park your vehicle in a visible place, preferably in a supervised park or at a private business that will allow it. Don't leave objects of value on a car seat, risking theft. If you can get someone to look after your vehicle, that's even better. Local outfitters may have an opinion on whether it is safe to park somewhere or not. On the St. Croix near Grantburg, the outfitter I worked with recommended parking my car nearby at their office.

Shuttles

A few of the paddle trips in this book can be done as out-and-back trips. But if you are going on a river of any discernible current, you are going to need a shuttle. Sometimes this is difficult. Outfitters often offer the service for a price similar to a canoe rental. But they may also allow you to leave your car in a secure setting. Call ahead and ask about prices, distances, and reservations. Also ask about camping and potential crowds, especially during weekends.

There are other alternatives, though often less desirable. I've had friends lock their canoe up with a bike lock and flag a fisherman down for a lift back to their car at the put-in. If you have a paddle partner, you might bring two vehicles. Always remember to go to the takeout point first, leaving a car there, with the put-in point car following. But if you are traveling across the state, two vehicles aren't exactly fuel efficient.

Another option is a bike shuttle. I've done many, deciding which direction to run them based on hills and my expected level of exhaustion. Pedal before paddle, or vice versa? Drop a bike off at your takeout point, and lock it to a tree or other fixed object. Go to the put-in, paddle down to your bicycle, lock the canoe this time, and pedal back to get your car. Whatever method you use, leave no valuables in your parked car. Take your keys with you, and store them securely while you are floating.

Paddling Safety

A safe paddler is a smart paddler. Be prepared before you get on the water and you will minimize the possibility of accidents. And if they do happen, you will be better prepared to deal with them.

Lightning

Lightning is a serious danger. When you sense a storm coming, have a plan as to what you will do when it hits. Most plans will involve getting off the water as quickly as possible. Seek shelter in a low area or in a grove of trees, not against a single tree, and wait it out.

Poisonous Plants

You already know poison ivy: Leaves of three, leave it be. Stinging nettles once found me as I made just a brief deadfall portage along the bank. If you are highly allergic to poisonous plants, check ahead for the area in which you will be paddling, then take the appropriate action, such as carrying Benadryl-based creams.

Bugs

Mosquitoes, blackflies, and deerflies are the most common aggressors of the Wisconsin insect world. Pack repellent with DEET, and wear light-colored clothing. Chiggers await in tall grasses—keep that in mind next time you portage along a bank. Deer ticks may carry Lyme disease.

Not specifically a nuisance to humans, the emerald ash borer destroys trees: The DNR has a rule that you cannot use firewood from farther away than 10 miles from whatever state park or forest you are visiting. Various aquatic invaders can hitch a ride on boats, so be sure your craft isn't their next bus to another waterway: rinse it off.

Snakes

There are only two venomous snakes in Wisconsin: the timber rattlesnake and the eastern massasauga rattlesnake. The latter is endangered. They may occur in southwestern Wisconsin but are not fans of the river, preferring rocky bluffs.

Sun and Heat

Bring sunscreen, a hat, and perhaps a bandanna. Wearing shorts in a canoe exposes your legs for a longer time than is typical. Use that sunscreen, or wear long pants. Clothes are your best defense. Put on the sunscreen before you get in the sun, and don't forget your hands and feet. Even your face under a hat is unprotected if there is reflected glare from the water. Sunstroke and heat exhaustion are more common than you think. Stay cool, and drink lots of fluids.

Cold

Be aware of the dangers of hypothermia. Getting wet and then being out in even a chilly evening for an extended time can take its toll. Waters are quite cold in spring due to winter meltwater, and the Great Lakes have claimed lives with hypothermia even at the height of summer. Stay dry, and stay warm.

First-aid Kit

First-aid kits have come a long way. Now you can find activity-specific kits that also come in different sizes for each activity, including paddling. First-aid kits designed for water sports come in waterproof pouches.

Camping

Overnight camping can add to your Wisconsin paddling experience. Where camping is a possibility, I have noted it in the paddling narratives. The Wisconsin River and Turtle-Flambeau are well known for paddle-up camping, but several other rivers offer it as well. Be sure to prepare a whole separate checklist if you are packing for a canoe-camping trip, and make preparations to keep your gear dry and secure in your craft. You may want to consider camping before or after your paddle rather than facing a long drive in the morning or back home in the evening. Check out the plethora of Wisconsin state park, national forest, or riverway rustic campgrounds, even county and city parks.

Legend

Symbol	Meaning	Symbol	Meaning
94	Interstate Highway		Airplane
61	US Highway		Boat Ramp
23	State Highway		Bridge
CR-A	County Road		Building/Point of Interest
	Local Road		Campground
	Unpaved Road		Campsite
	Railroad		Capital
	Utility/Power Line		Dam
	Trail		Horse Access
	State Line	1	Paddling Route
	Small River/Creek	P	Parking
	Intermittent Stream		Ranger Station/Headquarters
	Canal		Rapids
	Marsh/Swamp/Bog		Restrooms
	Body of Water		Scenic View/Viewpoint
	National/State Forest/Park		Spring
	Wilderness Area		Tower
	State/County Park		Town/City
	Miscellaneous Park	?	Visitor/Information Center
	Miscellaneous Area		

1 Wisconsin River–Boscobel to Woodman

This section of the Wisconsin, like the others below the final dam, is wide and steady. In medium to low flows, sandbars are abundant for stopping or even camping. But unlike areas upriver, this section is paddled less frequently; perhaps one in five paddlers choose this segment. Wooded to the banks, it shows abundant wildlife, especially birds—likely an eagle or two—and offers some narrower side channels among the islands for some more-intimate stretches. Though not far off the highways on either side, the forest of the Lower Wisconsin State Riverway keeps this section wild, and scenic bluffs are always on the horizon.

County: Grant
Start: Boscobel Boat Landing, N43 8.955' / W90 42.916'
End: Woodman Boat Landing, N43 4.573' / W90 50.651'
Length: 9.2 miles one-way
Float time: About 3 hours
Difficulty rating: Easy
Rapids: None
River type: Wide sandy and wooded pastoral river with lowlands
Current: Moderate
River gradient: 2.5 feet per mile
River gauge: USGS 05407000 Wisconsin River at Muscoda; always runnable due to minimum flow rates. Less than 3,000 cfs means lots of sandbars; greater than 20,000 cfs is dangerous and there are no sandbars for camping; 3,000–10,000 cfs is ideal for a balance between sandbars for stopping and easy channels for navigation.
Season: Spring through fall
Land status: Public boat landings, Wisconsin DNR, and some private
Fees and permits: No fees or permits required
Nearest city/town: Boscobel
Maps: USGS Boscobel, Long Hollow, Wauzeka East; *DeLorme: Wisconsin Atlas & Gazetteer*: Page 33 C5
Boats used: Canoes, kayaks, johnboats, motorized craft
Contacts: Lower Wisconsin State Riverway, Wisconsin DNR, 5808 CH C, Spring Green 53588; (608) 588-7723; dnr.wi.gov/topic/lands/lowerwisconsin
Outfitters: Wisconsin River Outings, 715 Wisconsin Ave., Boscobel 53805; (608) 375-5300; canoe-camping.com

Put-in/Takeout Information

To shuttle point/takeout: From Boscobel take WI 133 west 8.2 miles. Just after a hard left curve on the highway, take the next sharp right down to the Woodman Boat Landing. The takeout is a mud-and-gravel ramp. There are no facilities.

To put-in from takeout: From Woodman Boat Landing, travel east 8.2 miles on WI 133; turn left onto Elm Street and drive another 1.5 miles. The boat landing parking lot entrance is on the left, just before the bridge (river left downriver of the bridge). The put-in is a proper boat ramp. There are toilets and abundant parking.

River Overview

While it is known as the "hardest working river in America" because of the abundance of hydroelectric dams along its 430-mile length, the Wisconsin River takes play just about as seriously. From its humble headwaters at Lac Vieux Desert, straddling the border of Wisconsin and Michigan's Upper Peninsula, all the way down to its final flow into the Mississippi, the state river offers a variety of recreational opportunities. The final stretch, the Lower Wisconsin—from the last dam 1 mile above Prairie du Sac—runs 92 miles unimpeded to where it joins the Mississippi near Wyalusing State Park. The river is wide and the current steady but without rapids. Abundant sandbars and wooded islands allow for exploration, picnic stops, and even camping. Put-ins are generally improved and are frequent throughout the length on either bank. For all these reasons, this is the most paddled section of the entire river, indeed, of any river in Wisconsin. Anglers may find smallmouth bass, northern pike, and walleye, as well as crappie, bluegill, and rock bass.

Paddle Summary

Boscobel Boat Landing lies on a small backwater inlet just downriver left from the US 61 Bridge. As soon as you leave the landing's shelter and head left, the current picks you up. The river is wide here, well over 600 to 700 feet and as much as

The course of the Wisconsin River is wide and always changing with shifting sands.
PREAMTIP SATASUK

RIVER CAMPING

Sauk City native and regional author August Derleth called the Wisconsin the "River of a Thousand Isles." His book of that title tells stories of the local Native Americans, explorers, and more-recent historical figures such as Frank Lloyd Wright and their relationships with the river. You haven't paddled in Wisconsin until you've been on her river. And for those seeking a more personal and intimate experience, river camping is just the thing.

The final 92 miles of the Wisconsin River has no dams, solid current but no rapids, an abundance of protected forest along its banks, and a constantly changing assortment of large sandbars and wooded islands. For many day-trippers, a paddle of 2 to 6 hours starting out of Sauk City may be enough. This book offers a route that avoids those crowds and starts in Boscobel. But nothing is more memorable than a multiday trip. This can be done independently or with outfitters who can provide either just a shuttle or the complete package, including equipment.

Camping is allowed only on the islands and sandbars, but it is free and requires no reservations. Choose your route and the miles you want to paddle each day, arrange your shuttles, and pack your canoe with tent, sleeping bag, and plenty of food and water. Spend the night under the stars, cook over a fire, and fish for your dinner. No glass is allowed on the river, and everyone on board must have a personal flotation device.

The Wisconsin is hardly the only place for free paddle-up camping: Check out the St. Croix, Mississippi, Flambeau, and Namekagon Rivers and the Willow and Turtle-Flambeau Flowages as well.

1,000 feet at times. WI 60 passes close along the right bank, so you will hear some traffic noise. You'll pass a few islands along the way and views of bluffs. Remember the personal flotation device rule; it is often strictly enforced here, with fines for noncompliance.

As you pass under bridges, be aware of swirling currents and stay very clear of bridge supports. Strainers along shore are common but can be found anywhere in the river, as the depth fluctuates drastically. They say you never step in the same river twice. The expression is doubly true on this river with its constantly shifting sandbars. The right banks are low and thickly forested, with WI 60 often visible. At 1.3 miles you come to Allen Island, a large wooded isle that allows the main channel to pass it on the left, where you will also see Sanders Creek joining from river left. The right channel around Allen Island is slightly narrower but no less passable. But the channel's proximity to the highway gives favor to staying river left. However, watch river right on that main channel: Allen Island is split by a narrow cut that is often passable

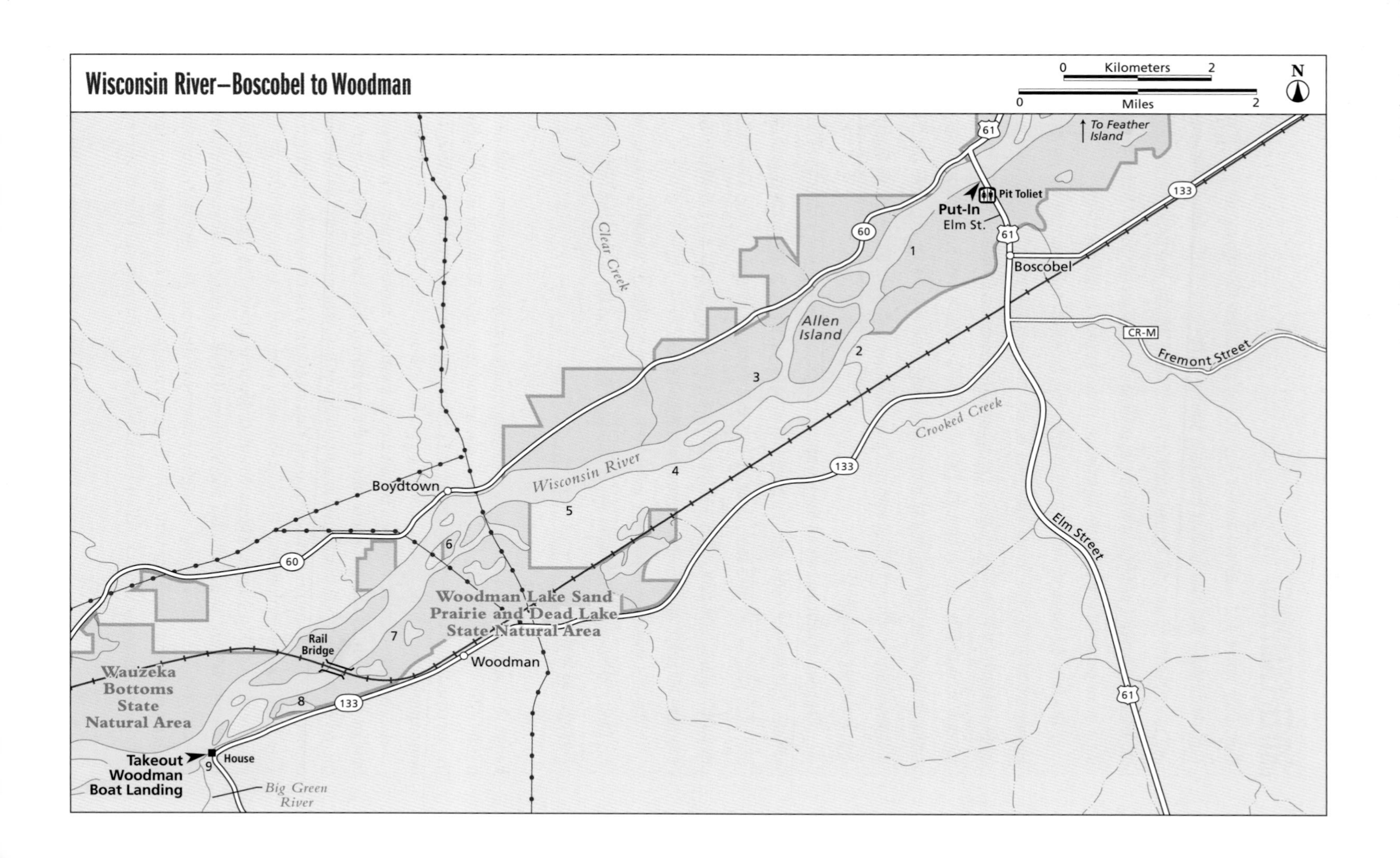
Wisconsin River—Boscobel to Woodman
0
Kilometers
2
0
Miles
2
N
To Feather Island
Pit Toliet
Put-In
Elm St.
Boscobel
CR-M
Fremont Street
Allen Island
Clear Creek
Crooked Creek
Wisconsin River
Elm Street
Boydtown
Woodman Lake Sand Prairie and Dead Lake State Natural Area
Rail Bridge
Woodman
Wauzeka Bottoms State Natural Area
Takeout Woodman Boat Landing
House
Big Green River
61
60
133
1
2
3
4
5
6
7
8
9

and worthy of exploration. Stay left after the island to avoid the long trail of sand downstream of it.

At 3.4 miles you come to another but shorter island, just about a third of a mile long. The passage to the left is shallow and quiet, affording good opportunities for birders. Beyond the island the river widens again, and at 4.2 miles Clear Creek enters on river right. Bluffs to the right are low, and in the distance you'll see some farm buildings. WI 60, which parted from the river near Allen Island, is over a quarter mile away until 5.2 miles, when it takes up its river-hugging course again.

Abundant sandbars on the Wisconsin are great places for taking a break or even camping.

At 5.7 miles, pass under power lines; unincorporated Boydtown lies just after that on river right as you come upon another small island. If you stay left of this island, you will see two channels. The main force of the river runs right through the middle here, but a narrower channel on river left skirts yet another island. The area to the left of that longer island is Woodman Lake Sand Prairie and Dead Lake State Natural Area. Midway down the left side of the island, before another set of power lines cross the Wisconsin at 6.2 miles, you can see a passage to the left headed back the direction you came. This narrow opening leads into 22-acre Woodman Lake, where you can find another boat landing.

At 7 miles is another large island, passable on either side. On the left channel you can see a railroad bridge in the distance. Pass under this on either side at 7.6 miles. Just past this island are some narrower channels through wooded isles. If you stay left the whole way, the far left channel will take you closer to WI 133 and the high banks there. This is a nice wooded and more-intimate paddle point, and being left ensures that you will not miss the takeout. Watch for a house at 9 miles up on the high left bank where WI 133 makes a curve left away from the river along the bluffs there. Just past here is a small sandy beach area and then an inlet where the Big Green River, a Class 1 trout stream, joins the Wisconsin. Paddle into here and you will see the gravel Woodman Boat Landing on river left. You can see a rusty metal bridge up the Big Green beyond the takeout.

Note: It is illegal to be in possession of glass (beer or wine bottles, jelly or condiment jars, etc.) on the Wisconsin River. The DNR is quite active with enforcement here. Fines for glass run up to $749. You are also required to carry a waterproof container for garbage, and don't forget the statewide personal flotation device law.

2 Grant River

This very scenic paddle starts on a winding path through agricultural fields offering an abundance of riffles and heading deeper into the typical bluffs of Wisconsin's glacially unaffected "Driftless Area." Patches of exposed rock—especially one impressive outcrop with multiple seeps drizzling down from it—provide a beautiful setting along a mostly wooded river with enough current to keep you at your paddle.

County: Grant
Start: Raiseback Bridge, N42 45.7071' / W90 51.8440'
End: Chaffie Hollow Bridge, N42 43.353' / W90 50.867'
Length: 8.9 miles one-way
Float time: About 3 hours
Difficulty rating: Easy
Rapids: Class I riffles
River type: Pastoral and woodland river with bluffs
Current: Slow to moderate
River gradient: 6.2 feet per mile
River gauge: USGS 05413500 Grant River at Burton; minimum runnable level 90 cfs
Season: Spring through fall
Land status: Private
Fees and permits: No fees or permits required; donation appreciated for landing upkeep
Nearest city/town: Lancaster
Maps: USGS Balltown, Beetown, Cassville, Hurricane; *DeLorme: Wisconsin Atlas & Gazetteer*: Page 24 B4
Boats used: Canoes, kayaks
Organizations: River Alliance of Wisconsin, 147 S. Butler St., Ste. 2, Madison 53703; (608) 257-2424; wisconsinrivers.org
Outfitters: Grant River Canoe and Kayak Rental, P.O. Box 23, Beetown 53802; (608) 794-2342; grantrivercanoerental.com

Put-in/Takeout Information

To shuttle point/takeout: From Lancaster head west on WI 81 for 1.7 miles. Turn left onto CR N and continue 7.8 miles. Turn right where CR N joins CR U and go 2.1 miles. Turn left onto CR N; after just 0.1 mile take the first right onto Chaffie Hollow Road. Follow that road for 2.4 miles; the takeout is on the right just before you reach the bridge. This is river right, upstream of the bridge. There are no facilities.
To put-in from takeout: From Chaffie Hollow Bridge, head northeast on Chaffie Hollow Road for 2.4 miles. Turn left onto CR N; go 0.1 mile, and then turn left onto CR U. Continue 2.6 miles, crossing Raiseback Bridge, and turn right on the other side on Blackjack Road. The put-in is on the right side of the road, down a gravel path where there's parking in the grass. This is river right, upstream from the bridge. There are no facilities.

River Overview

The Grant River is only 44 miles long, entirely within the county of the same name. The river flows south and east a bit as it comes to its juncture with the Mississippi

Seeps from a large rock outcrop on the Grant River PREAMTIP SATASUK

River just west of the town of Potosi. Much of the lower portion of the river shows riffles or low-grade rapids as it winds its way through bluffs untouched by the last period of the last ice age. The waters can muddy quickly just from the nature of the banks and the patches of agricultural fields tucked in along the river valley. The rock formations make this very scenic, and the forested bluffs are home to a lot of wildlife. Wildflowers are abundant, and fall colors are excellent along here. Most of the land all along the river's length is private, but at the outlet to the Mississippi you can find public camping at the Grant River Recreation Area, managed by the US Army Corps of Engineers.

Paddle Summary

The paddle begins from under the bridge or just downriver of it. This landing is on private land, and the local outfitter (listed above) maintains it. Leave space for them to move their van and trailer in here to drop off patrons. Also, consider making a donation to them for maintenance. They keep a set of steps down to the water, although you may also launch from the riprap along the bank.

The current is moderate and shows some riffles almost immediately. As this first couple miles touches on farmland, don't be surprised if you encounter bovine spectators. They may get into the water from time to time as well.

THE "DRIFTLESS AREA"

One may notice when looking at a map of Wisconsin that in this lake-filled state there are not many lakes in the southwest area, not natural ones anyway. Here an abundance of deep river valleys carve through tall, rolling hills. This is the Driftless Area, meaning that the most recent glaciers of the last ice age did not tread upon these bluffs and valleys and thus never deposited the rock, sand, silt, and boulders—collectively known as drift—that might have blocked rivers and isolated meltwater to create lakes.

Glacial lakes, held back by ice dams, occasionally burst and released massive amounts of rushing waters (such as those that formed the Dells, for example), but the terrain remained largely hilly. The bluffs around La Crosse are fine examples. If you paddle the Kickapoo, stop in at Wildcat Mountain State Park for some views of classic Driftless Area terrain. The last major advance of the most-recent ice age, known as the Wisconsin Glaciation, peaked about 21,000 to 25,000 years ago and retreated less than 11,000 years ago. About 85 percent of the Driftless Area lies in Wisconsin.

Banks are 6 feet high, and the water is 40 feet wide. Straight ahead you'll see the first tall, tree-covered ridge, which forces the river right. At about 0.3 mile you may encounter your first Class I rapids. The river runs straight here, and you'll see exposed rock on the tree-covered ridge to the left. Especially with flow changes, the depth comes and goes from 6 feet to scraping bottom in just a short distance.

At 1.2 miles the river hooks left and goes back toward the ridges. At 1.5 miles a smaller stream of muddy banks, the Beetown Branch, meanders through farm fields and joins here from behind on the right. The current picks up to riffles, perhaps Class I, and the turns are quicker and narrower, calling for some boat skills. Within 0.2 mile the river has narrowed to about 20 feet. At just about 2 miles, the river bears left and you can see power lines above the banks to the right and a farm in the distance. At 2.8 miles Rattlesnake Creek joins from the right, and the Grant bends left through a narrow section for a series of riffles before widening and slowing again through the last bit of farmland.

By 3 miles trees are hanging over the water, bluffs are close, and riffles are common. Boulders and rock formations show in the river but are not navigational concerns. At 3.4 miles the river comes to a rocky bluff and is forced to the right. At 4.9 miles the river curves gently to the left and you can see a farm on the left, a bluff to the right. The river runs straight for 0.25 mile. At 5.7 miles the river bends right and passes under power lines and then the Camel Ridge Road bridge, where there is an unimproved landing downriver on river right. You'll encounter tubers out in here on hot summer days, and they'll follow the rest of this paddle to the takeout point.

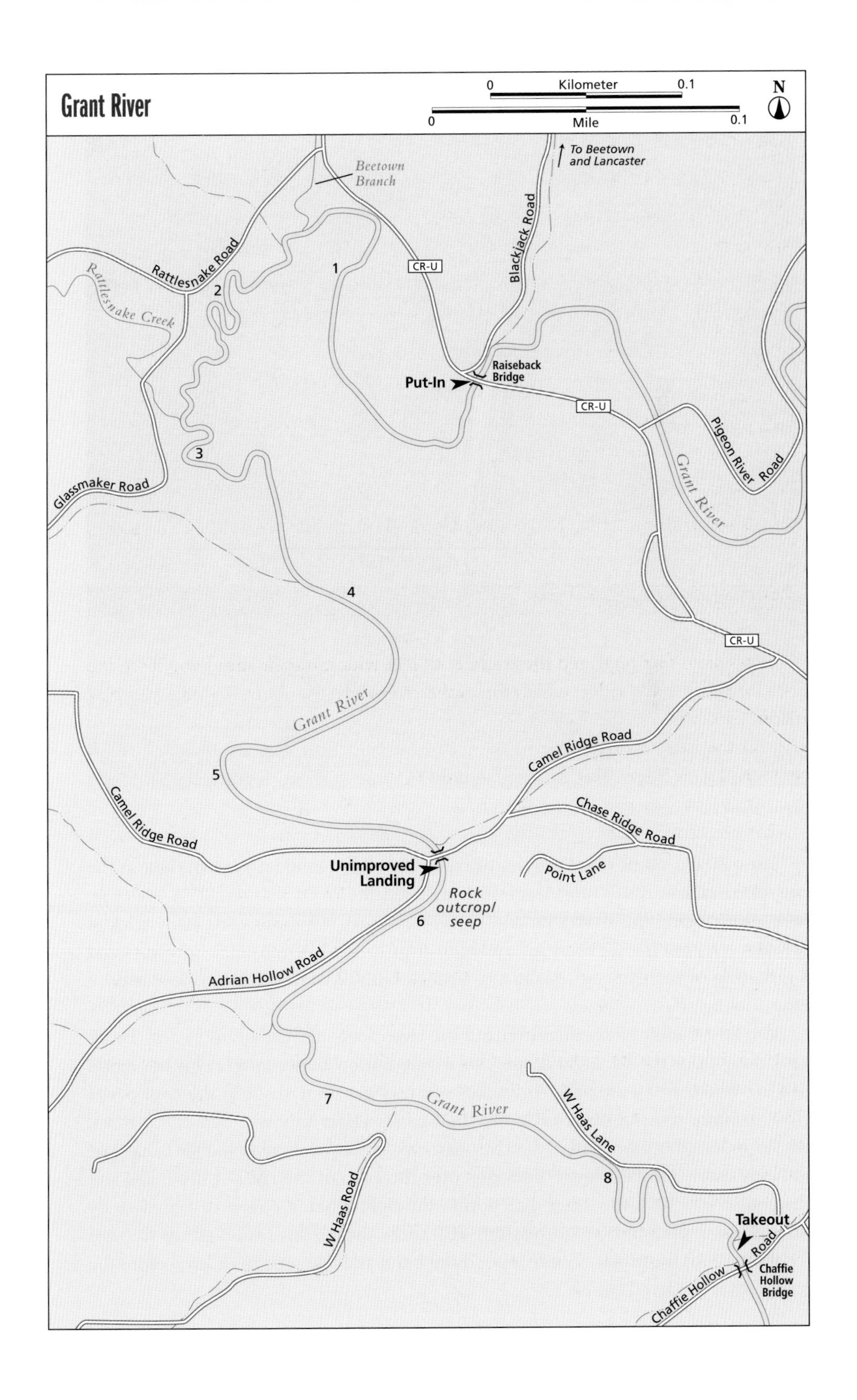
Grant River
0
Kilometer
0.1
0
Mile
0.1
N
To Beetown and Lancaster
Beetown Branch
Blackjack Road
Rattlesnake Road
Rattlesnake Creek
CR-U
1
2
Raiseback Bridge
Put-In
CR-U
Pigeon River Road
Grant River
3
Glassmaker Road
4
CR-U
Grant River
5
Camel Ridge Road
Camel Ridge Road
Chase Ridge Road
Point Lane
Unimproved Landing
Rock outcrop/ seep
6
Adrian Hollow Road
7
Grant River
W Haas Lane
W Haas Road
8
Takeout
Road
Chaffie Hollow
Chaffie Hollow Bridge

Seeps along the Grant River Preamtip Satasuk

Just past that point is a short run of rapids through a boulder garden; right at the end, on river left, is the most impressive sight on the river: a waterfall. A towering rock, overhanging the river a bit and covered in moss, lets loose with many trickles of water—seeps ranging from intermittent drips to long pencil-thick streams—and a gathering of such streams qualifies as a small but tall waterfall. Pass under it for a little cooling off.

You'll find a few riffles thereafter, but the river slows and widens to 50 feet. Bluffs back away from the banks, and you can see separation between trees on the banks and the woods along the hills. At 7 miles you may get some shade as the river passes close to more moss-covered rock and then passes under a power line at 7.2 miles. By 7.8 miles, after more riffles, the river narrows and slows, passing higher banks and showing more deadfall. Power lines pass over the edge of the river at 8.4 miles, and the course goes back the other direction to the right when it comes to a high sandy slope. With just 0.5 mile to go, pass through a very short Class I run and see the sign for the takeout for tubers. Come around the bend and take out river left, before the bridge, over mud and cobble.

3 Pecatonica River

An idyllic pastoral stream, the Pecatonica winds its way through farmland nearly always sheltered by trees or high banks to give the illusion that you are nowhere near a cornfield. The meandering course and occasional deadfall require some navigation but rarely much effort.

County: Lafayette
Start: CR G bridge, N42 44.4707' / W90 10.1532'
End: Black Bridge Park, N42 41.179' / W90 7.200'
Length: 8 miles one-way
Float time: About 3 hours
Difficulty rating: Easy
Rapids: None
River type: Narrow pastoral
Current: Gentle
River gradient: 1.2 feet per mile
River gauge: USGS 05432500 Pecatonica River at Darlington; minimum runnable level 100 cfs
Season: Spring through fall
Land status: Private, with public landings
Fees and permits: No fees or permits required
Nearest city/town: Darlington
Maps: USGS Calamine, Darlington; *DeLorme: Wisconsin Atlas & Gazetteer*: Page 26 C2
Boats used: Canoes, kayaks
Organizations: River Alliance of Wisconsin, 147 S. Butler St., Ste. 2, Madison 53703; (608) 257-2424; wisconsinrivers.org
Local information: Darlington Canoe Festival, Chamber of Commerce, 447 Main St., Darlington 53530; (608) 776-3067; darlingtoncanoefest.com. Held annually in June, this three-day fest includes a wealth of activities plus a canoe race.

Put-in/Takeout Information

To shuttle point/takeout: From where WI 81 and WI 23 join in downtown Darlington, head north 0.2 mile on WI 23 (Main Street); go left (west) on Harriet Street and right on the next street, Washington Street (this is still WI 23). The canoe landing is on the left at 0.2 mile, where a gravel road descends from the road to a grass-and-gravel lot right on the river. Coming into town from the north on WI 23, watch for the sign that reads Welcome to Darlington, Pearl of the Pecatonica. The landing has a portable toilet. This northernmost section of Black Bridge Park is not clearly marked as such. If you have gone to the camping area, you are in the wrong place.

To put-in from takeout: From the takeout, turn left (north) onto WI 23 and go 4.7 miles. Turn left (west) onto CR G and drive 2.8 miles, staying on CR G through Calamine. Cross the Pecatonica and turn right onto CR C. The landing is on the right side of the road, just upriver of the bridge on river right. No facilities here, but there's usually a portable toilet across the bridge near the -all-terrain-vehicle (ATV) trail.

Note: The multipurpose, packed-gravel Cheese Country Trail is a perfect bike shuttle route, directly connected to the takeout and to the put-in via a short stretch of the Pecatonica State Trail for a 30-minute ride.

River Overview

The Pecatonica River is a rather lengthy one for its modest size, stretching 120 miles from its southern Wisconsin origins into Illinois, where it passes Freeport and takes a turn to the northwest, eventually reaching the Rock River at Rockton. A 50-mile East Branch joins it just west of Browntown, Wisconsin. The origin of the name is Native American via the invariable mispronunciations of nonnative speakers. It may have meant "muddy river," "slow water," or "crooked stream." Take your pick—they are all accurate. Thanks to the river bottom and its muddy banks, the gentle, meandering river is generally as opaque as chocolate milk. Along its length in both states are excellent natural parks and preserves. Through the West Branch section, the river flows through hilly farmlands in the Driftless Area of Wisconsin. The Pecatonica and Cheese Country Trails are close by.

Paddle Summary

Put in upriver right of the CR G bridge. You can see Bonner Branch coming in from the right just upriver from the put-in point, but the current is nevertheless slow and steady. Pass under the highway bridge and the ATV trail bridge thereafter. The trees stand right up along the bank, often thickening into deeper patches of forest and in many places shading paddlers.

The river is 40 feet wide, and while there may be some deadfall, it is usually easy to navigate. Plus the locals take particular pride in keeping this stretch clear. Because of the tree shade along this corridor, birds are abundant, and it can feel nice and cool on a breezy summer day. At 1.6 miles a small creek comes in from river right and the Pecatonica bends gently to the left through some oak savanna. The tree cover opens up intermittently, and at 2.4 miles another stream joins from the left. Follow

THE BATTLE OF BLOODY LAKE AND THE EAST BRANCH

About a half-hour drive east from Darlington is Black Hawk Memorial Park, a lovely little county park situated on the East Branch of the Pecatonica. Even in high season, campsites are typically available here when other parks are fully booked, and the river and a backwater allow for some nice paddling and fishing. This was the site of the Battle of Bloody Lake (or the Battle of Horseshoe Bend).

On June 16, 1832, US militia under the command of Col. Henry Dodge caught up with a band of seventeen Kickapoo, loyal to Sauk warrior Black Hawk, who had ambushed them two days before. The Kickapoo took a stand at this bend in the river. The battle lasted only a few minutes, as the Kickapoo were able to get off only one rifle volley. In the end, the entire band was killed, while two of the four wounded militiamen perished.

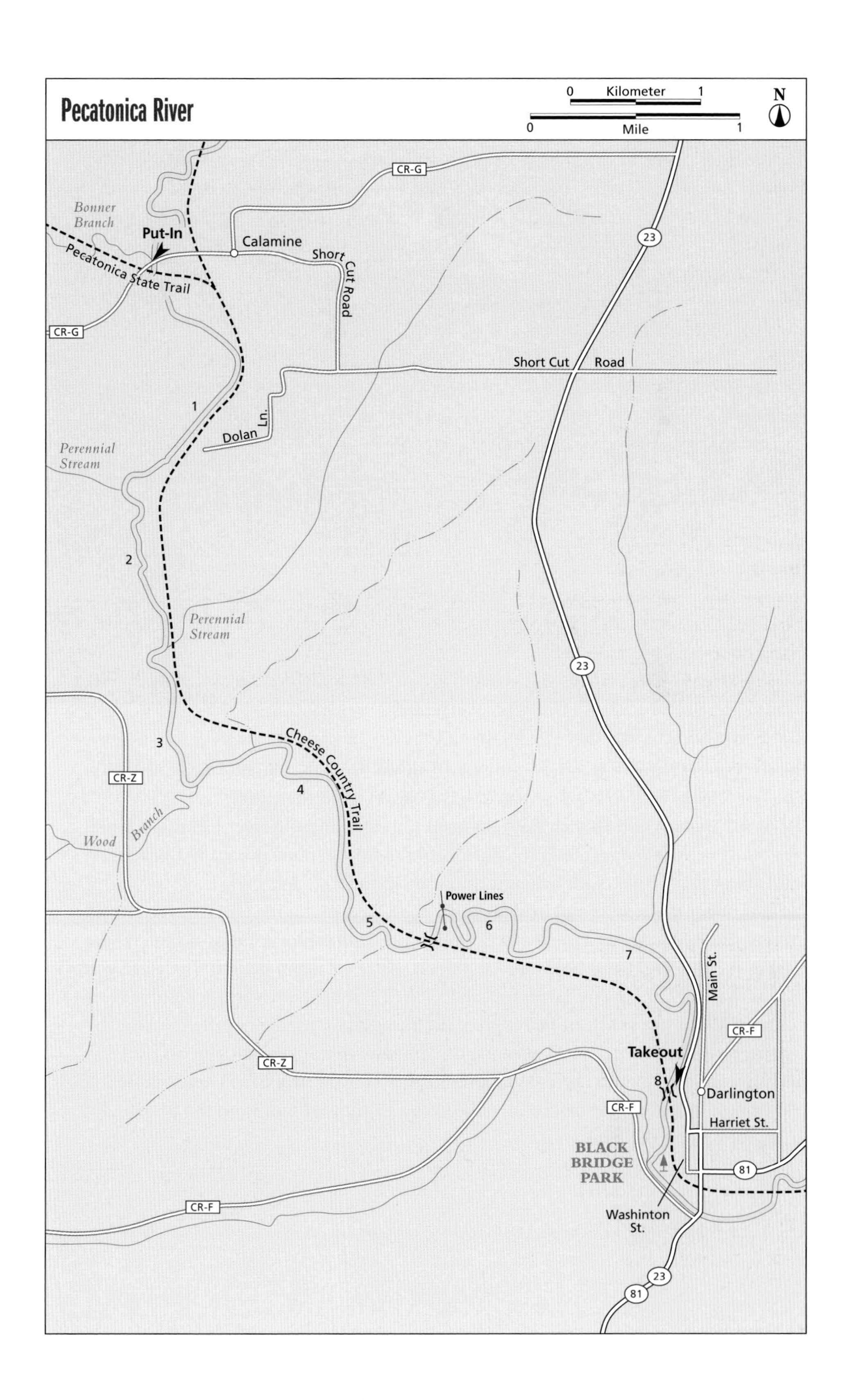

Pecatonica River
0 Kilometer 1
0 Mile 1
N
CR-G
Bonner
Branch
Put-In
Calamine
Short
Cut
Road
Pecatonica State Trail
CR-G
23
Short Cut Road
1
Dolan Ln.
Perennial
Stream
2
Perennial
Stream
23
3
CR-Z
Cheese Country Trail
4
Wood
Branch
Power Lines
5
6
7
Main St.
CR-F
Takeout
8
Darlington
CR-Z
CR-F
Harriet St.
BLACK
BRIDGE
PARK
81
CR-F
Washinton
St.
23
81

A relaxing paddle along the Pecatonica

the river's long bend to the right, and then you are heading straight south once again past farm fields, with low, grassy banks and a canal feel to the river.

At 3.2 miles Wood Branch flows in from the right and the river heads left. You'll see some low rock ledges along the right bank, and the canopy gradually thickens up until about the 5-mile mark, when it thins out again.

Pass under the former rail bridge—now the Cheese Country Trail—at 5.3 miles, putting the ATVs on river right. At 5.5 miles pass under power lines and follow the river as it bends right and heads into the open. After a hairpin bend in the river, you can catch a brief glimpse of farms on the left. At 7.6 miles the river reaches its closest point to WI 23 just north of Darlington and turns right, paralleling the road for the last stretch of the journey until reaching the muddy, unimproved landing on river left, upriver from the next trail bridge, another former railroad structure. There is a fishing platform on river left just before the takeout, and a mowed trail from the parking lot heads back along the bank to it.

4 Sugar River

A local favorite with paddlers, the Sugar flows through abundant mixed forest but with low banks and offering an abundance of backwaters along the route. Expect a lot of turns and twists and, with rising and falling water levels, some surprise channels that come and go. The trip ends with some flatwater paddling along a long impoundment and a takeout in a city park.

County: Green
Start: CR C bridge, N42 46.232' / W89 28.720'
End: Albany Park, N42 42.600' / W89 26.380'
Length: 8.7 miles one-way
Float time: About 2.5–3 hours
Difficulty rating: Easy
Rapids: Light riffles
River type: Wooded pastoral with marshy areas
Current: Gentle to moderate
River gradient: 2.7 feet per mile
River gauge: USGS 05436500 Sugar River near Brodhead; minimum runnable level 120 cfs
Season: Spring through fall
Land status: Private, with public landings
Fees and permits: No fees or permits required
Nearest city/town: Albany
Maps: USGS Albany, Attica; *DeLorme: Wisconsin Atlas & Gazetteer*: Page 28 B1
Boats used: Canoes, kayaks
Organizations: Lower Sugar River Watershed Association; lsrwa.org; e-mail: info@lsrwa.org
Outfitters: S&B Tubing, 100 E. Main St., Albany 53502; (608) 862-3933; sandbtubing.com. Offers shuttles, but only for their own craft.

Put-in/Takeout Information

To shuttle point/takeout: WI 59 passes right through downtown Albany. Coming into Albany from the north, take the first right in town onto Madison Street and go 1 block; the landing is just inside the park to the right. Coming into town from the south, WI 59 becomes Main Street. After crossing the Sugar River bridge, turn left onto Water Street and follow it all the way into the park. The landing is the first thing on the left when you enter the park area. There is a portable toilet here, and the library across the street has facilities when open.

To put-in from takeout: Exiting from the parking lot at the takeout, take the first left onto Madison Street. Go 1 block and turn left onto WI 59/Mechanic Street. Drive 0.6 mile and take a slight left onto CR E. Drive 3.9 miles, turn left onto Brooklyn-Albany Road, and drive 2.2 miles. Continue straight onto CR C and go 0.5 mile, just before the Sugar River bridge. The put-in is an unimproved landing on the right side of the road (river left, upstream of the bridge). There is off-road parking here and room to turn around with a trailer, but no facilities.

The Sugar River at the put-in site PREAMTIP SATASUK

River Overview

This 91-mile-long river in southern Wisconsin is a slow-flowing beauty with some riffle areas where it tightens up. While it is a tributary of the Pecatonica—joining it just south of the Wisconsin state line—it is not generally as muddy and has a couple of impoundments along the way, creating Lake Belle View and Albany Lake. The Sugar River flows through the Driftless Area, finding its headwaters right about where the last advance of the most recent glaciers ended. It connects a number of small towns and flows through rolling farmland in between. Its modest currents make it suitable for all skill levels. This particular stretch features a lot of low areas, and with even modest rains, the river can spread out from its banks and into backwaters and areas that were once the river's main channel. Though farmland lies on both sides, the river is in a very wide corridor of lowland forest, offering very few signs of development.

Paddle Summary

The put-in point is river left, upstream from the bridge on a low-grade, unimproved sand-and-mud landing. The river is 60 feet across at the bridge, showing steady current. Pass under the bridge and the river bends left, running parallel to the road 100 feet before turning south and leaving all signs of development behind—except for a couple views of distant farms—until you arrive in Albany Lake.

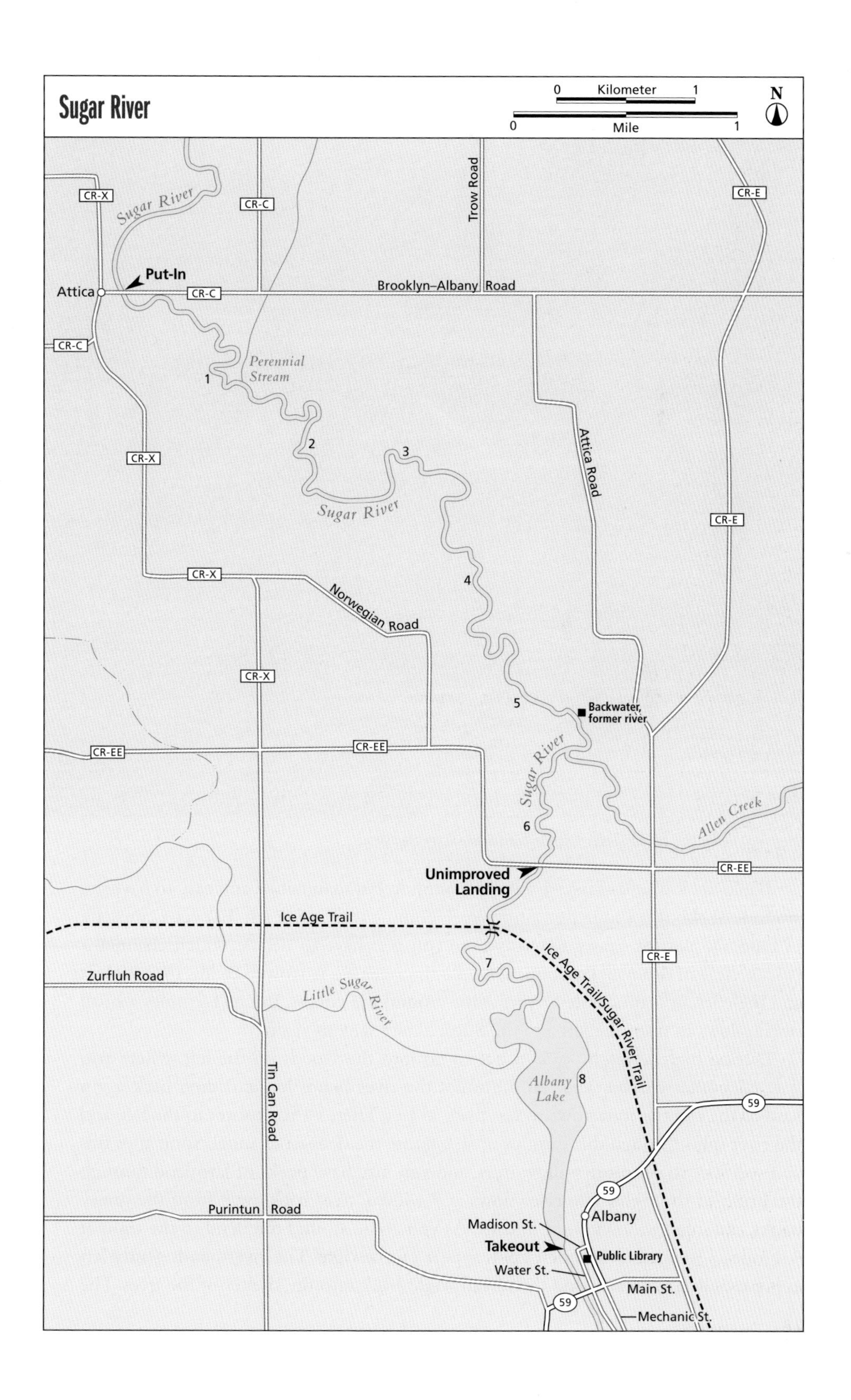

Sugar River
0 Kilometer 1
0 Mile 1
N
Sugar River
CR-X
CR-C
Trow Road
CR-E
Put-In
Attica
CR-C
Brooklyn–Albany Road
CR-C
Perennial Stream
1
2
3
Attica Road
CR-X
Sugar River
CR-E
CR-X
4
Norwegian Road
CR-X
5
Backwater, former river
CR-EE
CR-EE
Sugar River
Allen Creek
6
Unimproved Landing
CR-EE
Ice Age Trail
Ice Age Trail/Sugar River Trail
CR-E
7
Zurfluh Road
Little Sugar River
Albany Lake
8
Tin Can Road
59
59
Albany
Purintun Road
Madison St.
Takeout
Public Library
Water St.
Main St.
59
Mechanic St.

Passing along the Sugar River Bike Trail PREAMTIP SATASUK

Banks are low and grassy; deadfall is common but maintained and easy to navigate around. At about 0.4 mile pass a tiny creek coming in on river left. Expect a fair share of long and narrow grassy islands where you will have to decide which channel is best or clear of deadfall. By about 0.9 mile the river has narrowed to less than 40 feet and the current is moderate as you come around the curves. But at 1.2 miles a small stream flows in from the left and the Sugar River widens again.

During high water, be careful not to go into the woods on the left, where you may encounter barbed wire. At 3.8 miles the river bends left and then back again hard to the right as it narrows to less than 50 feet. There's a backwater to the left, and the river splits through this swampy area. Choose the deepest channel. Soon after this you will start to see more willow trees, and you may have peeks of farmland through the brush to the right. The river slows and widens; trees back away from the grassy banks, and small willows are abundant. As you come around the bend to the right at 4.2 miles, a barn, silo, and open fields appear on the right. The river bends gently left as it passes this open area and then heads right back into the shelter of the trees. The river doubles back, and now the barn is on your left. The river's course changes easily throughout, and satellite images show ghost images of where it once ran. Isolated patches of water may reconnect as backwaters in high-water periods. You will likely find them on either side at 5.3 miles. As you come around the bend to the right at 5.5 miles, Allen Creek flows in from river left.

The Sugar narrows to 20 feet and bends left at 5.7 miles. Pass under the CR EE bridge and some power lines at 6.3 miles; just past here on river right is a shallow, sandy, gentle slope takeout with parking. At 6.6 miles come to an old railroad bridge, now the Ice Age Trail/Sugar River Trail. The river approaches it from the side and the current is swift, making the passage through the two or three passable gates a little tricky sometimes. Be careful, as current may push into the pylons. Go far left to give yourself more time to line up, deadfall notwithstanding. After this bridge, the river is narrow and intimate. At the next backwater area, at about 7 miles, watch for the little orange sign indicating that the river goes left. There may be a split hereafter, with a narrow alternative channel; otherwise stay left again. Watch for saw-cut deadfall as a hint of maintained passages, but the little orange blaze with an arrow keeps you on course. Another 0.1 mile later, another sign points you left. The river narrows again to about 25 feet, and the current slows as you enter the upper reaches of Albany Lake.

At just about 7.6 miles, the river widens into the lake with a width more than 100 feet across. Stay left; as you paddle on another couple hundred feet, you should see the Little Sugar River coming in from the right. Go left past that, but stay center. Part of the lake swings out to the left at 7.7 miles, but you want to go straight across the open water and follow the opposite shore going right (south), passing some lake properties. On the left shore you'll see houses and cabins amid the trees, and just a few over on the right bank. The wide lake exposes you to the wind, and shallow, weedy spots might require some navigation to get around. Banks become steep rising ridges, and the impoundment is less than 200 feet across. When you see the maintained lawns of the park on the left, you are almost to the end. Stay left, passing the baseball diamond. The concrete ramp takeout is river left, upriver from the dam.

5 Badfish Creek

Known mostly by avid local paddlers, the narrow Badfish Creek is quite an alternative to the much wider and flatter rivers in the Madison area. It winds, it twists, and it might require some serious deadfall navigation. But it is delightfully playful and quick and has some of the clearest water you'll see—despite its origins. It passes under numerous bridges, offers only brief views of minimal development, and ends at a bridge on a country road, about 1.7 miles upstream from its juncture with the Yahara River.

County: Dane, Rock
Start: Old Stone Road Bridge, N42 52.815' / W89 16.548'
End: Casey Road Bridge, N42 50.013' / W89 11.475'
Length: 9.4 miles one-way
Float time: About 3 hours
Difficulty rating: Moderate to difficult due to tight maneuvering and occasional deadfall
Rapids: Class I riffles
River type: Narrow wooded pastoral creek
Current: Moderate to swift
River gradient: 6 feet per mile
River gauge: USGS 05430150 Badfish Creek at Cooksville; runnable even in drought due to daily discharges; avoid flood stage
Season: Spring through fall
Land status: Private, with public landings
Fees and permits: No fees or permits required
Nearest city/town: Edgerton
Maps: USGS Cooksville, Evansville, Rutland; *DeLorme: Wisconsin Atlas & Gazetteer*: Page 28 B2
Boats used: Canoes, kayaks
Organizations: Friends of Badfish Creek Watershed; rockrivercoalition.org/badfish
Outfitters: Outfitters tend to avoid this one for rentals due to the potential for a rough ride.
Local information: Watch for the Friends of Badfish Creek annual Canoe Tour, typically held in August.

Put-in/Takeout Information

To shuttle point/takeout: From the intersection of US 51 and WI 59 in downtown Edgerton, go west 5.6 miles on WI 59. Turn right (north) onto Casey Road and go 0.3 mile, crossing the bridge over Badfish Creek. The unimproved takeout is on the left side of the road, upstream and river left. Parking is on the roadside; there are no facilities.

To put-in from takeout: From the takeout, head south on Casey Road 0.3 mile to WI 59. Go right (west) 2.7 miles and turn right onto WI 138. Drive 2.7 miles and continue straight off a curve onto Bass Lake Road for another 0.7 mile. Turn left onto Old Stone Road, drive 1.6 miles, and cross the bridge. The gravel parking lot for the unimproved put-in is on the left. Carry your craft through the grass to get into the water.

The Badfish is typically crystal clear but muddies up in rainy periods.

River Overview

Badfish Creek is a favorite with local paddlers. It can run a little quick, with frequent riffles and turns, and narrow, especially in the upper reaches. The creek ends where it empties into the Yahara River. The water here is crystal clear, but there is a story behind that: Wastewater from the City of Madison keeps this little creek flowing even in the driest years. That water is treated by the Madison Metropolitan Sewerage District, so it's not as disturbing as it sounds, but there may be a faint chemical smell to it. Paddlers maintain the deadfall, but with the narrow path and the abundant woods, it is an endless task. If you are looking for a lazy river to sit back on and coast, this is not it. Beginners may do fine here if they are comfortable in their craft, but they might find the presence of deadfall on a narrow and swift section frustrating. In high water, this is recommended for more experienced paddlers.

Paddle Summary

From the put-in parking lot, carry your craft through the grass to find a comfortable place to slip into the river downstream of the bridge and any current there. The water is some of the clearest you will see, and the grassy banks show lots of wildflowers.

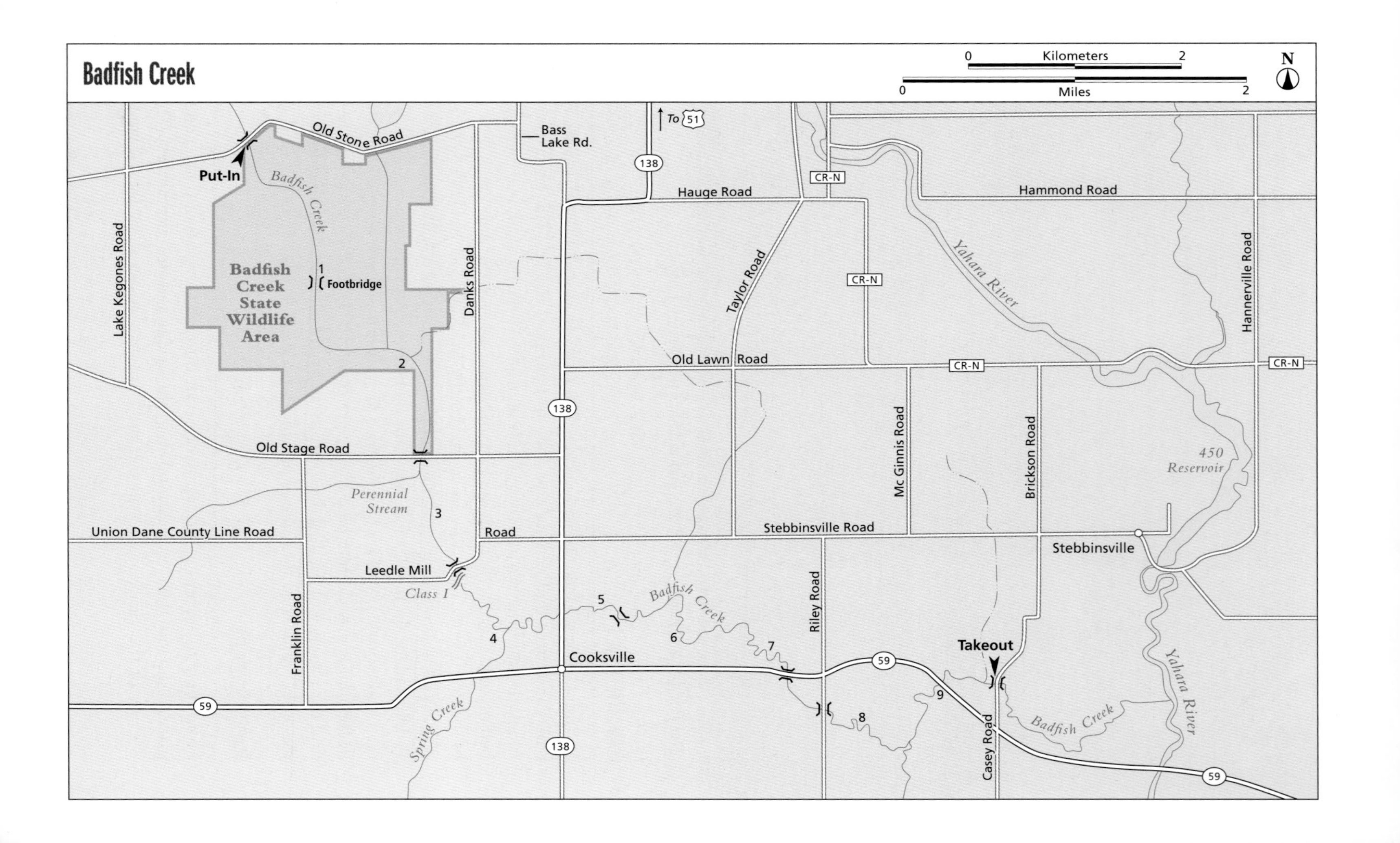
Badfish Creek
Kilometers
0
2
Miles
0
2
N
Old Stone Road
Bass
Lake Rd.
To 51
138
Put-In
Badfish Creek
Badfish Creek State Wildlife Area
1
Footbridge
Lake Kegones Road
Danks Road
2
Hauge Road
CR-N
Hammond Road
Taylor Road
Yahara River
Hanneville Road
Old Lawn Road
Old Stage Road
Perennial Stream
3
Union Dane County Line Road
Road
Stebbinsville Road
Mc Ginnis Road
Brickson Road
450 Reservoir
Stebbinsville
Leedle Mill
Class I
Franklin Road
4
5
6
7
8
9
Badfish Creek
Riley Road
Cooksville
59
Spring Creek
Takeout
Casey Road

THE WORLD'S LARGEST PADDLING EXPO

Held annually the second full weekend in March, Canoecopia (Canoecopia.com) is a paddler's dream. What began as a tent sale in the early 1980s was then only called "Meet the Folks Who Build the Boats." The Madison outfitter Rutabaga hosted it at their old location with the intention of bringing paddlers and the makers of their products together. What started with a speaker or two now features ninety presenters on over 150 topics from techniques to travel. The latest products and paddling destinations are featured in over one hundred booths.

The expo, held in the Exhibition Hall at the Alliant Energy Center in Madison, attracts over 20,000 attendees. Some of the proceeds go to nonprofit organizations dedicated to protecting our waterways. Whether you are looking to improve your skills, find a new faraway paddling vacation (or one in your backyard), or just get started, this is an event not to be missed.

Cottonwoods stand tall among the mixed forest. The river is only about 30 feet across. At 1.1 mile you pass under a footbridge. The Old Stage Road bridge is the next landmark at 2.6 miles. There is an unimproved put-in on river right downstream of the bridge and tiny stream coming in on the right. Another bridge awaits at 3.4 miles, and the narrowing of the creek forces the current up. The river takes a hard left into some riffles or Class I waves. You'll pass a house and yard on the left. Deadfall is less frequent at this point, and a widening hereafter gives you a break before the current ramps up again. At 3.6 miles a small island splits the flow; from there the creek snakes along with good current, requiring you to be at the paddle through this area of grassy banks and meadow. Pass another little island at 4 miles, and come to the WI 138 bridge at 4.7 miles. The trees move in closer, and at 5 miles there are a couple of short islands. On the left you'll see maintained lawn and lots of oak trees.

At 5.1 miles it may be necessary to duck a bit under a bridge of old rail ties. You'll see some cropland on the left and an area of oaks with mowed grass on the right. Less than 0.1 mile later you pass through a few waves or riffles. At 5.3 miles you come to a hairpin turn, which nature may be in the process of cutting through in high water, so watch for a shortened passage to the other side on the right. Banks are grassy through here, and you will see a few houses on the right, but the woods close in for a bit more cover by the 6-mile mark. At 7 miles pass a small island and a house up on the ridge. The river loops around to the right, passing through a long, gentle S-curve, and heads under the WI 59 bridge at 7.2 miles and the Riley Road bridge at 7.6 miles; you can expect some waves around the next bend there. The water flows back under WI 59 at 9 miles, and the takeout is on river left just before the Casey Road bridge 0.4 mile later. A drainage ditch makes a convenient place to slip into the bank and step up onto the mud and grass.

6 Yahara River

Take a paddle down the river that connects the chain of five lakes starting up in Madison. Freed from a former dam at Stebbinsville, this section of the Yahara—several miles south of Stoughton—makes its gentle way through a wooded corridor until its end at the Rock River. The land along its path is farmland, but the woods and some wetland patches leave this area undeveloped but for a brief pass along a village park in Fulton. The takeout point is actually beyond the river's end, a short distance down the much wider Rock River.

County: Rock
Start: Stebbinsville Road Bridge (former dam site), N42 50.619' / W89 10.348'
End: CR H (unmarked landing), N42 47.243' / W89 7.740'
Length: 9.2 miles one-way
Float time: About 2.5 hours
Difficulty rating: Easy
Rapids: Riffles
River type: Wooded pastoral
Current: Gentle with a few moderate spots
River gradient: 3.8 feet per mile
River gauge: USGS 05430175 Yahara River near Fulton; minimum runnable level 120 cfs
Season: Spring through fall
Land status: Private, with public landings
Fees and permits: No fees or permits required
Nearest city/town: Edgerton
Maps: USGS Cooksville, Edgerton; *DeLorme: Wisconsin Atlas & Gazetteer*: Page 28 B3
Boats used: Canoes, kayaks, johnboats
Organizations: River Alliance of Wisconsin, 147 S. Butler St., Ste. 2, Madison 53703; (608) 257-2424; wisconsinrivers.org
Outfitters: Rutabaga Paddlesports, 220 W. Broadway, Madison 53716; (608) 223-9300; rutabaga.com. Offers rentals but not shuttles.

Put-in/Takeout Information

To shuttle point/takeout: From the intersection of US 51 and WI 59 in downtown Edgerton, go west 3.7 miles on WI 59. At the second of two curves at this point on WI 59, stay straight onto CR H and continue south 0.7 mile. After a big curve take a right (south) to stay on CR H. Continue another 2.3 miles; the unimproved landing is on a half-circle turnout on the left side of the road. There are no facilities.
To put-in from takeout: From the takeout, backtrack north on CR H for 3 miles back to WI 59. Turn left (west) and go 1 mile on WI 59 to Wallin Road. Turn right and drive 1 mile. Turn left onto Stebbinsville Road and continue 1.2 miles to the bridge over the Yahara. This is a former dam site. Parking is off the side of the road on the right, just before the bridge. The unimproved landing is upriver from the bridge on river left. If the current there is intimidating so close to the bridge, there are trails across the road to put in downstream. There are no facilities.

Formerly an impoundment, the Yahara flows freely after a dam removal.

River Overview

The 45-mile-long Yahara River begins above Madison and passes through wetlands as it enters the lakes of Madison. The river enters Lake Mendota on its northeast side, flowing wide through wetlands that are slowly being reclaimed. From the lock at the southern end of Mendota, the river flows through Madison's famed isthmus as a canal-like stretch to Monona, and then continues through more wetlands and Lakes Waubesa and Kegonsa before becoming this wooded waterway for its last miles before joining the much wider Rock River. This stretch was once controlled by a dam right under the bridge where you put in. Since the dam's removal in 2010 and the 1993 removal of a dam at Fulton, fishing has improved, and the stretch of river from Dunkirk, north of here, to the Rock River is navigable without portages. This section of the river is excellent for birding, and anglers may find muskellunge, northern pike, walleye, bluegill, crappie, and perch.

Paddle Summary

Put in river left, upstream of the bridge. Be aware that the current is swift under the bridge (a former dam), and right after you pass under the structure, a grassy and wooded island forces you to quickly choose a channel. Give yourself a moment to get situated and have a look from the bridge before paddling. Some paddlers who jump right in and go can later be seen gathering their things from the water just past the island. An alternative put-in 100 feet downstream from the bridge can be reached down a trail across Stebbinsville Road.

After the island, the river zigzags a bit, with a width of about 40 to 50 feet before it widens out. Open fields are visible to the right. At 1.4 miles you enter a wide shallow area, marshy along the sides. Badfish Creek enters here from river right. The Yahara narrows for a short way, bends right, and then the current picks up. At 1.7

THE YAHARA AND MADISON'S LAKES

If you are lamenting not having a shuttle, there are some great areas for out-and-back flat-water paddling along the Yahara: Cherokee Marsh, Lake Mendota, Lake Monona, Upper Mud Lake, Lake Waubesa, Lower Mud Lake, and Lake Kegonsa line up from north to south, and Lake Wingra connects to Lake Monona via Wingra Creek.

The 3,200-acre Cherokee Marsh on Madison's north side makes for some good out-and-back excursions either upriver or down to Lake Mendota. Put in at Cherokee Marsh South off School Road.

Lake Mendota is the largest of the lakes, and popular paddle points include Picnic Point, Six-Mile Creek, and Governor's Island. Below the lock at Tenney Park, the Yahara is canal-like across the isthmus into Lake Monona. Paddle from Mendota's Tenney Park downriver and east along the Lake Monona shore to Starkweather Creek, and you can see Olbrich Botanical Gardens.

Lake Wingra, a small spring-fed lake just west of Lake Monona, is not part of the Yahara-joined chain of lakes. Shallow and bordered primarily by Vilas Park and the Arboretum, it is a nice lake paddle without the traffic and waves of the bigger lakes, plus there are some nooks and crannies to explore along the Arboretum shoreline. Put in at the boat ramp at Wingra Park, where there are rentals (Wingra [Madison] Boats; 608-233-5332; madisonboats.com), or at any point along the low shoreline at Vilas Park. This is a fantastic option for a moonlight paddle. Madison Boats also has rentals at Brittingham Park on Monona Bay of Lake Monona and at Marshall Park at the west end of Lake Mendota.

Rutabaga Paddlesports (220 W. Broadway, Madison; 608-223-9300; rutabaga.com) rents and sells craft and is situated on the short section of the Yahara between Lake Monona and Upper Mud Lake.

The Dane County Office of Lakes and Watersheds offers a free online Yahara Waterways Water Trail Guide, downloadable at danewaters.com. Go to "Get Involved," then click on "Discover Water-related Recreation," then "Boating."

miles there is a quick turn to the right with some riffles; 0.2 mile later you pass under the WI 59 bridge. Just past there the river widens to more than 80 feet, the trees back off from the banks, and you can see a barn to the right. A perennial stream may enter from the right here as well and get absorbed into a backwater.

Pass an island at 2.5 miles and another at 3 miles, then the banks and trees close in once again, narrowing the river to 40 feet. Pass under two sets of power lines and meet Gibbs Creek coming in from river right, before following a left-leading bend

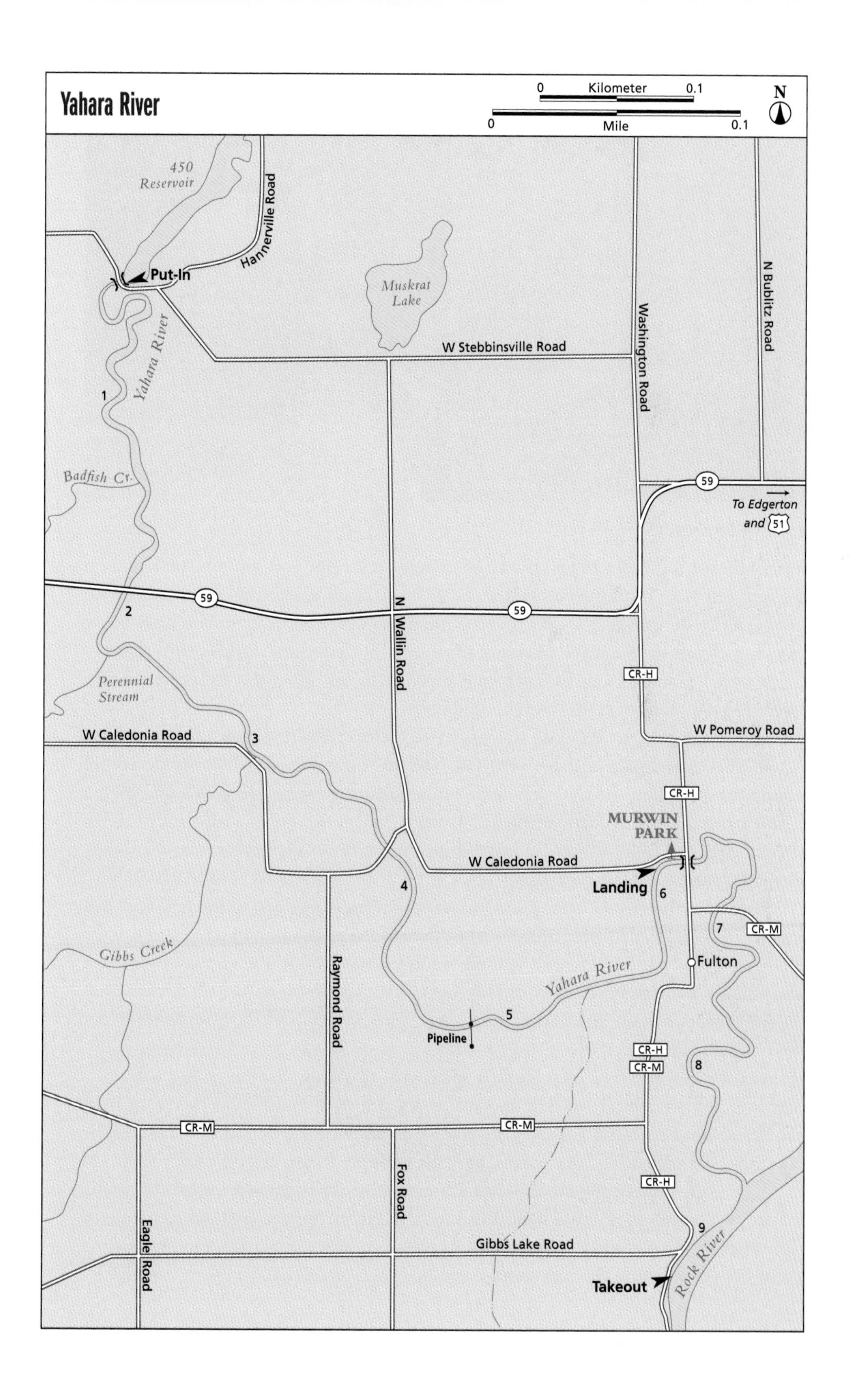
Yahara River
0
Kilometer
0.1
0
Mile
0.1
N
450 Reservoir
Hannerville Road
Put-In
Muskrat Lake
Yahara River
W Stebbinsville Road
Washington Road
N Bublitz Road
1
Badfish Cr.
59
To Edgerton and 51
2
59
N Wallin Road
59
Perennial Stream
CR-H
W Caledonia Road
3
W Pomeroy Road
CR-H
MURWIN PARK
W Caledonia Road
Landing
4
6
7
CR-M
Gibbs Creek
Raymond Road
Fulton
Yahara River
5
Pipeline
CR-H
CR-M
8
CR-M
CR-M
CR-H
Fox Road
9
Eagle Road
Gibbs Lake Road
Rock River
Takeout

Trees overhanging the Yahara River

in the river at 3.2 miles. When the river swings back right past some private land on the left, the current pushes up riffles. At 3.8 miles pass under the Caledonia Road bridge and some power lines. More residential property follows, and you'll see some wood-duck houses. Slip over an almost imperceptible ledge at 4.1 miles; riffles rise for the next few hundred feet. A petroleum pipeline passes under the river at 4.8 miles. ***Note:*** Do not anchor or dredge here, paddlers.

At 5.7 miles the river comes to a high ridge covered with riprap. Houses sit atop it, and the river makes a sharp turn left. You are now entering Fulton. Notice an unimproved landing on river left with some parking, just before you come to the curve to the right that takes you past Murwin Park at 6.1 miles with a bit of quick current. You can pull out here along the grassy left bank where there are pit toilets, picnic facilities, and a water pump.

Pass under the CR H bridge and follow the river's sharp turn to the left. This area is notorious for deadfall accumulation, but the river is wide enough to ensure passage if you don't let the current take you where it prefers. About 500 feet later the river again bends hard right. A high muddy bank with swallows' nests and thick woods lines the left, and open prairie unfolds on the right. At 6.9 miles the river flows under the CR M bridge.

At 7.4 miles the river may show a split, with the main channel going left and a narrower run straight ahead that also makes the left turn and rejoins the main river about 500 feet later if it is passable. The river remains wide and gentle, flowing into the lowlands around it when the waters are high enough. Farms are off to the right. At 8.7 miles you come to the Rock River, unmistakable for its great width at this point, making the Yahara look quite small. Go right, following the current, and stay close to river right. The takeout is just under 0.5 mile from here—a narrow, muddy landing a few steps down from the half-loop of crushed rock where you can park a vehicle.

7 Bark River

Another tributary to the Rock River, this stretch of the narrow and intimate Bark River runs amid farmland but remains well tucked into thick forest. Part of the Glacier Heritage Area's Water Trails, the Bark flows in its meandering course to the Rock; the paddle trip ends soon after in downtown Fort Atkinson.

County: Jefferson
Start: Burnt Village Park, N42 54.904' / W88 46.753'
End: Mechanic and Water Street Landing in Fort Atkinson, N42 55.752' / W88 50.327'
Length: 6.3 miles one-way
Float time: About 2.5 hours
Difficulty rating: Easy
Rapids: None
River type: Wooded pastoral
Current: Negligible
River gradient: 0.9 feet per mile
River gauge: USGS 05426250 Bark River near Rome; minimum runnable level 20 cfs
Season: Spring through fall
Land status: Private, with public landings
Fees and permits: No fees or permits required
Nearest city/town: Fort Atkinson
Maps: USGS Fort Atkinson; *DeLorme: Wisconsin Atlas & Gazetteer*: Page 29 A6
Boats used: Canoes, kayaks
Contacts: Jefferson County Parks, 311 S. Center Ave., Rm. 204, Jefferson 53549; (920) 674-7260; jeffersoncountywi.gov (go to Departments>Parks>Department Services and click Water Trails for links to Glacier Heritage Water Trails maps)
Outfitters: 2 Rivers Bicycle & Outdoor, 33 W. Sherman Ave., Fort Atkinson 53538; (920) 563-2222; 2riversbicycle.com

Put-in/Takeout Information

To shuttle point/takeout: US 12 and WI 89 pass through the center of Fort Atkinson and over the Rock River as Main Street. Two blocks north of the Rock River on Main Street, find Sherman Avenue/WI 106 and head west 1 block to Mechanic Street. Turn left (south); the city boat landing parking lot is on your right.
To put-in from takeout: From the takeout, backtrack to Sherman Avenue/WI 106 and turn right (east). Follow it 2.8 miles to CR N east of town. Turn right (south) onto CR N and drive 1.7 miles, crossing the bridge over the Bark River. Watch for the driveway on the left. Enter and drive back parallel to the highway to the unimproved, crushed-gravel launch. There is a picnic table, grill, and ample room for parking.

Note: Bike shuttles should cross the Rock River headed south on the US 12 bridge. Turn left onto Milwaukee Avenue/Rock River Road, ride east to Bark River Road, and turn right, following Bark River Road all the way to CR N. Turn right; the put-in is 0.5 mile on the left.

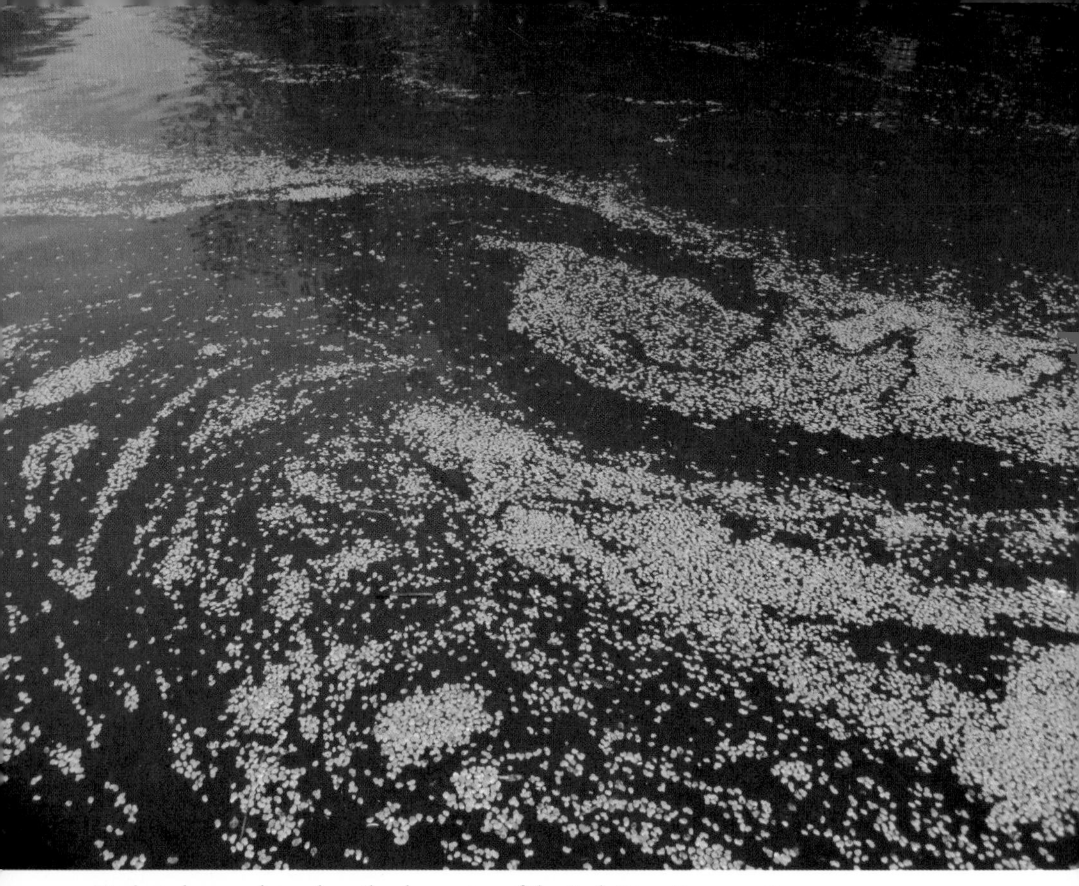

Duckweed accumulates along the slow waters of the Bark River. Preamtip Satasuk

River Overview

A tributary of the Rock River, the Bark River flows just over 67 miles until it joins the bigger river just outside Fort Atkinson. Generally inside a wooded corridor, the small river starts near Menomonee Falls at Bark Lake, passes through larger lakes in the Delafield area as it crosses I-94, and then meanders through farmland and smaller lakes on its way southwest. To the east of Fort Atkinson, the river passes through Prince's Point Wildlife Area, where it takes in the Scuppernong River and becomes part of the Glacier Heritage Area Water Trails.

Paddle Summary

Note: About a mile upstream from the put-in is Whitewater Creek, a possible extension of this trip if it's too short for your day.

Launch from Burnt Village County Park and follow the current left. Paddle 300 feet and pass under the CR N bridge. Beyond there, the river is about 50 feet wide and the view is open to farmland that slopes down to the river basin. A drainage canal runs in from the fields on river left. But you need not paddle far before the river tucks in among the trees, hiding the developed world. Herons and kingfishers abound through here. In summer duckweed is abundant, and in periods of high water, when

Back in the 1700s the area near the put-in was the site of a Ho-Chunk village. After a confrontation between tribes, the community was destroyed by fire. US soldiers, chasing the famed warrior Black Hawk and his people in the 1830s, camped here and named it Burnt Village.

the path is unclear as the river overruns its banks into the forest, that duckweed forms a trail that gives away the almost imperceptible current.

At 1 mile, as the river bends a bit to the right, you will see a large backwater on river right. This is actually a former oxbow on the river. The river's more recent course just goes straight across the opening, but with enough water, it's possible to paddle back into part of that old loop of river.

As you paddle farther downstream, the river narrows a bit and snakes through the woods dominated by maples and often shaded by them. At 2.6 miles pass a house on river right, the first you'll see up close. At 3.5 miles is an old private boat landing and a shed facing the river from the left bank. Beyond here the river makes a couple of long hairpins before its final run to the Rock River. The trees are old and tall here. Pass the first hairpin and enter a straight stretch to the next. As you enter the second, you will see a small, shallow channel on the left at 4.6 miles; a footbridge passes over it. This channel is typically impassable, but it does offer a shortcut across the inside of the next hairpin. The switchback point on the second hairpin comes rather close to

GLACIER HERITAGE AREA

The GHA (glacialheritagearea.org) is a system of natural reserves spread across a large area between Madison and Milwaukee. Its mission is to "reconnect people to the land through recreation, conservation and tourism." A variety of wildlife areas, waterway access points, trails, wetlands, and cultural heritage sites are strung together to make a rich natural corridor amid small towns and agricultural fields. Included waters are the Bark, Beaver Dam, Crawfish, Maunesha, Rock, and Scuppernong Rivers; Koshkonong and Rock Creeks; and Blue Spring, Koshkonong, Lower Spring, Marsh, Mud, Red Cedar, Ripley, Rock, Spence, and Storrs Lakes.

One of the most intimate waterways, however, is the Bark, offering some excellent wildlife viewing—especially birds—and a variety of plant life. Highlights include Rome Pond and Prince's Point Wildlife Areas, where the Scuppernong flows into the Bark. These sections, above Burnt Village Park where this book's Bark River segment begins, are wilder and thus sometimes more challenging in terms of deadfall. Rustic campsites throughout the GHA are in planning. You can get a downloadable guide and maps from the Jefferson County website (Jefferson County Parks, Courthouse, Rm. 204, 320 S. Center Ave., Jefferson 53549; 920-674-7260; jeffersoncountywi.gov).

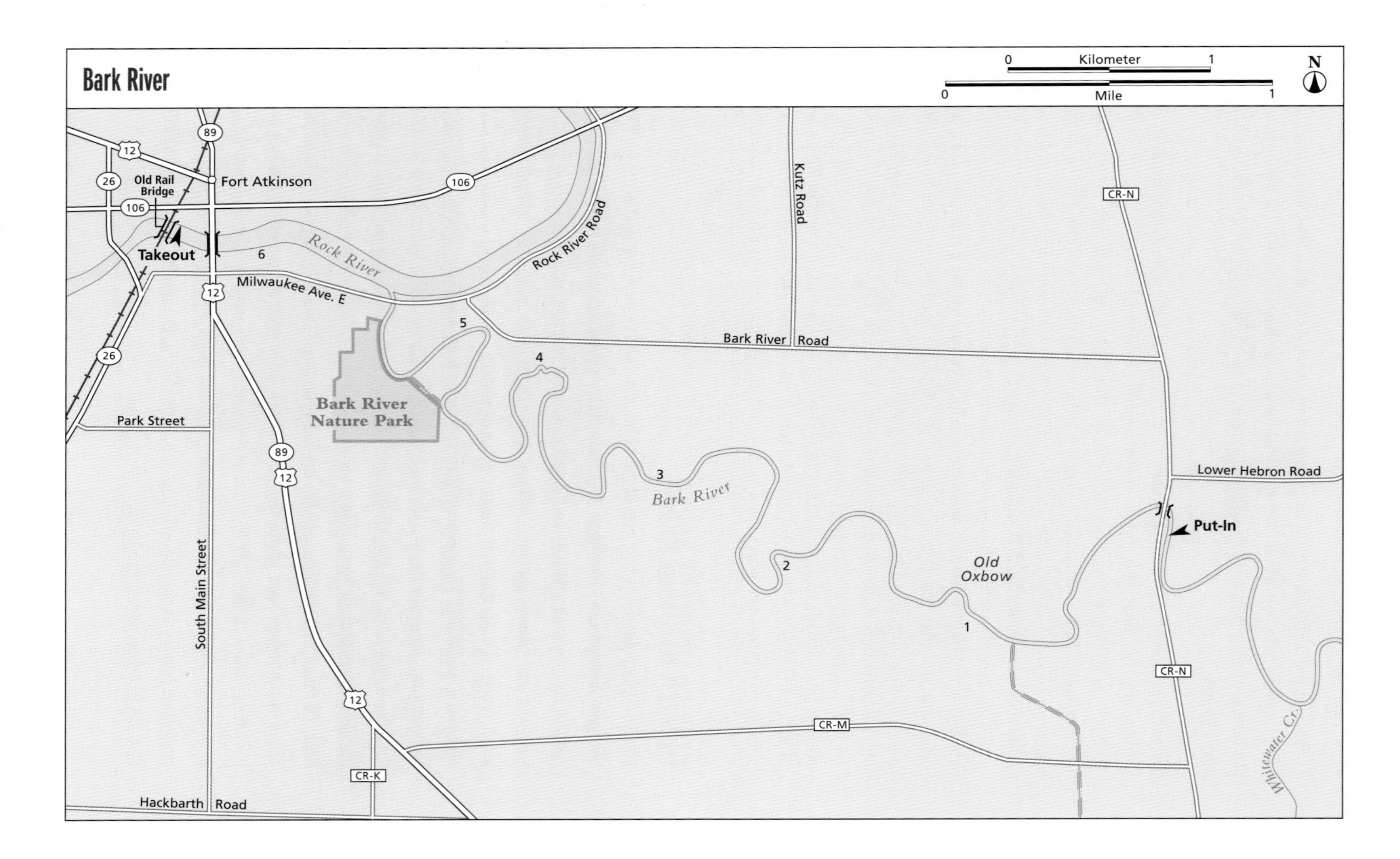
Bark River
Kilometer
0
1
Mile
0
1
N
Fort Atkinson
Old Rail Bridge
Takeout
Rock River
Rock River Road
Milwaukee Ave. E
Kutz Road
Bark River Road
CR-N
Bark River Nature Park
Park Street
South Main Street
Hackbarth Road
CR-K
CR-M
Bark River
Old Oxbow
Put-In
Lower Hebron Road
Whitewater Cr.
89
12
26
106
1
2
3
4
5
6

Bark River Road. As you come back along the second leg of the long turn, you will pass the outlet of that shortcut.

The land along the left bank is part of Bark River Nature Park, and there may be a fishing platform there. Haumerson Pond lies just on the other side of the bank before you arrive at the first residences there on the left. At 5.5 miles pass under the last bridge before the Rock River, then head left with the current into downtown Fort Atkinson. For the final 0.8 mile, pass boathouses, residences, and apartment buildings on this much-wider river. Pass under the Main Street bridge; as soon as you come through, exit river right at a concrete ramp or one of the docks, just before an old rail bridge turned trail bridge. There are no facilities at the takeout, but you can use restrooms inside the municipal building on weekdays from 8 a.m. to 5 p.m.

Waters sometime overflow the banks on the Bark, creating swamplike forests. PREAMTIP SATASUK

8 Root River

Just a short drive south of Milwaukee, the Root River Parkway is a natural space preserved amid suburban development. The river starts narrow and snakes its way south toward the edge of the city of Racine, where it reaches an impoundment for the last mile of the paddle.

County: Racine
Start: Linwood Park, 5 Mile Road Bridge, N42 47.974' / W87 52.217'
End: Horlick Park, N42 45.243' / W87 49.371'
Length: 7.7 miles one-way
Float time: About 3 hours
Difficulty rating: Easy
Rapids: None
River type: Wooded pastoral
Current: Gentle
River gradient: 3.5 feet per mile
River gauge: USGS 04087240 Root River at Racine. Levels below 2 feet may mean scraping in the first 2 miles. Above 6 feet the river is fast, though still runnable, but the landing area at Horlick Park may be closed if the level approaches 8 feet, leaving you without a takeout point. Water levels rise and fall rapidly with rain.
Season: Spring, summer, rainy periods
Land status: Private, with public landings and some public land along the parkway
Fees and permits: No fees or permits required
Nearest city/town: Racine
Maps: USGS Racine North; *DeLorme: Wisconsin Atlas & Gazetteer*: Page 31 B7
Boats used: Canoes, kayaks
Organizations: Root River Council; rootrivercouncil.org (occasionally sponsors a free summer paddle)
Contacts: Root River Environmental Education Community Center (REC), University of Wisconsin-Parkside, 1301 W. 6th St., Racine 53144; (262) 818-4200

River Bend Nature Center, 3600 N. Green Bay Rd., Racine 53404; (262) 639-1515; riverbendnaturecenterracine.org
Outfitters: The REC offers rentals on summer weekends.
Local information: Watch for the Root River Spring Paddle in late May/early June, organized by the Root-Pike Watershed Initiative Network; rootpikewin.org.

Put-in/Takeout Information

To shuttle point/takeout: From downtown Racine at State (WI 38) and Main (WI 32) Streets, go west on State (which becomes Northwestern Avenue) for 2.5 miles. Turn right onto Rapids Drive and take another quick left onto Rapids Court. The park entrance is 0.1 mile on the right. Pass the first lot where the restrooms are, and follow the park road 0.1 mile to the parking lot and its concrete boat ramp and floating dock.
To put-in from takeout: From the takeout, turn left onto Rapids Court and drive 0.1 mile. Take the sharp right onto Rapids Drive and continue 0.1 mile to Northwestern Avenue/WI 38, following that for 2.2 miles. Turn right (north) at the traffic circle to stay on WI 38, and go 3 miles. Turn right onto 5 Mile Road and go 0.3 mile

Much of the Root River is still, peaceful, and shaded. Preamtip Satasuk

to the park on the left, just before the bridge over the river. Make a U-turn and park on the north side of the road, where there is ample parking on a widened asphalt shoulder. Carry your craft through the wood fence and find the put-in spot through the grass along the riverbank upstream from the bridge. The park has benches, a trash receptacle, and a grill; 200 feet to the west there is a portable toilet in season and a gravel parking lot.

River Overview

The city of Racine is actually named for this river: The name is from the French for "root." The 43.7-mile-long Root River rises up north of the city and then makes its way south-southeast from the Milwaukee area through Racine before emptying into Lake Michigan. The Horlick Dam creates an impoundment where the river enters Racine. The Root River Parkway is a county project to protect 1,650 acres of green space on either side of the river. This would not only offer environmental and recreational opportunities but also create some flood protection for the area. The Root is a green haven in an increasingly urban area of the state, and for paddlers it is an easily accessible wild space with paddling conditions suitable for all skill levels. The area is renowned for its bird diversity.

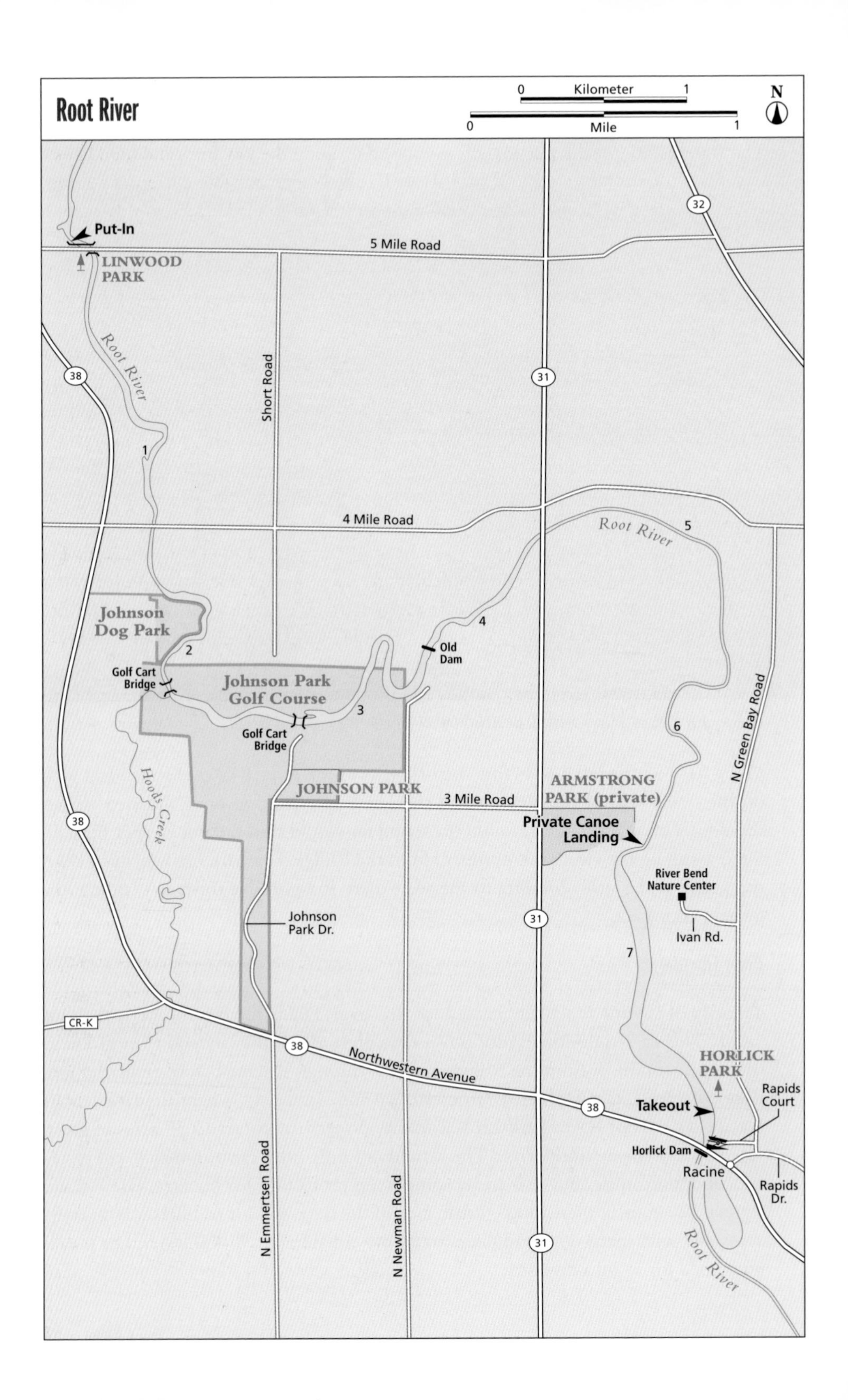
Root River
0
Kilometer
1
0
Mile
1
N
Put-In
5 Mile Road
LINWOOD PARK
32
Root River
38
Short Road
31
1
4 Mile Road
Root River
5
Johnson Dog Park
2
4
Old Dam
Golf Cart Bridge
Johnson Park Golf Course
3
Golf Cart Bridge
6
N Green Bay Road
Hoods Creek
JOHNSON PARK
3 Mile Road
ARMSTRONG PARK (private)
38
Private Canoe Landing
River Bend Nature Center
Johnson Park Dr.
31
Ivan Rd.
7
CR-K
38
Northwestern Avenue
HORLICK PARK
Rapids Court
Takeout
38
Horlick Dam
Racine
Rapids Dr.
N Emmertsen Road
N Newman Road
31
Root River

Paddle Summary

The water is slow at the put-in, where you slip in along the low grass and mud banks, possibly with a mesh to step off of. Pass under the bridge on slow current. The river is about 50 feet wide and immediately closed in by large shade trees, mostly maples at this point.

The river comes around a curve that starts left and comes back around right at 0.9 mile; there's a backwater to the left there. You may glimpse some farm properties through the trees, but mostly this is secluded and the canopy closes in a bit. You may see some small riffles just before and after the 4 Mile Road bridge at 1.3 miles. The river bottom is sand and gravel, and in low water you may scrape a bit here. At 1.6 miles are some more riffles and a few boulders, nothing a beginner can't handle but something you might bounce along in low water as the river zigzags through. At 2.1 miles you'll get another several hundred feet of light riffles and low banks with park benches—Johnson Dog Park on river right—before passing under power lines and then a small footbridge at 2.2 miles. Riffles rise up as Hoods Creek joins from river right.

The bridge is for golf carts, and the next 0.5 mile is through the middle of the Johnson Park Golf Course, with manicured greens on either side and turtles sunning themselves along this wider and shallower section of the river. After the next cart bridge, the current picks up with some riffles and the river heads back into the cover of trees.

At 2.9 miles the river runs deeper and the waters are still. Banks to the right are steep; the left side is low and swampy. Pass under power lines 0.2 mile later. At 3.3

RIVER BEND NATURE CENTER

Situated on 78 wooded acres along the banks of the Root River, this excellent environmental education facility has been around since the late 1950s, operating as a day camp for kids, an animal rehab facility, and finally this nature center. The grounds are open every day for hikers and birders. The network of trails remains open in winter for snowshoeing and cross-country skiing (the facility rents equipment for those activities). The lands were purchased incrementally over the years using funds from private and corporate donations. Racine County purchased the property, formerly owned by the YWCA, and set it up as a nonprofit facility. Its operation is funded not with tax dollars but with more private donations and revenue earned from special events and rental of the facilities. Volunteers contribute a great deal as well.

The birding here is exceptional; many of the native species of Wisconsin have been spotted within the varied terrain. Watch for the tapping of maple trees, pancake breakfasts, guided hikes and birding, book discussions and lectures, volunteer clean-ups, summer camp for kids, book clubs, and other family-friendly events.

miles the high banks switch sides and the river takes a hairpin turn back south into a short stretch of riffles and under the power lines once more. The river is 40 feet wide here, and at 3.7 miles, after another turn under the power lines, you pass old concrete dam remains on either side.

At 4.4 miles, pass under the dual bridges of WI 31. Beyond that, the river is wide and shallow, with slow current over a sandy bottom until the river takes a right turn at a high bank with oaks along the top. Then it's a straight shot south in a wide and canal-like stretch for 0.5 mile, then another sharp bend west. At 5.9 miles pass under more power lines and paddle through a gentle S-curve, passing backwaters on the left at 6.3 miles. Houses start to appear more often, though mixed hardwood forest and brush still keep this area quite green. Armstrong Park appears on river right, with a large pavilion, picnic area, playground, and a small canoe landing; this is a private park, exclusive for employees of SC Johnson.

The river slows to nearly a standstill, and passable marshy areas may open up to either side. At 6.8 miles you enter the impoundment. There is wide water to the left, but head right (south) into the long, wide water. Beyond the trees and brush on the left (east) bank is the River Bend Nature Center. From where the river comes out into the wider water of the impoundment, there is still 0.9 mile of paddling left to get to the takeout. This is clearly marked on river left and features an asphalt ramp and small dock, all comfortably far from the Horlick Dam, which can be dangerous. (***Note:*** By 2024 Racine County authorities will be required by the Wisconsin DNR to modify or completely remove the dam, which may affect the paddling here.)

Coming around the bend into the final stretch above Horlick Dam.

9 Milwaukee River—Urban Paddle

This urban paddle starts in one of Milwaukee's many excellent city parks and follows an unlikely green corridor all the way into downtown. From your viewpoint on the river, there is little more than a couple high-rises and bridges to reveal the larger city surrounding. That soon changes as the city skyline takes over and you pass among historic buildings and neighborhoods before ending just past the confluence of the city's three rivers and right before the outlet to Lake Michigan.

County: Milwaukee
Start: Hubbard Park, N43 4.969' / W87 53.516'
End: Riverfront Launching Site/Bruce Street, N43 1.515' / W87 54.261'
Length: 4.9 miles one-way
Float time: About 2.5 hours
Difficulty rating: Easy
Rapids: A few riffles and one Class II chute
River type: Urban river with a greenway
Current: Gentle to nil
River gradient: 0.6 feet per mile downtown; 1.2 feet per mile upriver
River gauge: USGS 04087000 Milwaukee River at Milwaukee; consistently runnable below North Avenue bridge; dragging at the put-in at Hubbard Park likely when flows drop below 200 cfs
Season: Spring through fall
Land status: Public
Fees and permits: Launch fee if you take out at Riverfront Launch
Nearest city/town: Milwaukee
Maps: USGS Milwaukee; *DeLorme: Wisconsin Atlas & Gazetteer*: Page 39 D6
Boats used: Canoes, kayaks
Organizations: Milwaukee Riverkeeper, 1845 N. Farwell Ave., Ste. 100, Milwaukee 53202; (414) 287-0207; milwaukeeriverkeeper.org
Project Paddle Milwaukee; meetup.com/ProjectPaddleMilwaukee
Contacts: Visit Milwaukee, 648 N. Plankinton Ave. #425, Milwaukee 53203; (414) 273-3950; visitmilwaukee.org
Outfitters: Milwaukee Kayak Company, 318 S. Water St., Milwaukee 53204; (414) 301-2240; milwaukeekayak.com

Put-in/Takeout Information

To shuttle point/takeout: From Water Street in the Third Ward, head south and cross the Milwaukee River on the Water Street bridge. Take the first left across the bridge on South Water Street. Continue 0.5 mile and turn left into the boat launch area at Bruce Street.

To put-in from takeout: From the takeout, head north 0.5 mile on Water Street; turn right and cross the Water Street bridge. At 0.4 mile turn left onto Clybourn Street and take the ramp to I-43 North. Use exit 1C for I-43 toward Green Bay. Drive 3.5 miles and take exit 76A for Capitol Drive, taking Capitol 1.6 miles and then turning right onto Morris Boulevard. Drive 0.4 mile and turn right where Morris meets Menlo at a four-way stop. Follow that road right into Hubbard Park, passing the parking lot (where you'll park) on your right and going through two stone tunnels that lead to a cul-de-sac by the river. Drop your craft here and go back through the tunnels for parking.

River Overview

The Milwaukee River starts over 100 miles north, rising up through surprisingly wild surroundings before it ends up here in Wisconsin's largest city. Once it goes urban, however, there is still a good natural quality to it. Parks run one into the next along the river, indistinguishable to the paddler, who simply sees an awesome greenway. Then, as the river enters downtown, the architecture of the city skyline and its numerous bridges take over. This is a nice day trip if you start farther up the greenway—below Estabrook Park, where no portages are required. Alternatively, if you only want to paddle around downtown, you can put in and take out at Riverfront Launch, as the current in the downtown section is negligible.

Paddle Summary

Put in at Hubbard Park, but be sure to park your vehicle outside the tunnels into the park; there is no parking allowed at the put-in. Carry to the water's edge (less than 100 feet) and find a short trail down to the shoreline. In low water, this area can be shallow and cause scraping (or require stepping out of the craft) until you are clear into the middle of the river. Scraping here is not an indication that the rest of the journey will be the same.

At times there are few signs you are in the middle of Wisconsin's largest city. PREAMTIP SATASUK

FROM DIRTY RIVER TO PADDLING WATERWAY

The three rivers of Milwaukee—the Menomonee, the Kinnickinnic, and the Milwaukee—were not always the pleasant, accessible riverways we see today. In fact, in the late nineteenth century, all sewer systems simply dumped right into the Milwaukee River. The problem was so bad that the Milwaukee River Flushing Station was built in 1888 with the ability to pump up to 500 million gallons of Lake Michigan into the river to move the problem downstream and into the lake. The sewer system is much improved since those times, but the pump still operates in summer to keep a current in the last stretch of the river and to flush out some of the inevitable pollutants of such a large city.

The Milwaukee Riverkeeper is a nonprofit organization dedicated to protecting, improving, and restoring the rivers so that they may be used safely by all. Check out their 25-mile Milwaukee Urban Water Trail by going to their website (milwaukeeriverkeeper.org) to download a detailed map of the system and its takeouts and portages.

Paddle south and at 0.7 mile pass over the remains of the former Schlitz Brewery's ice house dam, which puts up some modest waves in higher water and in low water is easiest passed on the right. At 0.9 mile you may encounter a simple wave train passing two ledges as you reach the high Locust Street bridge. Stay right, keeping away from the sides. You can't always hear the traffic noise, and at some points birdsong and the breeze in the trees are enough to eliminate it. A few high-rise apartments poking up on the skyline may be the only things to dispel the illusion that you are paddling a rural waterway.

At 1.1 miles you pass Riverside Park and its landing on the left. Oak savanna is visible up the hillside, part of the Milwaukee Rotary Centennial Arboretum, a patchwork of woods within Riverside Park and along the river. A wheelchair-accessible canoe launch is here as well. Notice the trails on either side of the river: On river right is the Beerline Trail; on the left is Oak Leaf Trail.

In 2018, the Estabrook Dam to the north was removed, meaning the next dam is 14 miles north in Thiensville. Otherwise, only Estabrook Falls and Kletzsch Falls—north of here 1.5 and 5.2 miles, respectively—still require portages.

At 1.6 miles you come to the high, concrete North Avenue bridge, with lampposts along the top. Formerly a dam site, the channel beneath is a straight shot of surprising Class I–II rapids. Typically this is a sizable wave train that's easily run. Keep center and straight. If waters are too high or you prefer to skip this section, take out on either side before the bridge and portage. The channel runs a couple hundred feet and ends in a wide shallow area at the North Avenue Dam Pedestrian Bridge, which connects the Oak Leaf Trail to the start of the Beerline Trail on river right.

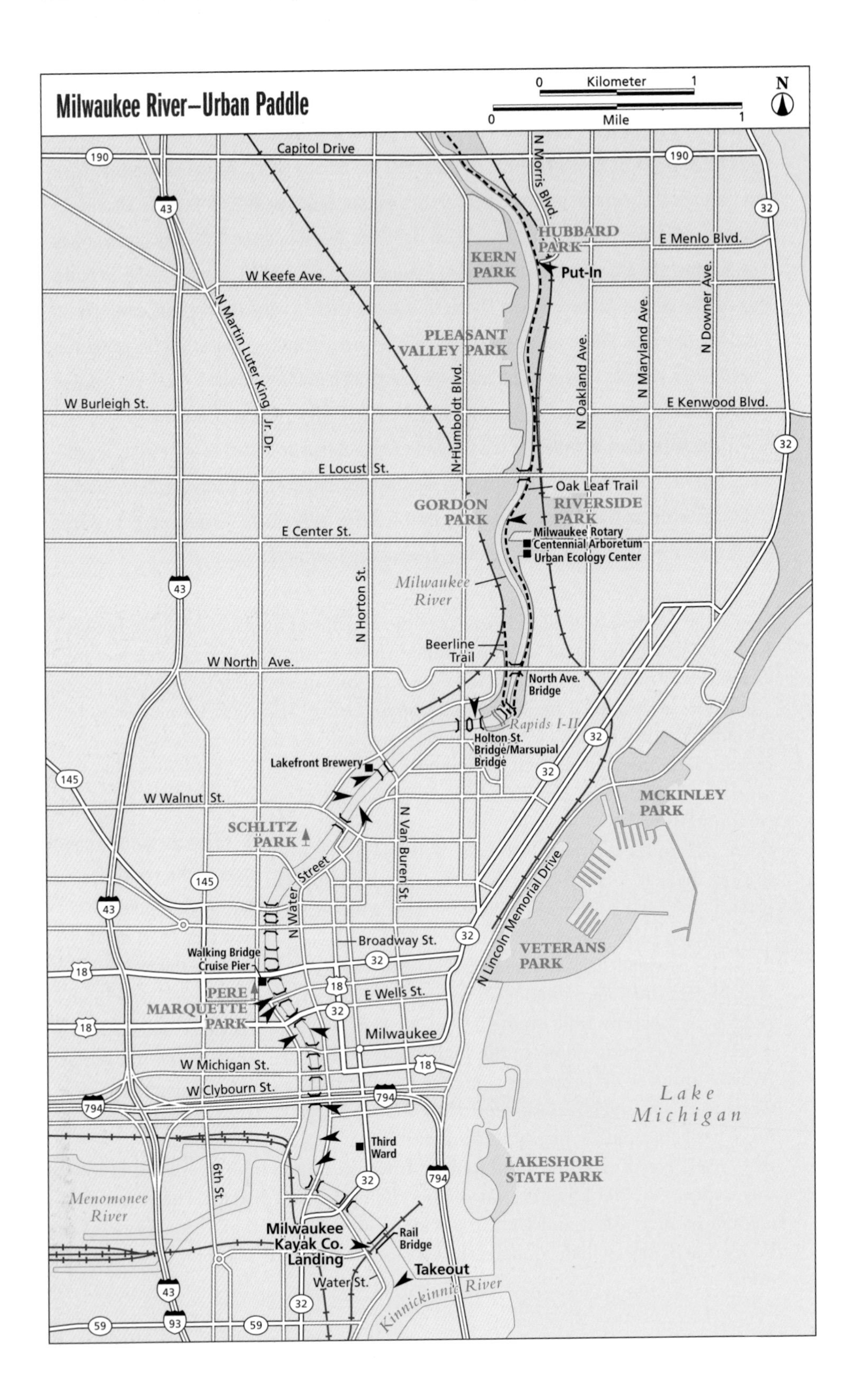

Milwaukee River—Urban Paddle
0 Kilometer 1
0 Mile 1
N
Capitol Drive
190
43
N Morris Blvd.
HUBBARD PARK
E Menlo Blvd.
32
KERN PARK
Put-In
W Keefe Ave.
N Martin Luter King Jr. Dr.
PLEASANT VALLEY PARK
N Oakland Ave.
N Maryland Ave.
N Downer Ave.
N Humboldt Blvd.
W Burleigh St.
E Kenwood Blvd.
E Locust St.
Oak Leaf Trail
GORDON PARK
RIVERSIDE PARK
E Center St.
Milwaukee Rotary Centennial Arboretum
Urban Ecology Center
Milwaukee River
N Horton St.
Beerline Trail
W North Ave.
North Ave. Bridge
Rapids I-II
Holton St. Bridge/Marsupial Bridge
Lakefront Brewery
145
W Walnut St.
N Van Buren St.
SCHLITZ PARK
MCKINLEY PARK
N Water Street
N Lincoln Memorial Drive
Broadway St.
Walking Bridge Cruise Pier
VETERANS PARK
18
PERE MARQUETTE PARK
E Wells St.
Milwaukee
W Michigan St.
W Clybourn St.
794
Lake Michigan
Third Ward
6th St.
LAKESHORE STATE PARK
Menomonee River
Milwaukee Kayak Co. Landing
Rail Bridge
Takeout
Water St.
Kinnickinnic River
93
59

An old swing bridge on the Milwaukee River Preamtip Satasuk

At 2 miles pass a storm sewer pipe on river right—along with a takeout for restaurant/bar access above the bank—then pass under the Humboldt Avenue bridge. The green space begins to give way to condos. You are now paddling through historical brewery territory. At 2.4 miles pass under the Holton Street Viaduct with its special Marsupial Bridge—a multiuse path hanging under the roadway—and reach Lakefront Brewery on river right. Find a landing and parking there, and consider a brewery tour. Just past here is public access amid clearly marked private berths on either bank. The landing on river left is walking distance from Brady Street, a popular neighborhood for food, drink, and eclectic shops. There is a 4-hour mooring time limit.

Now begins the litany of bridges. At 2.7 miles you'll see the Pleasant Street bridge with its Cream City brick towers. Just past it on river right is Schlitz Park with a canoe landing. The river current is minimal, and retaining walls on either side make it more like a canal. Natural water outflow enters through pipes on river right, just before the Art Deco Cherry Street bridge at 2.9 miles. Downtown, with all its tall buildings, is now in plain view. Then follows the Knapp Street bridge at 3.1 miles, the Juneau Avenue bridge at 3.2 miles, a pedestrian bridge at 3.3 miles, and a drawbridge for State Street at 3.4 miles, just past Usinger's, the famous sausage maker. After State Street is Pere Marquette Park, with a private pier for river cruises; just downriver, before the Kilbourn Avenue bridge, is a canoe/kayak launch—all on river right.

The Riverwalk is on both sides of the river here. The tubes on either side downriver of the bridge are sewer discharge pipes for overflow periods—not a place to be when there's water coming out of them. Pass the Wells Street bridge at 3.6 miles and find Rock Bottom Brewpub on river right with its own dock. Pass under an enclosed bridge between two office buildings, then under the Wisconsin Avenue bridge at 3.7 miles. The Michigan Street bridge follows, then in quick succession come the Clybourn Street bridge, I-794 bridges, and the St. Paul Avenue bridge into the Historic Third Ward, a revitalized area of shops, bars, and restaurants.

At the end of Buffalo Street on river left is more docking space for visiting restaurants and bars along here. At 4.2 miles the Menomonee River comes in from the right under a large steel railroad bridge. (You can paddle upstream with no visible current almost 2 miles before it becomes too shallow.) Just before the Water Street bridge at 4.3 miles, there is a kayak launch—a step down to the water—on the end of South 1st Place in the wide area on river right.

At 4.4 miles pass the Broadway Street bridge. The outfitter's dock is on river right, just before giant concrete towers at 4.6 miles. See the now-abandoned swing bridge permanently swung open in the middle of the river. Past this, the Kinnickinnic River meets the Milwaukee, and beyond it to the left is the passage to Lake Michigan. Lake paddling is not very good, although the area is behind a breakwater. The Kinnickinnic, like the Menomonee, is navigable almost 2 miles upstream. Finally, the Riverfront Launching Site, at a bend in Water Street that intersects Bruce Street, is just ahead on river right at 4.9 miles. There is a daily launch fee for a nonmotorized boat.

Downtown Milwaukee

10 Milwaukee River–Newburg to Fredonia

This rural stretch of the Milwaukee actually runs north before it turns south to its urban destination. Thanks in part to the Riveredge Nature Center, this section is wooded and wild. A challenge of riffles of the scraping variety and sometimes deadfall navigation, the river is nonetheless wide enough to find a channel and is divided frequently by small islands. Most paddlers are pleasantly surprised by the amount of wildlife on a river more often associated with the city. After a brief pass through a small town, the river widens and slows for the last straight shot to a county park.

County: Washington
Start: Fireman's Park in Newburg, N43 25.990' / W88 2.627'
End: Waubedonia Park, N43 28.104' / W87 58.390'
Length: 10.6 miles one-way
Float time: About 4 hours
Difficulty rating: Easy; moderate due to scraping when water levels are low
Rapids: Riffles
River type: Wooded pastoral
Current: Gentle to moderate
River gradient: 7 feet per mile
River gauge: USGS 04086600 Milwaukee River near Cedarburg; runnable at levels as low as 200 cfs, but dragging becomes frequent below 300 cfs
Season: Spring, midsummer, after a good rain
Land status: Private, with public landings
Fees and permits: No fees or permits required
Nearest city/town: Saukville
Maps: USGS Newburg, Port Washington West; *DeLorme: Wisconsin Atlas & Gazetteer*: Page 39 5A
Boats used: Canoes, kayaks
Organizations: River Alliance of Wisconsin, 147 S. Butler St., Ste. 2, Madison 53703; (608) 257-2424; wisconsinrivers.org
Outfitters: Sherper's, 128 N. Franklin St., Port Washington 53074; (262) 536-4210; sherpers.com
Local information: Riveredge Nature Center, 4458 Hawthorne Dr., Saukville 53080; (262) 375-2715; riveredgenaturecenter.org

Put-in/Takeout Information

To shuttle point/takeout: From WI 57 on the east side of Fredonia, take the Highland Drive exit and go west 1.6 miles; Waubedonia Park is on the left. The takeout is an old asphalt boat landing. The park has restrooms and parking.
To put-in from takeout: From the takeout, turn left onto CR A and CR H (Fredonia Avenue); at 0.3 mile, go left on CR I. Drive 2 miles, turn right onto Hawthorne Drive, and continue 3.4 miles to Newburg. Turn right onto Main Street and drive 0.3 mile; the park entrance is on the right. Drive down the hill; the put-in is anywhere along the river here to the right. Parking and some in-season portable toilets are available.

A deer crosses downriver on the Milwaukee.

River Overview

The Milwaukee River is best known for the section that runs through the city of the same name, an urban river. But the upper reaches may as well be a hundred miles away—in fact, its headwaters are. Development along its banks is often very limited, and it can seem as though you are very far from civilization. Clear waters run, often with riffles, over a sand and gravel bottom, and wildlife is abundant. Dam removal over the years has done much to restore the riparian environment and make the river more navigable. In this stretch, the best paddling is when the waters are high; later in summer, this can become a challenging run due to frequent shallow spots that may require getting out of your craft. Even then, if you don't mind the extra effort, it may still be worth it. Deadfall is common, as is aquatic grass, but the abundance of herons is notable, and we have seen deer cross right in front of us and eagles feed along a rocky shore. Anglers will find smallmouth bass and northern pike in deeper areas.

Paddle Summary

From the put-in through the grassy bank downriver of the old mill race at the opposite end of the park, the river heads into the woods with a high bank on the townside on river right. After that first left turn at the tall bank, the banks are low and brushy. Low water will mean choosing the best path. At 1.1 miles the river finds three (or more) paths through a low spot, creating some islands in the middle. Deadfall and water levels may force your decision on which way to go here, and in dry seasons, this is the most likely place you may drag on this journey. If you are clear here, the rest of the ride should be fine.

At 1.8 miles, the river breaks from its westerly course and heads north. Look for the shale shelves in the shallows. At 2.7 miles the river bends left; you can see an old barn beyond the banks in front of you. The river goes west, with some views of fields on the right after that; a short distance later you'll pass a small drop over a row of boulders all the way across the river. At 3.8 miles the river splits around a few wooded islands. Beyond that the river takes a slow curve left, passing some residences set back from the banks on the right.

At 5 miles at another bend, the river shallows out a bit and passes some nice houses on river right. At 5.5 miles pass under the CR A bridge and the river switches back east again; Riverside Road begins to follow on the left. The water widens out; it gets grassy late in summer, sometimes adding work to the paddling if the grass is thick enough. At 6.3 miles you can see on river left where Riverside Road comes to a right-angle turn and bends away from the river headed due north. At 6.9 miles the North Branch of the Milwaukee River joins from the left. At about 8 miles the river gets wide and slow as it enters the Waubeka area. Power lines span the river at 8.2 miles, and River Road follows along beyond the brush to the left. You'll pass a low, grassy island at 8.7 miles; the left channel may be the deeper here. An access point for a takeout is posted "Private," but an easement gives access to anglers and hikers.

RIVEREDGE NATURE CENTER

Established in 1968 on a 380-acre parcel of land just outside Newburg, the center has hosted a variety of scientific studies. It is part of a sturgeon project with the Wisconsin Department of Natural Resources, aiming to produce a self-sustaining population of sturgeon in the river. Visitors can explore ponds and prairie, forest and wetland, and of course the Milwaukee River, which runs past its northern edge. The property offers over 10 miles of trails for hiking (or skiing and snowshoeing in winter) and a natural play area for children. Watch their events calendar for special programs and presentations. The center is open daily, with special hours on holidays. There is a trail fee for nonmembers, and no dogs are allowed (Riveredge Nature Center, 4458 Hawthorne Dr., Saukville 53080; 262-375-2715; riveredgenaturecenter.org).

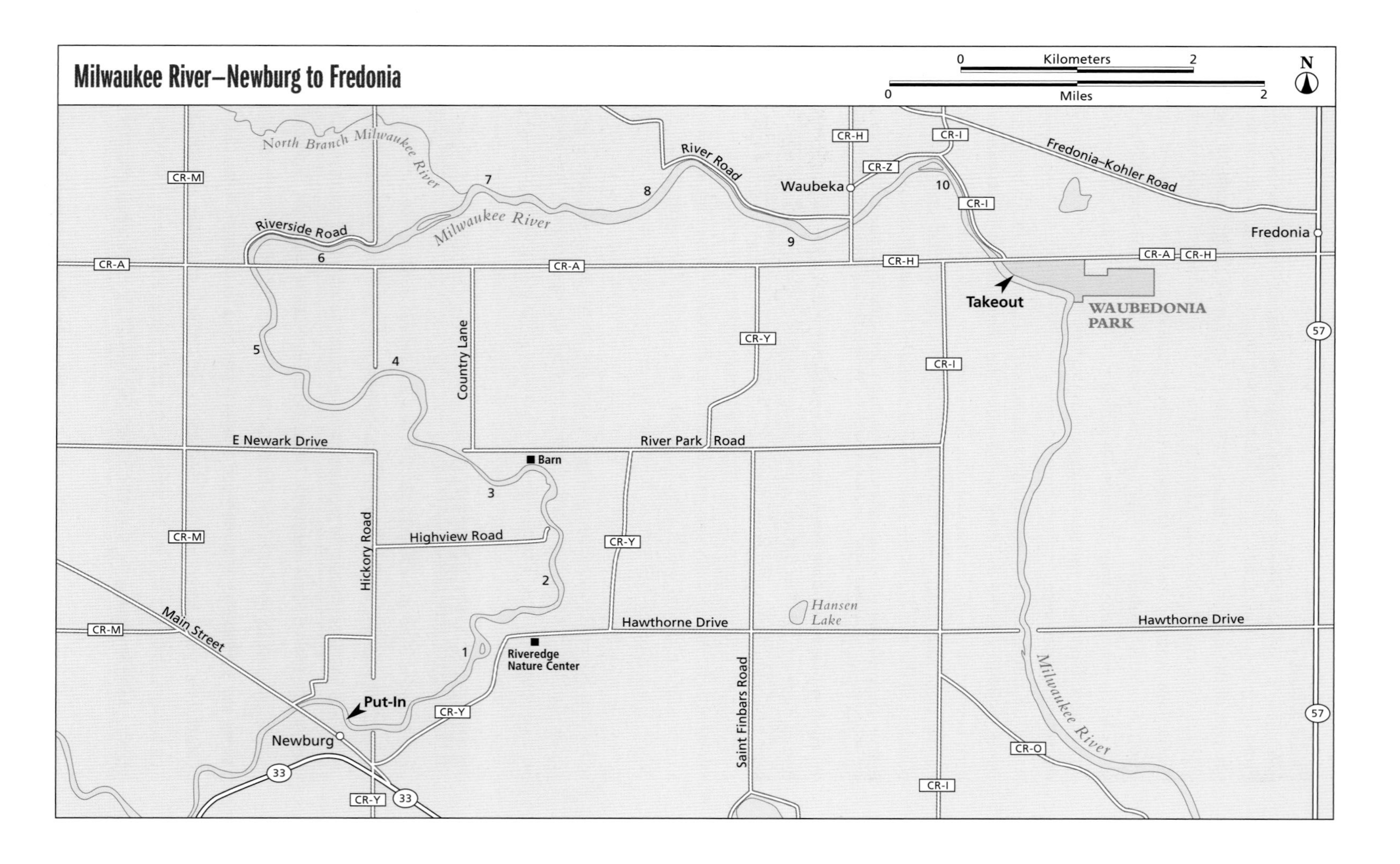
Milwaukee River—Newburg to Fredonia
Kilometers
Miles
0
2
N
North Branch Milwaukee River
Milwaukee River
Riverside Road
River Road
Waubeka
Fredonia–Kohler Road
Fredonia
WAUBEDONIA PARK
Takeout
Put-In
Newburg
Main Street
Country Lane
E Newark Drive
River Park Road
Barn
Highview Road
Hickory Road
Hawthorne Drive
Riveredge Nature Center
Saint Finbars Road
Hansen Lake
CR-A
CR-H
CR-I
CR-M
CR-O
CR-Y
CR-Z
33
57
1
2
3
4
5
6
7
8
9
10

Thick grasses in the Milwaukee River

At 9.3 miles, just before the WI 84 bridge, the river bends left and passes through a modest boulder garden that requires steering in low water and can show riffles in higher water. Pass under the bridge and you are in the center of Waubeka. On the other side of town, the river comes right up to CR I at 9.9 miles, where there are some concrete stairs up. The river turns south, with the highway following above the left bank. Just before this bend in the river, a sort of shortcut across the corner on river right opens up when water levels are high. Pass under the power lines after the turn; the river widens out to over 100 feet. This final stretch is straight all the way to the CR A bridge. Just before the bridge, you could pull out at the park on river left. Pass under the bridge at 10.5 miles, and Waubedonia Park shows up on river left. The takeout is shallow and a mix of broken asphalt, sand, and mud.

11 Horicon Marsh Canoe Trail

Starting in a narrow segment of the Rock River, this trip begins in a wooded marsh. Then the canoe trail emerges into vast open wetlands, following channels through cattails and grasses. A haven for birders, Horicon Marsh has national and state protection. There is rarely any current here; it is a paddle trip for lingering and wildlife viewing. The journey ends in the town of Horicon.

County: Dodge
Start: Greenhead Boat Landing, N43 30.339' / W88 35.486'
End: Legion Auxiliary Park, N43 26.966' / W88 37.854'
Length: 7.2 miles one-way
Float time: About 4 hours
Difficulty rating: Easy
Rapids: None
River type: Marsh river and channels
Current: None
River gradient: Less than 1 foot per mile
River gauge: USGS 05424057 Rock River at Horicon; runnable at all times
Season: Spring through fall; best for birding during migration periods
Land status: Public
Fees and permits: No fees or permits required
Nearest city/town: Horicon
Maps: USGS Horicon, Mayville North, Mayville South; PDF online at horiconmarsh.org; *DeLorme: Wisconsin Atlas & Gazetteer*: Page 46 D1
Boats used: Canoes, kayaks, johnboats
Contacts: Horicon Marsh National Wildlife Refuge, W4279 Headquarters Rd., Mayville 53050; (920) 387-2658; fws.gov/midwest/horicon

Horicon Marsh State Wildlife Area, N7725 Hwy 28, Horicon 53032; (920) 387-7860; dnr.wi.gov/topic/lands/WildlifeAreas/horicon
Outfitters: Horicon Marsh Boat Tours, Blue Heron Landing, 305 Mill St., Horicon 53032; (920) 485-4663; horiconmarsh.com
Local information: Watch for paddling events hosted by the Horicon Marsh International Education Center; N7725 WI Hwy. 28, Horicon 53032; (920) 387-7890; horiconmarsh.org.

Put-in/Takeout Information

To shuttle point/takeout: Come into Horicon on WI 33 from the west, and follow the road to just before the bridge over the Rock River. Turn right onto Barstow Street and drive 1 block to its end. The takeout is a crumbling asphalt boat landing next to a gravel parking lot with no facilities.
To put-in from takeout: From the takeout, drive out on Barstow Street; turn right onto Vine Street to cross the Rock River bridge. Drive 2 blocks and turn right (east) onto Lake Street. Go 0.5 mile and turn left onto WI 28/Clason Street; continue 3.3 miles. Turn left onto Bay View Road, drive 0.8 mile, then take the second left onto Green Head Road. Follow it 1 mile to its end, making a right-angle turn at the halfway mark to stay on the road. Park in the gravel lot and use the simple sloping gravel entry to the water. There are no facilities.

River Overview

This paddle trip is part of the Rock River, the 300-mile river that becomes wide and slow as it crosses through Wisconsin and heads to the Mississippi down through Illinois. But that fact is secondary; Horicon Marsh, through which it flows at this point, is a natural site of great importance. The 32,000 acres of wetlands are divided into the Horicon National Wildlife Refuge to the north and the Horicon State Wildlife Area to the south, where this canoe trail is located. This is the largest freshwater cattail marsh in the United States and a significant birding site known for its abundance of feathered visitors during migration periods. The paddling is entirely flatwater.

Paddle Summary

This can also be done as an out-and-back paddle, as the current is negligible throughout, and often it's the wind that determines how hard you'll need to paddle. Landmarks are very few, so these instructions may seem a little loose.

From the Greenhead Boat Landing, go left with just the tiniest bit of current on a channel that is 60 feet wide. You can also paddle upstream a bit to explore. Orange arrow signs mark the trail throughout. The canoe trail at this point is sheltered; bordered by swampy areas, abundant willows, and tall grasses; and showing occasional deadfall but nothing that hinders your passing. Right after the put-in, pass a small wooden observation platform surrounded by rock. The trail goes right and snakes through some trees, mostly willows.

AND THEN THERE WAS MARSH

As with many things in Wisconsin, we have the glaciers to thank for Horicon Marsh. Once the site of a glacial lake, the marsh is now the largest freshwater cattail marsh in the United States. Part of the Wisconsinan glacier known as the Green Bay Lobe ground its way into the neighborhood about 70,000 years ago, carving out this basin. When the lobe retreated—that is, melted—12,000 years ago, it deposited rock and sediment (glacial drift) to form a sort of ridge called a moraine. Water gathered behind it, creating Glacial Lake Horicon. The Rock River eventually wore the moraine away and drained the lake, but not before silt and peat filled in the lake's former basin, which eventually became the marsh.

As fast as the ice fled, humans moved in. An arrowhead found here dates back to around 11,200 years ago. A nineteenth-century dam brought back the lake for a short while, but local landowners fought it. Attempts were made to drain the marsh for farming, but that plan didn't work out either. Finally, the State of Wisconsin established the Horicon Marsh Refuge to protect the area.

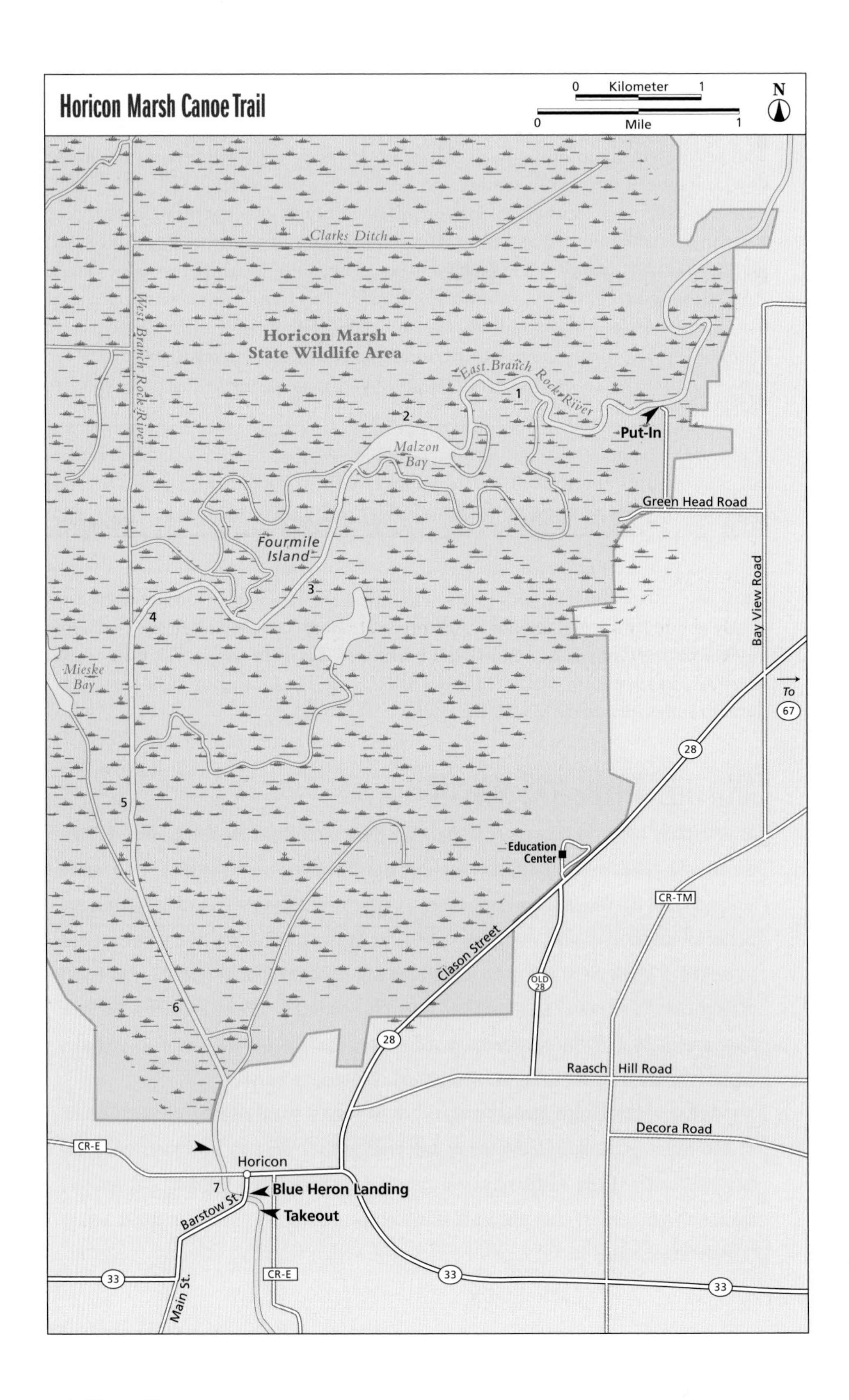
Horicon Marsh Canoe Trail
0 Kilometer 1
0 Mile 1
N
Clarks Ditch
Horicon Marsh
State Wildlife Area
West Branch Rock River
East Branch Rock River
1
2
Put-In
Malzon Bay
Green Head Road
Fourmile Island
3
4
Bay View Road
Mieske Bay
To 67
28
5
Education Center
CR-TM
Clason Street
OLD 28
6
28
Raasch Hill Road
Decora Road
CR-E
Horicon
7
Blue Heron Landing
Barstow St.
Takeout
33
CR-E
Main St.
33
33

Before you reach the open spaces of Horicon Marsh, the Rock River is narrow and sheltered.
PREAMTIP SATASUK

By about 1 mile you are out in the open, although cattails and grasses may often block your view of the horizon. Wind becomes a factor from this point on. At 1.2 miles pass another bend to the left (southwest) and pass a clump of willows on river right. Despite your being out in the open, deadfall is still possible.

At 1.5 miles a few willows rise on either side of the channel, and straight ahead you'll see a water tower far away in the town of Horicon. At 1.9 miles the flow splits around a grassy island; bear right, following the little orange canoe trail sign. The water doubles in width and stretches into a long, narrow, and shallow pond known as Malzon Bay. Pass a couple grassy islands as your course bends gradually southward. You can see farms off in the distance before you and wind turbines far behind you. You may see openings in the grass to the right, but stay straight through here on a south-southwest course.

A long collection of trees off to the left runs parallel to your course, and in the distance is Fourmile Island. At 3.3 miles, when you've about passed the end of that island, look for a canoe trail sign. Turn right here, heading northwest for about 1,000 feet before the trail switches back left and southwest again. The wide-open water here may be intimidating, but just stay right, look straight ahead to a grassy island, and scan the grasses for another little orange canoe trail sign. As you paddle forward, you will see one that may have been hidden in the grass. As long as you are heading west and southwest, you are on course.

At 4.1 miles the channel joins a rather straight north–south canal, shown on the map as Main Ditch. You are coming at a southwest angle and then taking a gentle left to head due south. The channel narrows and heads toward a water tower far in the distance. At 4.3 miles you enter more wide water; stay along the right on this long

A blue-flag iris in Horicon Marsh PREAMTIP SATASUK

straight cut (human-made). There are trees straight ahead in the distance, and at about 4.7 miles they are as close as the banks. As you come up on 5 miles you'll see large cottonwoods, likely candidates for eagle nests. At 5.1 miles the banks on the right end and you have open water there. Stay straight, hugging the left bank and using the trees and the distant water tower as your guide.

Check with the Horicon Marsh International Education Center for bird and wildflower checklists.

By 5.5 miles the course is bending a bit to the left, putting you on a southeasterly path that heads just slightly left of a lollipop water tower now on the horizon. Keep following the line of trees. At 6.1 miles there is open water to the left; again, keep straight, using the right bank to guide you now. Another sign appears at 6.4 miles, directing you to the right. Follow it and you will see an industrial site ahead. At 6.7 miles there is a boat landing on river right. At 6.9 miles you pass under the Lake Street bridge, the first of two. Beyond that is a park with a fishing pier on river right. The river turns to the left a bit and passes under the concrete Vine Street bridge. On the left are the local outfitter and Blue Heron Landing. As the river comes around to the right, you will see the takeout on river right and a Dam Ahead sign. The water here is slow and high. Step out at the asphalt ramp on the right.

12 Mecan River

A long and winding paddle, the Mecan passes through banks that are high and then low, grassy and then wooded, narrow and then wide. The tight windy stretches through thick forest at the center of this trip can challenge your navigation skills, while much of the rest is lazy and peaceful with few signs of development. The final couple miles are mostly wetlands, with some tree coverage.

County: Marquette
Start: Germania Dam, N43 53.609' / W89 15.529'
End: CR C bridge, N43 48.905' / W89 12.365'
Length: 10.7 miles one-way
Float time: About 4.5 hours
Difficulty rating: Moderate for boat control; difficult when deadfall isn't maintained
Rapids: Some riffles, one short Class I
River type: Wooded pastoral then marshland
Current: Moderate
River gradient: 2.6 feet per mile
River gauge: None; always runnable, but avoid paddling when water exceeds the banks
Season: Spring through fall
Land status: Private, with public landings/access
Fees and permits: No fees or permits required
Nearest city/town: Montello
Maps: USGS Neshkoro, Princeton West; *DeLorme: Wisconsin Atlas & Gazetteer*: Page 44 A2
Boats used: Canoes, kayaks
Organizations: River Alliance of Wisconsin, 147 S. Butler St., Ste. 2, Madison 53703; (608) 257-2424; wisconsinrivers.org
Contacts: Germania Marsh Wildlife Area; dnr.wi.gov/topic/lands/WildlifeAreas/germania.html
Outfitters: Mecan River Outfitters & Lodge, W720 Hwy. 23, Princeton 54968; (920) 295-3439; mecanriveroutfitters.com

Put-in/Takeout Information

To shuttle point/takeout: From Montello head east on WI 23 for 7.3 miles. Turn right onto CR C and drive 1.3 miles. Cross the Mecan River; the takeout drive is immediately on the right, a half circle of dirt and gravel. The unimproved landing is a gentle slope of grass and mud upriver of the bridge. Park along the side of the turnout. There are no facilities.

To put-in from takeout: From the takeout, backtrack north on CR C to WI 23. Go left (west) for 2 miles and turn right onto CR N. Stay on the marked CR N as it makes frequent turns onto other roads. Where it joins with CR J, turn right; at 0.5 mile it parts with J and goes left. Drive another 1.7 miles on CR N. At Eagle Road turn left and go 0.1 mile. Take the dirt road on your right to the left of the church there—it's public, despite signs and appearances—and go straight to the end, where there is a gravel parking lot. You must carry your craft on a grassy trail to the dam and take the trail down to the right out onto a sloping triangle of land between the spillway and a flatwater overflow area. Launch from the sand-and-gravel point, taking care to be out of the current from the dam. There is an alternative parking area on the north side of the dam, reachable via CR N if you continue through Germania, but it is less convenient for the carry to the water.

River Overview

The Mecan (pronounced "McCann") is a lesson in boat control. The upper stretches are spring-fed and popular with trout anglers. A dam at Germania helps maintain the Germania Marsh, a state wildlife area and prime area for birders. But below the Germania dam, the waters are dark and clear as the Mecan winds its way to where it empties into the Fox River, about 0.8 river mile beyond the takeout for this segment. Water levels have never gone too low to run, thanks to the springs upriver. Deadfall is common, and though outfitters maintain it, the task sometimes overwhelms. The bottom is sandy in places, and sandbars rise up at river bends, especially in low water. Anglers can expect walleye, northern pike, and even catfish, plus smallmouth bass in July.

Paddle Summary

Push off from the flatwater side of the point and paddle into the current from the dam. The river is 55 feet wide here, with grassy banks full of wildflowers backed by thick brush and trees. Within 500 feet pass some residences on the right. At 0.3 mile the river narrows at a bend to the right, sending you through a 40-foot run of riffles/Class I rapids as you pass under the CR N bridge as you are leaving the little village of Germania. The mud and grass banks are about 5 feet high, and the trees stand off

THE ENDANGERED BLUES

While you are out paddling the Mecan, keep an eye out for something very rare and special: the Karner blue butterfly. Classified as an endangered species, the Karner blue—or *Lycaeides melissa samuelis*, as it's known to biologists—appears only in isolated locations in the upper Midwest and in New York. The largest population in the world can be found in Necedah National Wildlife Refuge in central Wisconsin, but another good place to find them is Germania Marsh, just above the dam on the Mecan, where the Wisconsin DNR is trying to restore upland dry prairie. What brings them to these places is an abundance of blue lupine. Scientists are still trying to determine how the combination of shade and open spaces, and the wild lupine in each, affect the butterflies, but there is little doubt that loss of habitat is the species' greatest threat.

Interestingly, this butterfly was first identified by Vladimir Nabokov, the author of the controversial novel *Lolita*. The name comes from a town in New York where the species was first spotted.

The put-in below the dam on the Mecan River PREAMTIP SATASUK

from the river, giving no shade. At 0.8 mile a narrow flatwater channel of the river joins from river right.

The river becomes serpentine here until it widens out and straightens, taking on a canal-like look by the 2-mile mark. Even in this open area, there is more deadfall than you might expect, but the wide river makes it easy to avoid. By 2.7 miles the river narrows to 35 feet and there is very little sign of development. Pass under the low, concrete CR J bridge at 3.3 miles. The canopy closes in at this point.

Old (and not so old) maps of the river show quite different pathways for the Mecan. The river is constantly changing and branching out to create grassy islands. You will encounter several diverging points where you will need to choose what looks best under the conditions. Right before another bridge at 5 miles, the river does a tricky turn through some possible deadfall and sandbar before coming under the road. This is CR N again, and the bridge, with a "#7" on it, is rather low. In high water be prepared to portage here. Just after this point the river splits through the forest. Stay left; this branch may be better maintained. The river is very narrow here, often down to about 10 feet across, with abundant twists and turns. The faster current and the potential for deadfall can give paddlers a challenge. This 0.8 mile makes the Kickapoo River look straight as an arrow.

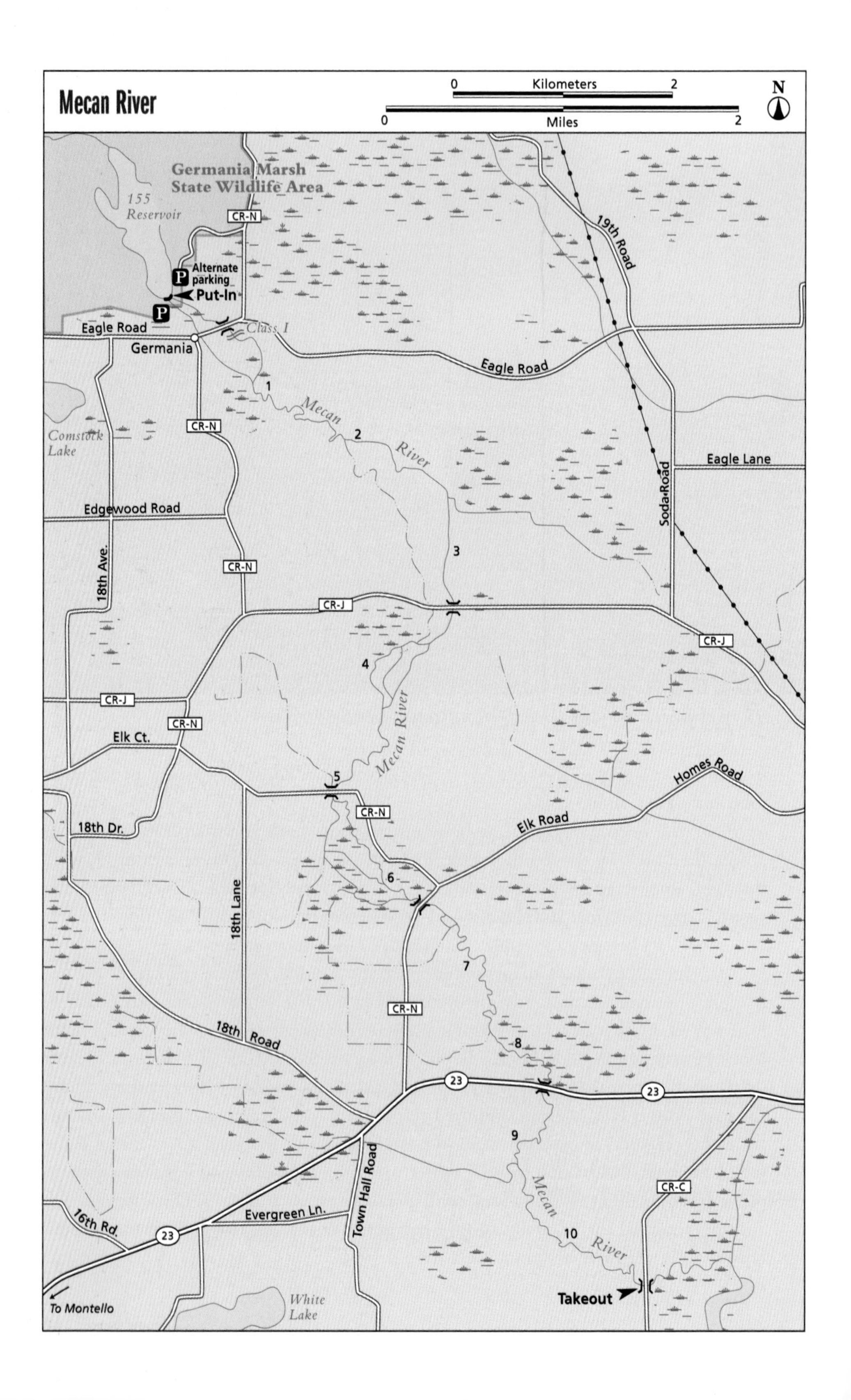

Mecan River
0
Kilometers
2
0
Miles
2
N
Germania Marsh
State Wildlife Area
155
Reservoir
CR-N
Alternate parking
Put-In
Eagle Road
Class I
Germania
19th Road
Eagle Road
1
Mecan
2
River
CR-N
Comstock
Lake
Eagle Lane
Soda Road
Edgewood Road
18th Ave.
3
CR-N
CR-J
CR-J
4
CR-J
Mecan River
CR-N
Elk Ct.
5
Homes Road
CR-N
Elk Road
18th Dr.
6
18th Lane
7
CR-N
18th
Road
8
23
23
9
Town Hall Road
Mecan
CR-C
16th Rd.
Evergreen Ln.
10
River
23
Takeout
To Montello
White
Lake

A small drop beneath the first bridge on the Mecan River Preamtip Satasuk

At 5.9 miles you leave the trees and enter a grassy marsh area. The current remains strong, and a branch not taken joins from the left just before you reach the juncture with a branch on the right (which you parted from back near the bridge). The river has widened out to 40 feet. Trees come closer along the edges, potentially offering some shade. At 6.2 miles pass under bridge #8, again on CR N. There is an unimproved landing on river right if the bridge is too low to get under. The river splits again just 0.2 mile past the bridge, coming together again about 0.2 mile later. Pines start to appear in the tree coverage, and the river widens on a big turn and bends left as you approach WI 23 and pass under bridge #9 at 8.4 miles.

At 9.1 miles another stream comes in from the right; keep with the current, heading left. The river slows as it passes through a wide-open grassy area, and as you near the landing, you are likely to encounter anglers in canoes or johnboats. At 10.6 miles the river forms a sort of Y, with a backwater to the right and the continuing river to the left. Follow a little fishhook turn and you'll see the sign for the takeout on river right, just before the CR C bridge.

13 Wisconsin River—Lower Dells to Pine Island

Beginning at the very end of the sandstone formations, this segment of the Wisconsin comes out of a mile of sculpted outcrops and then follows a wide path full of shifting sandbars and occasional side channels that are explorable when water levels allow. Its southerly course avoids much of the tourist and "duck" boat (amphibious vehicle) traffic and finds a wide but suddenly quiet and secluded river.

County: Columbia, Sauk
Start: Newport Park in Lake Delton, N43 36.174' / W89 45.683'
End: Pine Island Boat Landing, N43 32.580' / W89 34.939'
Length: 13.7 miles one-way
Float time: About 4 hours
Difficulty rating: Easy; moderate when windy
Rapids: None
River type: Wide pastoral with shifting sandbars
Current: Slow to moderate
River gradient: 1.3 feet per mile
River gauge: USGS 05404000 Wisconsin River at Wisconsin Dells; minimum runnable level 3,000 cfs
Season: Spring, summer, rainy periods in fall
Land status: Private, with public landings
Fees and permits: Municipal boat launch fee at Newport Park
Nearest city/town: Lake Delton
Maps: USGS Lewiston, Pine Island, Wisconsin Dells South; *DeLorme: Wisconsin Atlas & Gazetteer*: Page 43 D5
Boats used: Canoes, kayaks, johnboats; small motorized craft before Aug
Organizations: River Alliance of Wisconsin, 147 S. Butler St., Ste. 2, Madison 53703; (608) 257-2424; wisconsinrivers.org
Contacts: Pine Island Wildlife Area; dnr.wi.gov/topic/lands/wildlifeareas/pineisland.html
Outfitters: Rivers Edge Resort, 30 CR A, Wisconsin Dells 53965; (608) 253-6600; riversedgeresort.com

Put-in/Takeout Information

To shuttle point/takeout: From Wisconsin Dells Parkway/US 12 in Lake Delton, take CR A east 4.7 miles. Turn left onto CR T and drive 2.8 miles. Turn left onto Levee Road and go 5.4 miles; the gravel road to the landing is on the left. A gravel lot is next to the river; there are no facilities.

To put-in from takeout: From the takeout, backtrack on Levee Road and go right on CR T for 2.8 miles. Turn right onto CR A and continue 3.1 miles to Newport Park, on the right. There are restrooms, water, and ample parking. The boat ramp is concrete, and there is a self-pay station for fees.

River Overview

This portion of the 430-mile Wisconsin River is far from its humble origins and here takes on the great width and frequent sandbars the Lower Wisconsin is known for. But what makes this part of the river special is its geology as it passes through the famous Wisconsin Dells. This is where Wisconsin's most touristy element meets one of its most amazing natural places. The river narrows as it runs through beautiful sandstone formations. The Kilbourn Dam in downtown Wisconsin Dells separates the Upper Dells from the Lower Dells. Both are extraordinary, and both are popular with tour boats, duck boats, pleasure craft, and paddlers. The Lower Dells, however, lose the crowds within a mile of their start, and once you pass the last of the most dramatic rock formations, the river opens up, showing sandbars, islands, a couple side channels, and more wildlife. It can get quite shallow, often restricting passage to paddlers and even then requiring some river reading and navigation to get through without having to step out of your craft. The scenery is arguably better in the Upper Dells, but the abundance of boats and their wakes there detracts from the experience, and higher than average water levels can create dangerous currents. This section is good for fall colors; decent for fishing, especially bass; and nice for spotting shorebirds and waterfowl. Pine Island Wildlife Area, at the end of the paddle, is designated an Important Bird Area. Odds are good you'll see an eagle or some deer. The size and location of the levee running along the river should give some indication of where the river can go in flood periods.

THE FORMATION OF THE DELLS

The Dells of Wisconsin—the river gorge, canyons, cliffs, and rock outcrops—run along 5 miles of the Wisconsin River. Looking at the eroded rock, you might expect that they took eons to form, much like the Grand Canyon. But actually, their formation happened in a geological heartbeat. The stone itself is what took eons to form, the result of sediments from a warm, shallow sea that covered the region over 510 million years ago.

During the end of the Wisconsin Glacial Episode, the most recent phase of the latest ice age, the ice sheets stopped just before they reached where the Dells are today. This was still part of the untouched Driftless Area. As the ice melted, water became trapped behind ice dams. In this case, the meltwater formed Glacial Lake Wisconsin. When the ice dam eventually burst, it released a massive and sudden torrent of water, which carved the gorge and its features from the relatively soft sandstone.

The Dells are part of a state natural area under the protection of the Wisconsin Department of Natural Resources, and while boat tours—especially the amphibious "duck" tours—are popular for viewing them from the water, certain areas are closed to the public to protect delicate formations and rare species of plants. How rare? Cliff cudweed (*Gnaphalium obtusifolium* var. *saxicola*) has only been identified in two places on Earth: here and in the Kickapoo Valley.

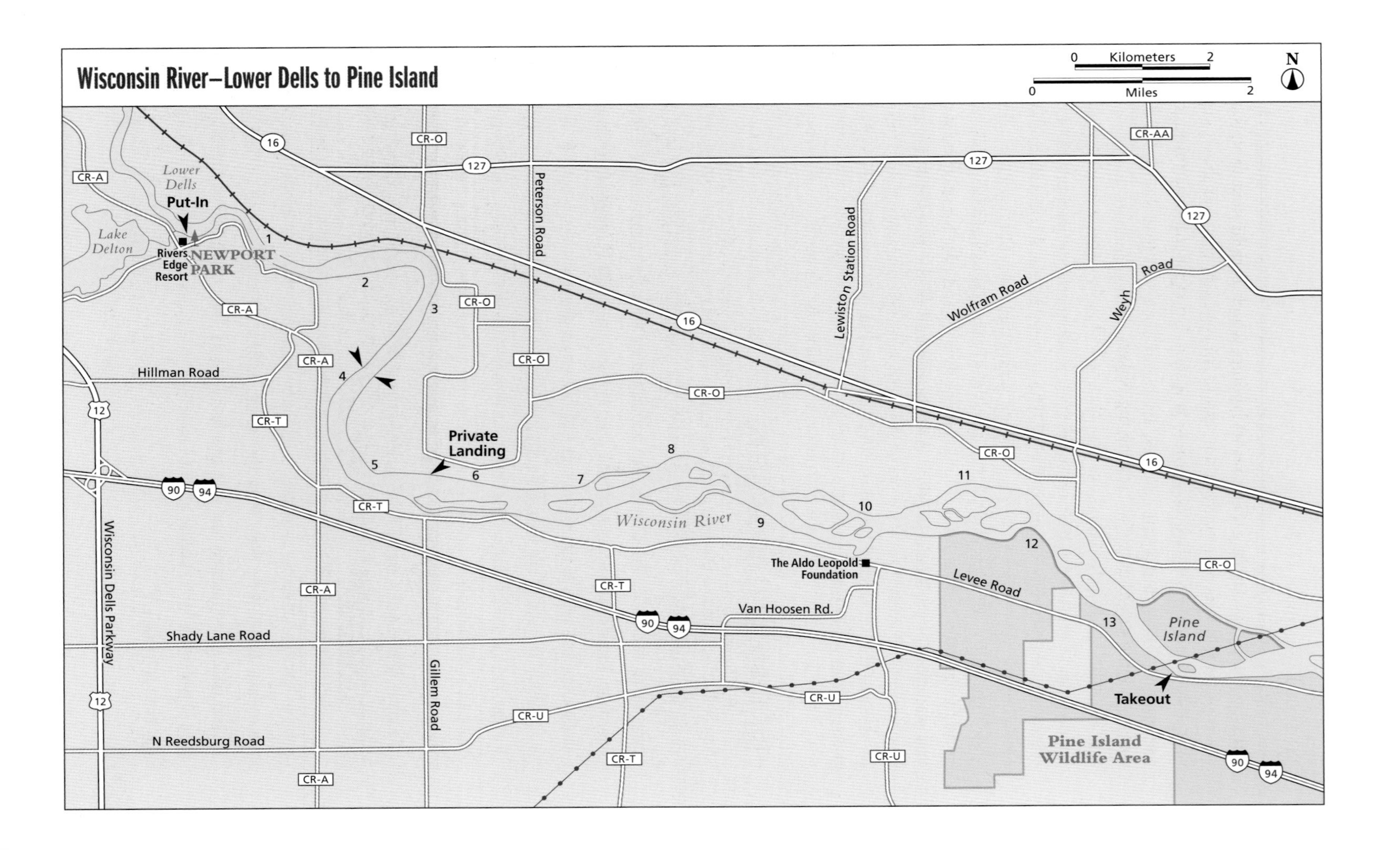

Wisconsin River—Lower Dells to Pine Island
0 Kilometers 2
0 Miles 2
N
Lower Dells
Lake Delton
Put-In
Rivers Edge Resort
NEWPORT PARK
Private Landing
Takeout
Wisconsin River
Pine Island
Pine Island Wildlife Area
The Aldo Leopold Foundation
Peterson Road
Lewiston Station Road
Wolfram Road
Weyh Road
Hillman Road
Levee Road
Van Hoosen Rd.
Shady Lane Road
Gillem Road
N Reedsburg Road
Wisconsin Dells Parkway
CR-A
CR-O
CR-T
CR-U
CR-AA
16
127
12
90
94
1
2
3
4
5
6
7
8
9
10
11
12
13

Paddle Summary

Put in at the public landing. (The resort landing, which is right next to it, is only for guests or for paddlers renting from the resort's livery.) Here the river shows sandstone rock across from the sandy beach where you start. Go right and head through a narrow passage in the rocks. You may encounter tour boats—be especially alert for the jet boats doing doughnuts and creating big wakes.

Nevertheless, this first stretch—less than a mile—has the only display of rock formations. Linger here and paddle around the rock columns and along the shores. Just past the sandstone cliffs on river right is the road where the amphibious vehicles known as "ducks" roll into the river. They are rather slow boats, so not much of a nuisance. By 0.8 mile downriver, the rock formations end and the river really widens up—to over 200 feet across. You pass under some power lines here. At 1.5 miles a sign indicates that rental boats should not pass this point. Paddlers rule from here on out. Train tracks follow along river left, and you may hear and see the occasional train.

This section of the river may not have rapids, but it is not without some areas of riffles where constricting sandbars and a shallow river bottom may push up the current. You'll encounter one such point at 1.7 miles. At about 3.7 miles you can see some islands hugging the banks on river right. Narrow passages through and behind these islands may be runnable in higher water. At 3.8 miles there is a landing on river left. There's another landing on river right, but you need to paddle back up the

Paddling past picturesque sculpted sandstone in the Lower Dells on the Wisconsin

Rock formations were carved by a massive flood from a glacial lake.

narrow passage behind the final island to get to it. The river has a rocky bottom here, and if you see sandbars to the left or center, you have a chance of scraping. At 5.5 miles a resort's private landing is on river left. At this point the river has widened even more, reaching 300 feet. A channel on river right may be passable in high water. At 6.8 miles pass a large island on either side.

Because of its massive volume of moving water and the sandy nature of its riverbed, the Wisconsin River is constantly shifting. Keep that in mind when maps don't show what you see. This area in particular morphs within a season, moving significant sandbars and erasing islands. At 7.6 miles is another example of a runnable narrow side channel, this one on river right. I've paddled this one even with low water levels. Within it, the current bumps up a bit, and there may be some deadfall to navigate. It is a welcome mile-long break from the exposed wider river and a chance to sneak up on some wildlife. At 9.2 miles another large island divides the river into two wide channels. If you stay right, you will see some cabins on river right at 9.6 miles. The Aldo Leopold Foundation is beyond here off Levee Road.

You will see power lines, located at about 13.6 miles, well in advance; these cross the river right before your takeout, and they are the first such wires on this segment of the river after the Dells. Paddle along the right bank. Pine Island is right across from the simple gravel ramp on river right.

14 Mirror Lake

The natural counterpoint to the touristy mecca nearby at Wisconsin Dells, this dam-formed lake in a state park is a scenic out-and-back paddle venture amid the carved sandstone of Dell Creek.

County: Sauk
Start/End: Mirror Lake State Park boat landing, N43 34.221' / W89 48.633'
Length: Up to 7.6 miles
Float time: About 3-4 hours
Difficulty rating: Easy
Rapids: None
River type: Lake
Current: None
Season: Spring through fall
Land status: Wisconsin DNR and some private
Fees and permits: State park vehicle fee if using park boat landings and parking
Nearest city/town: Lake Delton
Maps: In park office; USGS Wisconsin Dells South; *DeLorme: Wisconsin Atlas & Gazetteer*: Page 43 D5
Boats used: Canoes, kayaks, johnboats
Contacts: Mirror Lake State Park, E10320 Fern Dell Rd., Baraboo 53913; (608) 254-2333; dnr.wi.gov/topic/parks/name/mirrorlake
Outfitters: Mirror Lake Boat Rentals, E10320 Fern Dell Rd, Baraboo 53913; (608) 254-4104; mirrorlakeboatrentals.com
Camping: Mirror Lake State Park has 151 campsites. Contact wisconsin.goingtocamp.com or call (888) 947-2757.

Put-in/Takeout Information

To put-in/takeout: From Lake Delton take US 12 south, crossing under I-90/94 and continuing another 0.5 mile to exit 212 toward Mirror Lake State Park. Continue on Fern Dell Road for 2.6 miles to the park entrance on the right. Pay fees at the ranger office and continue on the park road following signs for the boat launch, a concrete ramp with abundant parking nearby. The state park has restrooms, water, showers, and campgrounds.

Lake Overview

Designated as a state park in 1966, Mirror Lake is actually a 139-acre impoundment on modest Dell Creek. On a map it appears to have northern, southern, and western lobes, and much of the park terrain is forested. The shoreline in the creek gorge also shows exposed sandstone that was formed in the Cambrian period 500 million years ago when this was the loose sand at the bottom of a warm sea. At the end of the comparatively recent Wisconsin Glacial Episode of the last ice age, this rocky land lay under the edge of the melting ice while a lake of meltwater grew behind an ice dam. Eventually that dam gave way, sending a thundering torrent of water that carved this sandstone in a geological heartbeat. The far west end of the lake features abundant wild rice and a more typical-looking lake area that's popular with anglers, while the narrow creek gorge is impressively quiet and beautiful with abundant animal and plant life. Heading north toward the highway is popular with kayak rentals and pontoon tours; after the interstate the water narrows to a creek gorge again. It's a popular park, but even on a summer Saturday it can be a peaceful paddle if you go west or simply get on the water earlier in the day. Blue and green herons, and other waterfowl, are common throughout. Anglers find bluegill, crappie, largemouth bass, northern pike, and walleye.

Paddle Summary

The Mirror Lake State Park boat landing is a wide concrete ramp with an accessible fishing pier. The concessionaire-outfitter has its own special kayak launch to the left for its rentals. Set off from the put-in heading left (south) along the shore. This is the lower lobe of the lake, with large pine and oak trees along banks that sit low on the west side but rise steeply on the east. Paddle around a swimming area on your left at 0.3 mile, and at 0.6 mile you're already at the southernmost point. Take a wide turn to the opposite shore and head back north. Note the abundant deadfall—large trees stretching out into the water like the ribs of old shipwrecks, giving perches to green herons.

A tree makes an arch over The Narrows on Mirror Lake.

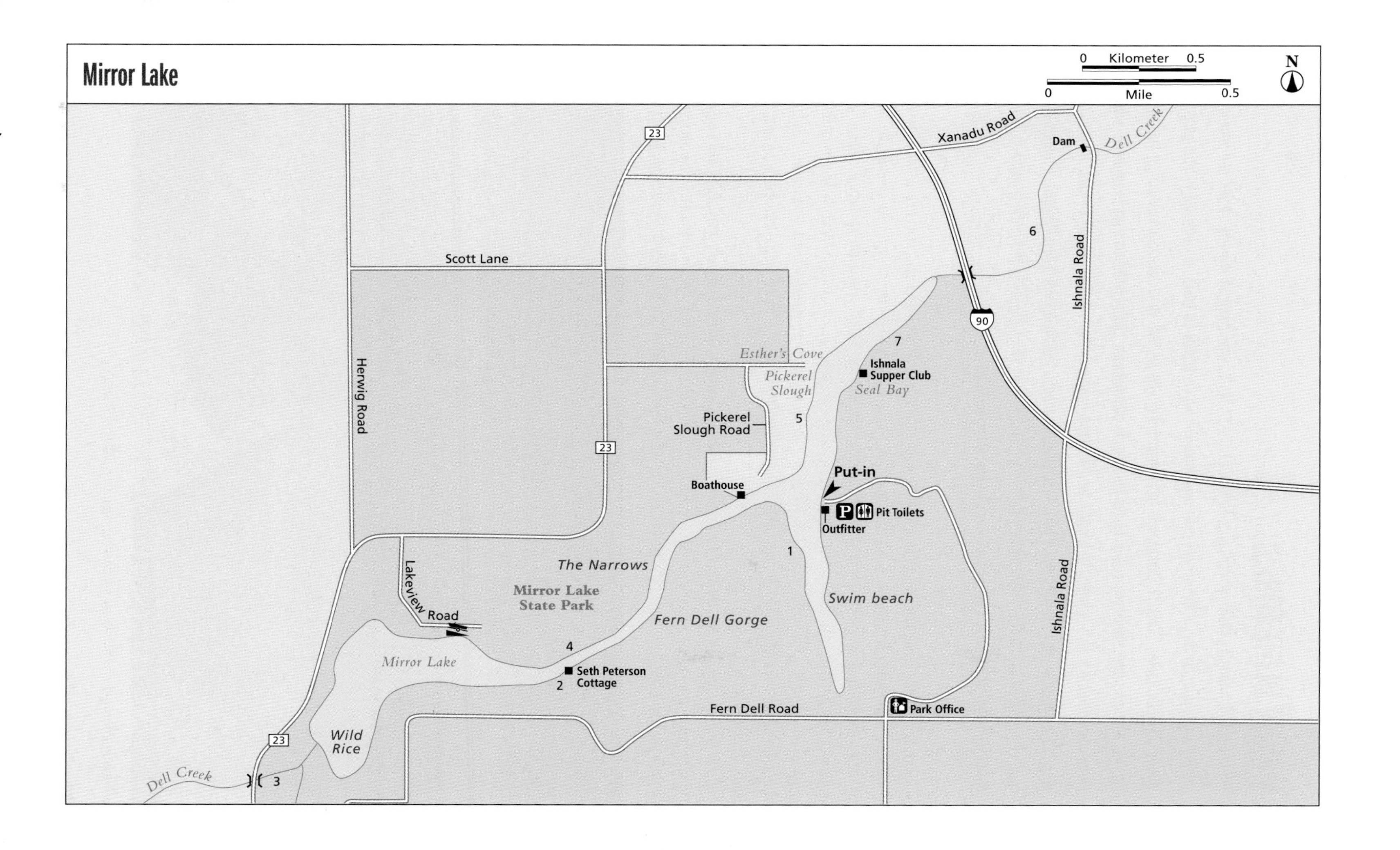
Mirror Lake
0 Kilometer 0.5
0 Mile 0.5
N
Xanadu Road
Dam
Dell Creek
23
6
Scott Lane
Ishnala Road
90
Esther's Cove
7
Ishnala
Supper Club
Pickerel
Slough
Seal Bay
Herwig Road
Pickerel
Slough Road
5
Put-in
Boathouse
Pit Toilets
Outfitter
1
The Narrows
Lakeview Road
Mirror Lake
State Park
Swim beach
Fern Dell Gorge
4
Mirror Lake
Seth Peterson
Cottage
2
Fern Dell Road
Park Office
Wild
Rice
Dell Creek
3

WRIGHT IN THE FOREST

Wisconsin's most famous architect, Frank Lloyd Wright, was almost ninety years old when a young man named Seth Peterson commissioned him in 1958 to build a cottage in the woods above Mirror Lake. Wright designed his structures to blend into the surrounding natural world, and as such this two-room cottage shows sandstone construction and expansive windows overlooking the gorge. It would be his last commission, yet neither he nor Peterson would live to see its completion. Peterson, who shared a birthday with Mr. Wright, died at the age of twenty-four. Today, the state park owns the property and opens it for tours the second Sunday of each month. Guests may also rent it overnight.

At 1.2 miles pass the boat launch across the water to the right and turn west into a narrower channel known as The Narrows. A large boathouse stands to the right. The passage becomes a deep gorge of eroded sandstone with abundant large pines and hardwoods adding shade to an already sheltered stretch of water. Watch for perching eagles. As these are still waters, you can expect a lot of duckweed at times, turning the lake into a brilliant blanket of bright green that sizzles like soda bubbles along the hull of your craft as you pass.

At 1.7 miles on the left is Fern Dell Gorge, often with a sandy patch at its mouth where you could step out of the canoe a moment or even venture into the gorge a ways on foot. At the top of the bluffs on the left is the historic Seth Peterson Cottage

Duckweed makes a brilliant green surface on Mirror Lake.

High sandstone wall along Mirror Lake's shore

at 1.9 miles, though the bluffs' height and foliage make it difficult to see. Beyond here the water opens up wide to a more typical lake, with a few private properties in several places along the shore and a boat landing on the north (right) side. This lacks the intimacy of the gorge you just left, but if you continue west about 2.4 miles, look as the lake bends south and find the cleared path through an abundance of wild rice. Enter there and you can get a close-up look at the plants. Continue into the channel; it gradually narrows to Dell Creek. At 3 miles is the Highway 23 bridge, which makes a good turnaround point.

Backtrack to the gorge at 3.9 miles, and out again to the boathouse at the other end at 4.7 miles. Stay to the left shore as it curves to the north. This part of the lake is busier with other paddlers, day-trippers, and anglers. At 5.1 miles pass Pickerel Slough on the left, and Esther's Cove not 100 feet after that. Across the water to the right is Ishnala, a historic supper club with a lakeside view, and Seal Bay, another narrow thrust of water into the shoreline. On a map these three inlets and the lake form the star of Mirror Lake. Highway noise is prominent now, and at 5.6 miles you pass under the towering double bridge of the interstate. The gorge narrows again, showing more sandstone formations and some old cabins, and even at midday some of the water is shaded. At 6.2 miles lies the dam. It is possible to portage down steps on the left to continue on Dell Creek into Lake Delton and on to the Wisconsin River, but that's a much more intensive trip.

Backtrack to the interstate bridges at 6.8 miles and keep to the left shoreline to see some impressive sculpted walls of sandstone. Pass Ishnala Supper Club at 7.2 miles and round the exposed rock faces on the left as you make the turn into the southern lobe where the landing is on your left.

15 Baraboo River

Beavers, eagles, herons, deer—you might see anything here, and it will be close when you surprise it coming around a bend. The river is narrow as it winds from the edge of a golf course and into patches of trees amid farmland. But the centerpiece of the paddle trip is the towering and photogenic sandstone cliff toward the end. In a few places thereafter, the undercut stone is close enough to touch.

County: Juneau
Start: WI 33 bridge, N43 40.857' / W90 16.080'
End: Wonewoc municipal canoe landing, N43 39.203' / W90 13.579'
Length: 6.3 miles one-way
Float time: About 3 hours
Difficulty rating: Easy
Rapids: None
River type: Wooded pastoral
Current: Gentle
River gradient: 2.7 feet per mile
River gauge: USGS 054041665 Baraboo River at Reedsburg; minimum runnable level 100 cfs; avoid at flood stage
Season: Spring, summer, rainy periods in fall
Land status: Private, with one public landing
Fees and permits: No fees or permits required; daily trail fee if using state trail for bike shuttle
Nearest city/town: Wonewoc
Maps: USGS Hillsboro, Wonewoc; *DeLorme: Wisconsin Atlas & Gazetteer*: Page 42 C1
Boats used: Canoes, kayaks
Organizations: River Alliance of Wisconsin, 147 S. Butler St., Ste. 2, Madison 53703; (608) 257-2424; wisconsinrivers.org
Outfitters: Beyond Boundaries, 113 Center St., Wonewoc 53968; (608) 464-7433; goingfarbeyond.com
Local information: 400 State Trail; 400statetrail.org or dnr.wi.gov/topic/parks/name/400

Put-in/Takeout Information

To shuttle point/takeout: WI 33 passes right through Wonewoc. In the heart of town, head west on Washington Street about 0.1 mile to where the road forks. Bear left; the entrance to the landing is right there at the fork. The takeout—upriver from the Washington Street bridge, downriver of the CR FF bridge—is a simple opening in the mud-and-grass bank, a few steps from a gravel circle for gathering boats and a shelter with picnic table and grill. Parking is across the street in a grassy lot. There's a portable toilet here in season.

To put-in from takeout: From the takeout, take Washington Street east, back into Wonewoc. Turn left (north) onto WI 33 and continue 3.7 miles, through Union Center, to the highway bridge over the Baraboo River. On the right you can see a golf course. Cross the bridge and park alongside the road. Carry your craft to the simple muddy bank put-in on river right, upstream from the bridge. This is private property, and there are no facilities here.

Paddling under the Third Castle, a towering rock outcrop over the Baraboo River

River Overview

A tributary of the Wisconsin River, the Baraboo flows about 70 miles, picking up the Little Baraboo River and the West Branch Baraboo River along the way. For much of the journey it is a narrow and winding, intimate river, often wooded and rich with wildlife, especially birds. You can see occasional sandstone rock formations, but much of any nearby development is out of sight. Odds are good for seeing deer and beavers, as well as blue herons and the occasional eagle. The Baraboo shows some rapids as it passes through the town of the same name, but for this stretch the current is smooth and gentle, although it still requires attentive paddling as it winds back and forth, much like the famously crooked Kickapoo but with narrower passages. The Third Castle, a towering rock outcrop that descends right to the river's edge, is the highlight of the journey.

Paddle Summary

Put in on a short step down from a muddy bank with a piece of treadmill. The river passes through a private golf course before this point and is narrow, about 20 feet wide, with lazy current. Pass under the highway bridge and some power lines, and off you go. Just 500 feet beyond is the narrow bridge for the Hillsboro State Trail, which connects to the longer 400 State Trail to the east in Union Center and takes you all the way to Wonewoc for an easy bike shuttle option.

Don't let this straight canal-like first look fool you. This river is twisty. Trees close in, roots emerge from the banks, and you can see the tracks of deer and other critters in the mud. Beavers are common here, but the outfitters keep this stretch free of their

The Third Castle is a massive rock formation looming over the Baraboo River. PREAMTIP SATASUK

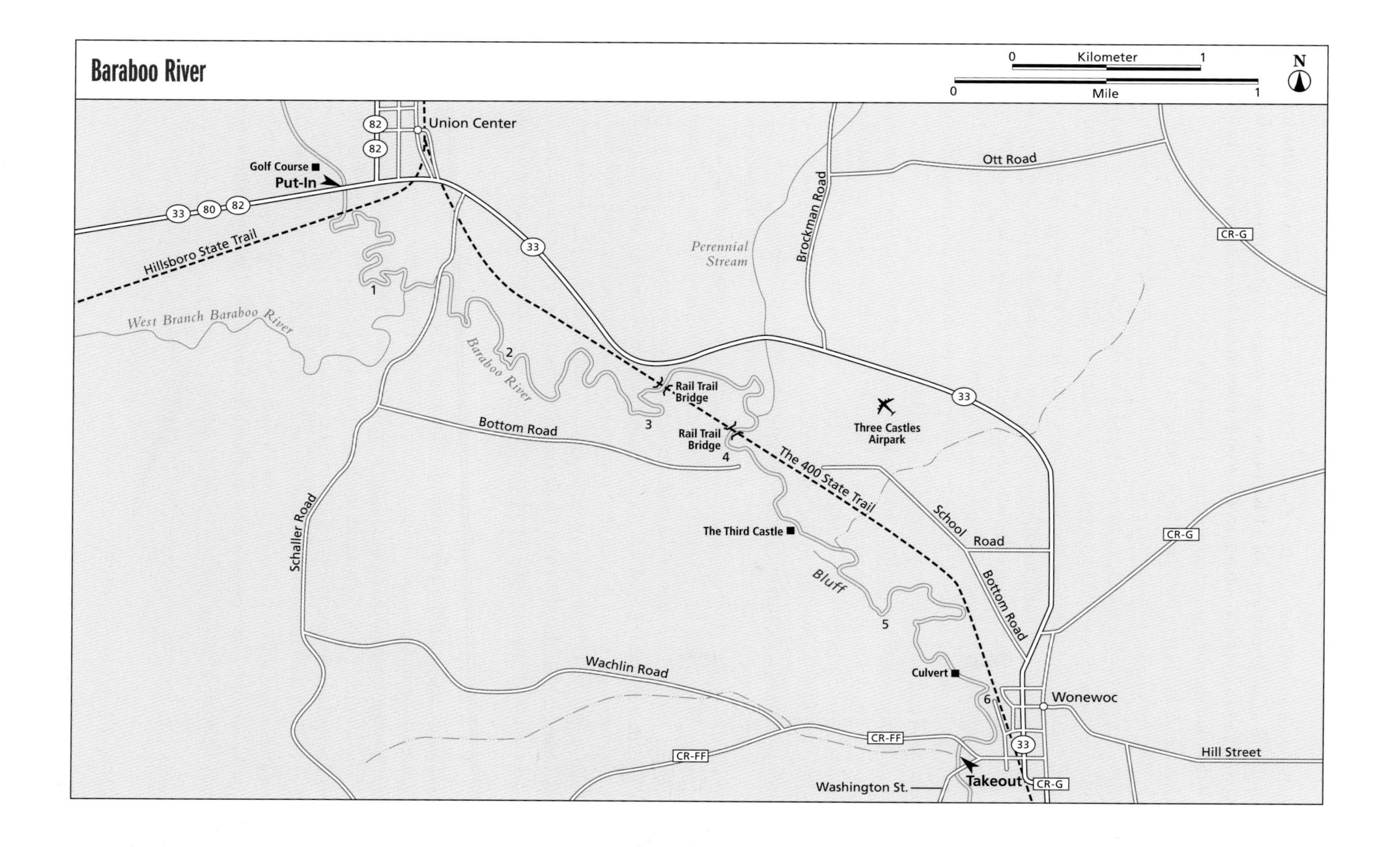
Baraboo River
0
Kilometer
1
0
Mile
1
N
Union Center
82
82
Golf Course
Put-In
33
80
82
Hillsboro State Trail
1
West Branch Baraboo River
33
Baraboo River
2
Rail Trail Bridge
3
Bottom Road
Rail Trail Bridge
4
The 400 State Trail
Perennial Stream
Brockman Road
Ott Road
CR-G
Three Castles Airpark
33
School Road
Bottom Road
CR-G
The Third Castle
Bluff
5
Schaller Road
Wachlin Road
Culvert
6
Wonewoc
33
CR-FF
CR-FF
Takeout
CR-G
Hill Street
Washington St.

handiwork and frequent deadfall. Farmland lies beyond the banks and the trees and is visible in many places here. At 1.1 miles the river makes a right-angle turn to the left as the West Branch of the Baraboo joins from river right. After the left turn, the river widens and deepens just a bit, slowing up. Pass under some power lines, and then the river bends left before the Hann Street bridge at 1.3 miles.

The river really starts to zigzag now. You'll see a barn a few times with the switchbacks, but now you leave the farmland behind. Little feeder creeks trickle in throughout. The river can be muddy, especially right after rainfall, because of the sand and mud bottom; but much of the silt it once held has washed away since the dam removal. Occasional sandbars still rise up around the bends and may drag at you in low-water periods. At 3.2 miles pass under the old rail bridge; this is now the 400 Trail before it reaches the Hillsboro Trail. The highway is visible ahead, and swallows' nests riddle the muddy bank. There are power lines on the left, and a large bluff covered with pine and some exposed rock is visible.

The river hooks around left and back in a small oxbow and then passes a small seasonal stream on the left and widens to 30 to 40 feet as it comes up on another rail-trail bridge—an 1899 structure from Lassig Bridge & Iron Works in Chicago—at 3.9 miles. The river curves left on the other side, and 500 feet later you pass a concrete wall on river left. A stream comes in opposite, on the right bank.

As you come around the corner, you'll get your first glimpse of the geologic star of the show today: the Third Castle—a massive rock outcrop rising up 182 feet and showing pine across its crown. It's shadowed in the morning, but in late afternoon the sun warms the colors of the rock. At 4.4 miles the river comes right up against the formation and is forced left. Paddle along the base of this wall and look up at the sandstone to see trees clinging to the steep rock face. After the rock face, the river bends right. At 4.7 miles you come up close to another exposed sandstone cliff, part of the larger bluff that the Third Castle stands out from. You'll hear the gurgling water of a small creek joining from the right at the turn here and then slip along the foot of the rock on river right.

At 5.8 miles pass a large culvert on river left. The river bends right; trees approach the water again, and the river starts to widen and become shallower. As you enter Wonewoc at about 6 miles, houses appear on the left bank. Paddle a few hundred feet, passing the remains of an old brick wall and then a culvert and a storm runoff. The river then bends right again and leaves the yards behind. Pass under the CR FF bridge at 6.3 miles; the takeout is just past the bridge, on river left. A couple hundred feet beyond the takeout is the Washington Street bridge, and beneath it are a few sandstone formations you may choose to ogle a bit before paddling back upstream for the takeout. The current is a bit quicker here, though, and in high water it would take quite an effort.

16 Pine River (Richland Center)

From its auspicious start under a natural sandstone "bridge," the Pine River continues to impress on its winding course through part of the unglaciated Driftless Area. Expect impressive exposed sandstone and rock outcrops in the upper stretches, with sections that are tree-lined and shaded and others where farmland is visible. For paddlers looking for a full day of paddling, this route can be extended 5 miles for a fun finish in Richland Center, where the river narrows for an easy, unobstructed Class II drop before another takeout.

County: Richland
Start: Pier Natural Bridge Park, N43 26.850' / W90 21.864'
End: Bowen's Mill Landing/CR AA bridge, N43 22.387' / W90 23.034'
Length: 10.1 miles one-way
Float time: About 4 hours
Difficulty rating: Easy; advanced boat control on upper portion with canoes
Rapids: None
River type: Pastoral with rock formations
Current: Gentle
River gradient: 1.5 feet per mile
River gauge: Contact the outfitter for current river levels. High water makes bridges in the first 2 miles dangerously low.
Season: Spring through fall
Land status: Private and public, with public landings
Fees and permits: No fees or permits required
Nearest city/town: Richland Center
Maps: USGS Richland Center; *DeLorme: Wisconsin Atlas & Gazetteer*: Page 33 B7
Boats used: Kayaks preferred, canoes possible with great boat control
Contacts: Richland Center Parks & Recreation, 1100 N. Jefferson St., Richland Center 53581; (608) 647-8108, ext. 2; ci.richland-center.wi.us
Outfitters: Pine River Paddle and Tube, Richland Center 53581; (608) 475-2199; facebook.com/PineRiverPaddleAndTubeLlc
Note: Glass containers are prohibited on the Pine River. Contact the outfitter to find out the current state of deadfall on the river.

Put-in/Takeout Information

To shuttle point/takeout: From Richland Center head north on WI 80 about 2.5 miles and turn right onto CR AA. Continue 0.4 mile; the landing is on the right side of the road, just before the bridge over the Pine River. There are no facilities here but room enough to park off the shoulder of the highway.

To put-in from takeout: From the CR AA bridge/Bowen's Mill Landing, travel north 0.4 mile and turn right on WI 80. Drive 5.5 miles and look for the entry to Pier Park on the left. Follow the park road to the end (notice the exposed sandstone on your left) and put in near the rock bridge. There are toilets and parking in this park. A walking bridge crosses the water along the sandstone ridge and leads to a short tunnel through to the other side, the West Branch of the Pine River. Paddlers have the option to carry through to the western side, launch there, and paddle north

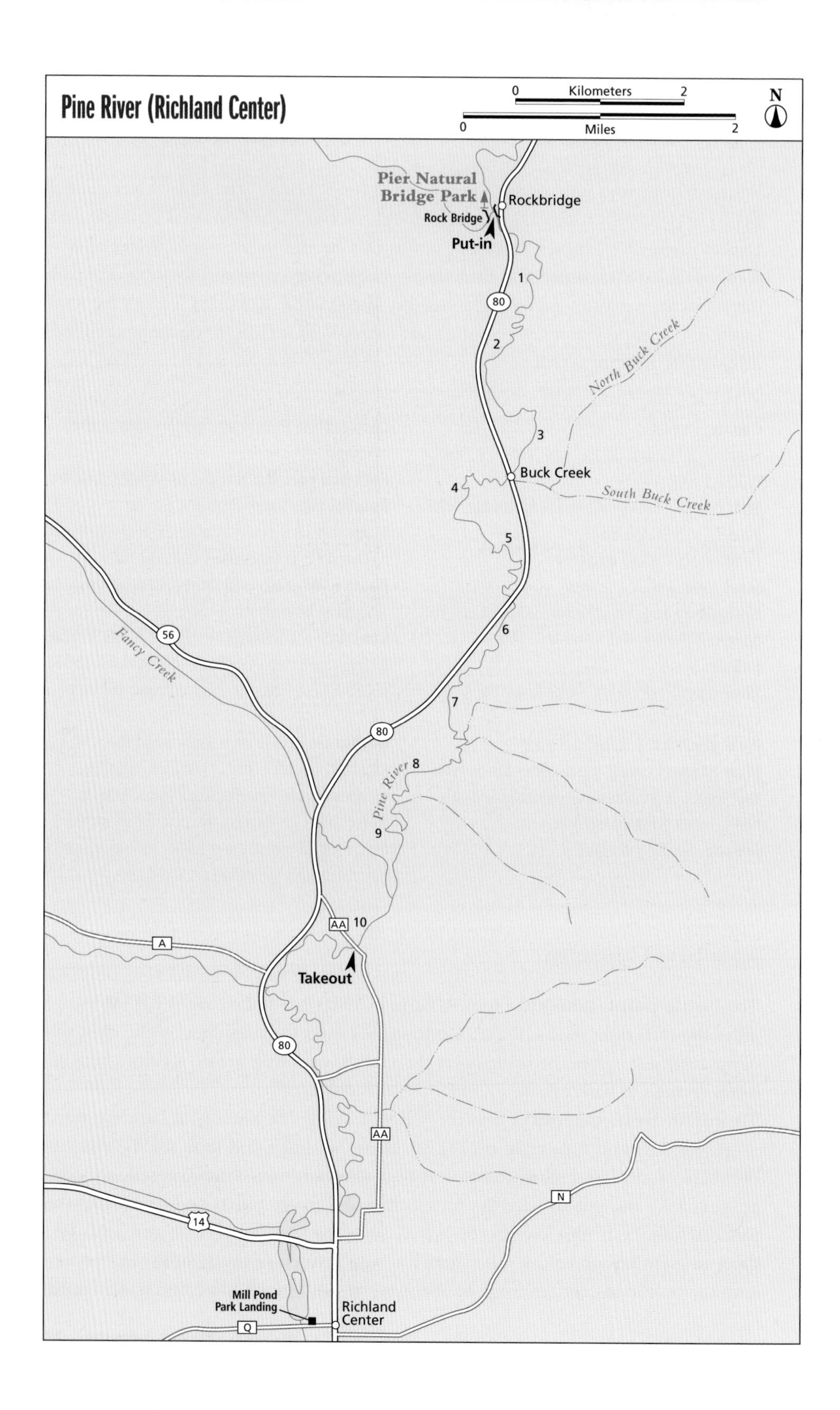

Pine River (Richland Center)
0
Kilometers
2
0
Miles
2
N
Pier Natural
Bridge Park
Rockbridge
Rock Bridge
Put-in
1
80
2
North Buck Creek
3
Buck Creek
4
South Buck Creek
5
6
56
Fancy Creek
7
80
Pine River
8
9
AA
10
A
Takeout
80
AA
N
14
Mill Pond
Park Landing
Richland
Center
Q

Sandstone, such as this formation near the put-in, is abundant along the upper reaches of the Pine River.

about 60 feet to where the water flows to the right through the rock passage. The trip begins there.

River Overview

Not to be confused with the Pine River of northeastern Wisconsin, this Pine wends its way through the Driftless Area from its natural spring source in Vernon County southward to where it feeds into the Wisconsin River near Gotham. Closer to the headwaters, it is actually a Class 2 trout stream. North of Richland Center, the course

winds enough to make the Kickapoo jealous, and frequent carved sandstone right up along the bank gives it some character. The river flows through the former mill pond in Richland Center, a community that has provided five canoe landings along the river's passage near and through town. Then it widens and slows as it gets closer to the Wisconsin and a sixth canoe landing at Gotham. Arguably the best segment is the one described here, which gives paddlers a chance to slip through a short passage in the rock, and offers views of several rock outcrops thereafter.

Paddle Summary

Put in near the opening in the sandstone rock—the rock bridge—at the end of the parking lot where it meets the Pine River, or follow the hiking bridge to put in on the western side of the sandstone formation, or simply paddle up through the passage to have a look and then paddle back to begin heading down the Pine. From the put-in the river bends to the south, running alongside WI 80 for 1,000 feet before passing under it to the left. At 0.6 mile you encounter more sandstone on the left. At 1 mile pass under the bridge at Cunningham Lane; the rock formations continue on the left as the river continues switching back and forth. At 2.4 miles is another bridge at Albert Lane. At 2.6 miles the river bends to the east, and when it turns right again 0.3 mile later to continue south, more sandstone adorns the banks.

At 3.4 miles Buck Creek enters from the left just before you pass under another WI 80 bridge. The course does some serious twisting from this point, but at 4.5 miles it makes another 90-degree turn, turning east and passing before a very tall rock outcrop on the right. At 5.8 miles the river heads east under another WI 80 bridge, then swings south running parallel to the highway for 0.4 mile through another winding stretch. At 6.9 miles the river flows straighter for 1,500 feet, goes through some gentle switchbacks, and heads west passing the last of the outcrops, these along the left bank. At the next bend you might see a backwater or a former path of the river; bear left.

The winding path opens up bit by bit until at 9.1 miles the course is more direct. Pass Fancy Creek coming in on river right at 9.6 miles; the final 0.5 mile is a gentle direct run to the CR AA bridge where you'll find a floating paddler's pier on river right, just downstream of the bridge. This is your takeout.

Option: While this trip has no rapids or riffles, you might consider adding 5 more miles to the end of this paddle by continuing to Mill Pond Park Landing in Richland Center. Right before the takeout on river right, the banks narrow up and provide a short, unobstructed rush of Class I–II rapids. It's short enough that many take out and carry their craft back above the run to do it again.

◀ *An easy chute ends at the takeout on the Pine River; paddlers frequently carry their craft upriver 100 feet to run it again.*

17 Kickapoo River

Commonly referred to as "the Most Crooked River in the World"—certainly a contender anyway—the Kickapoo is a serpentine delight for paddlers, passing before and behind numerous exposed sandstone bluffs and enjoying a steady current. Abundant tree cover and the shade of the undercut cliffs keep this paddle pleasant even on a hot summer day. This segment also avoids the tubers and the quick in-and-out paddlers upstream in Ontario, plus much of the deadfall farther downstream. It starts within the Kickapoo Valley Reserve but ends at the edge of town in La Farge.

County: Vernon
Start: Bridge #10 on WI 131, N43 38.978' / W90 35.594'
End: WI 82 bridge/Andrews Canoe Landing in La Farge, N43 34.495' / W90 38.609'
Length: 12 miles one-way
Float time: About 3.5–4 hours
Difficulty rating: Easy
Rapids: Riffles only
River type: Wooded pastoral with sandstone bluffs and ledges
Current: Gentle to moderate
River gradient: 2 feet per mile
River gauge: USGS 05408000 Kickapoo River at WI 33 at Ontario; minimum runnable level 70 cfs; avoid at high or rising levels. It is strongly advised that you contact an outfitter regarding the water levels. Readings are frequently deceptive, and the local outfitters know how to read the tributaries upriver to judge whether it will still be safe a couple hours later.
Season: Spring through fall
Land status: Public
Fees and permits: Self-pay parking fee required at put-in; additional fee for river camping
Nearest city/town: La Farge
Maps: USGS Dell, La Farge, Ontario, West Lima; maps available at Kickapoo Valley Reserve Visitor Center; *DeLorme: Wisconsin Atlas & Gazetteer*: Page 41 C6
Boats used: Canoes, kayaks
Contacts: Kickapoo Valley Reserve Visitor Center, Hwy. 131, La Farge 54639; (608) 625-2960; kvr.state.wi.us
Outfitters: Drifty's Complete Canoe Rental, Hwys. 33 and 131 North, Ontario 54651; (608) 337-4288; driftyscanoerental.net

Mr. Ducks Canoe Rental, 100 Main St., Ontario 54651; (608) 337-4711; mrduckscanoerental.com

Titanic Canoe Rental, 300 Hwy. 131, Ontario 54651; (877) 438-7865; titaniccanoerental.com

Put-in/Takeout Information

To shuttle point/takeout: WI 131 and WI 82 meet on Main Street in La Farge. Go west on Main Street to the edge of town, just before the bridge over the Kickapoo. The takeout, Andrews Canoe Landing, is on the north side of the road, upriver of the bridge on river left. A short dirt road leads to a grass parking lot and an unimproved put-in along the mud-and-grass bank. There's a portable toilet here in season.

To put-in from takeout: From the takeout, turn left onto Main Street; drive 0.1 mile and turn left (north) onto WI 131/Mill Street. Drive 6.7 miles, staying on WI

131 as it crosses left over a large bridge high above the river and then turns right, passing through Rockton. Take the first right on CR P; the entrance to the put-in point is 0.2 mile on the right, below bridge #10. Pay the day-use fee at the self-pay tube and park in the large gravel lot. There's a portable toilet here in season.

River Overview

The Kickapoo is a paddler's delight, with fantastic geological features in abundance, a meandering course with steady current, and natural, wild surroundings in an accessible location. The name is Algonquin for "it goes here, it goes there." The Kickapoo flows 126 miles to join the Wisconsin River, and there are various places to paddle throughout its length. The lower section is wide and slow, but up around Ontario is the most popular section, within the Kickapoo Valley Reserve. Even the section above Ontario can be done, risking deadfall; below La Farge the river can also show obstructions, keeping you out of your craft more often than is enjoyable. But the stretch from Ontario to La Farge is as scenic as they come and thus popular, even with tubers.

The whole section could make for a very long day of paddling, but the route described here skips the tubers and most paddlers and starts at a good midpoint for an easy day trip. For paddlers looking to spend more time with the river, rustic first-come, first-served campsites are available along the banks, managed by the Kickapoo Valley Reserve. The river is susceptible to flooding, and a good rain can quickly raise the levels, so pay close attention to the weather. No glass is allowed on the river.

THE DAM THAT NEVER WAS

While Kickapoo might mean "it goes here, it goes there," the US Army Corps of Engineers would have redefined it as "doesn't go anywhere at all." The river fills dangerously in strong rainfall, and floods are rather common. Gay Mills, just downstream, was nearly wiped out by the Kickapoo as recently as 2008. So the Corps made plans to dam the whole thing and prevent such events in the future.

The government bought out 149 farms using eminent domain and set to work on a large dam at La Farge, which would have flooded everything here today. Construction began in 1971—you can still see the concrete control tower and an earthen dam—but angry former landowners and environmentalists took the matter to the courts, tying the project up until finally defeating it in 1975. In 1996 the Corps was forced to return part of the land to the Ho-Chunk Nation, while 8,569 acres between Ontario and La Farge went to the State of Wisconsin. The state created the Kickapoo Valley Reserve to preserve the natural state of the river and its surroundings, which are now enjoyed by all.

Sandstone bluffs are common along the winding Kickapoo. PREAMTIP SATASUK

Paddle Summary

Put in at the concrete ramp and follow the current left, where you're immediately confronted with the first of what will be many sandstone walls. Mere riffles await here, but they're enough to push the unwary toward that wall. The water is clear and the bottom sandy. At the beginning the river is 30 feet across and winds like spaghetti. You'll paddle almost double the straight-line distance between put-in and takeout. The sandstone along the river is colorful and often covered with patches of bright green moss.

At 0.3 mile Warner Creek comes in from river left. At 0.6 mile the river bends hard left as it comes up against another sandstone wall. On turns watch for sand accumulation on the banks opposite the rock walls; sandbars often lurk there in shallow waters. Banks are high—over 10 feet—and grassy, but with many trees hanging over. The river widens out to 40 to 50 feet, so while there may be some deadfall, there's room to get around. Plus this stretch is consistently maintained. At 0.9 mile there's

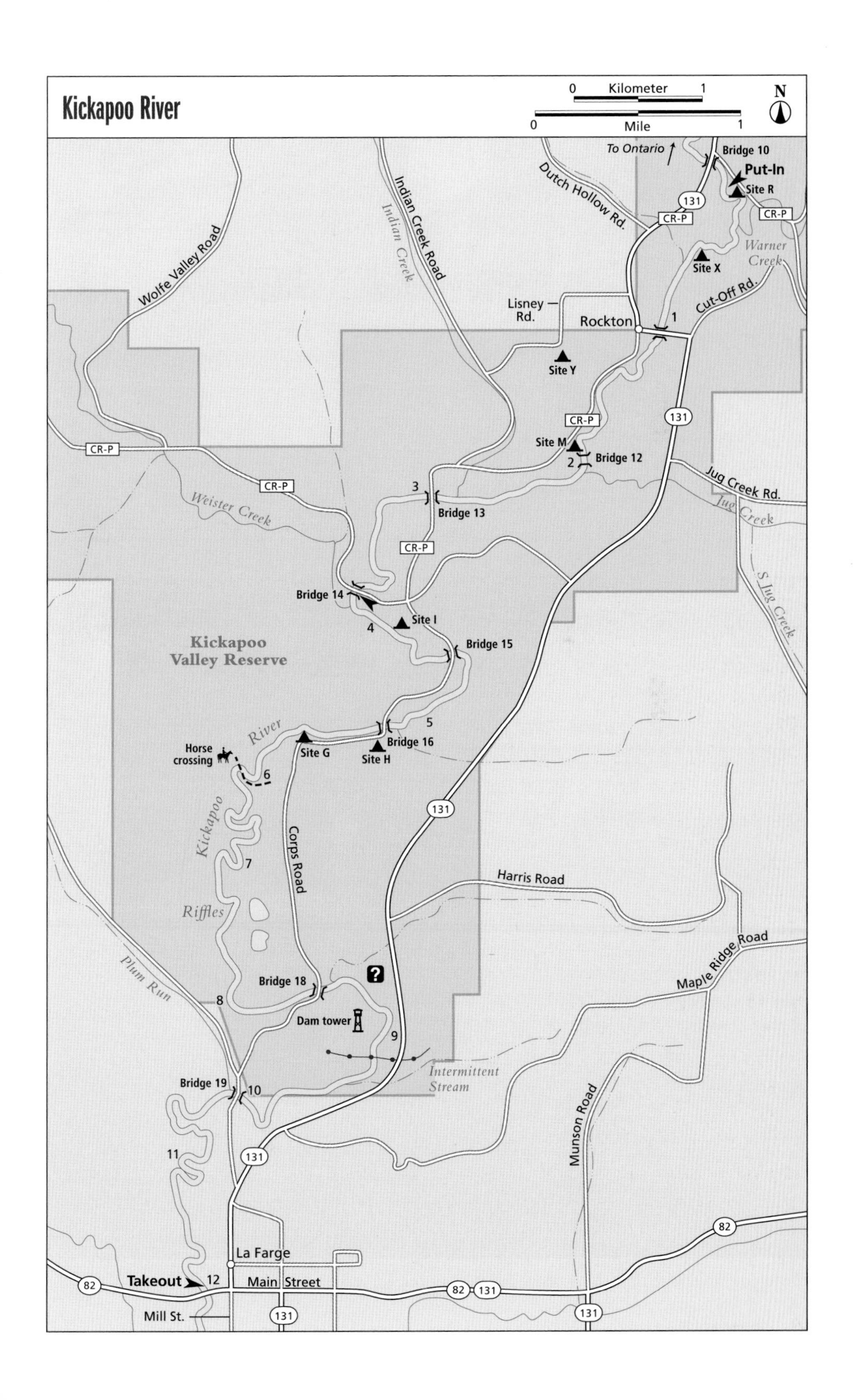
Kickapoo River
0 Kilometer 1
0 Mile 1
N
To Ontario
Bridge 10
Put-In
Site R
CR-P
131
Dutch Hollow Rd.
Warner Creek
Site X
Cut-Off Rd.
Indian Creek Road
Indian Creek
Wolfe Valley Road
Lisney Rd.
Rockton
1
Site Y
CR-P
Site M
2
Bridge 12
131
Jug Creek Rd.
Jug Creek
S Jug Creek
CR-P
3
Bridge 13
Weister Creek
CR-P
Bridge 14
4
Site I
Bridge 15
Kickapoo Valley Reserve
5
Bridge 16
Site G
Site H
River
Horse crossing
6
Kickapoo
7
Riffles
Corps Road
131
Harris Road
Maple Ridge Road
Plum Run
Bridge 18
8
Dam tower
9
Intermittent Stream
Bridge 19
10
11
131
Munson Road
82
La Farge
Takeout
12
Main Street
82
131
Mill St.
131
131

Photogenic sandstone cliffs tower above paddlers on the Kickapoo.

more moss-covered sandstone, undercut by the river and with a stand of pine and cedars on top.

At 1.1 miles you pass under towering bridge #11 with its concrete pillars. Then the river bends right. Another bluff pushes the river to the left. Soon after, the river hits another exposed rock and goes right. Just before that point, on river right, is a landing on a high pile of sand; Campsite Y is on river left. Around the next bend, at 2 miles, Campsite M is up the sandy bank. About 300 feet later are the two metal foundations of bridge #12 on the left; just beyond that, Jug Creek joins from river left. Continue ping-ponging down the river; there's always an exposed rock face forcing the river one way or the other and a sandy area on the opposite side of the river. You'll see bright patches where recent chunks of sandstone have fallen away.

At 2.7 miles tiny Indian Creek flows in from the right; 0.1 mile later, pass under bridge #13. The twisting lessens a bit. At 3.8 miles, just downriver of the metal bridge #14 is a concrete landing and parking on river left. Paddle another 300 feet from the bridge and find Weister Creek flowing in from the right. Come to an S-curve with good current and pass unsheltered Campsite I, set back from the bank on river left. Then you head straight into another bluff; sandbars and deadfall are common here.

At 4.5 miles pass the wooden bridge #15. Beyond here is another granddaddy of a bluff, rising up over 60 feet. Bridge #16 is another wooden trail bridge at 5.2 miles, with Campsite H up on river left. At 6.1 miles the river swings around left in a curve and passes through sand and mud where the equestrian Willow Trail crosses from river left through the water to reach the multiuse trail on river right. You'll then pass through a series of tight curves created by the sandstone impediments. At 7.4 miles, as you come around a tight curve to the right, you can see the gravel bottom; the shallow current kicks up riffles for 100 feet, with some possible dragging in very dry periods. Just past 8.2 miles is another fantastic stretch of exposed rock; the river runs in the shade of it on its north side heading east. At 8.4 miles the Old Highway 131 Trail crosses on bridge #18.

At 8.9 miles the river comes to high rocks on the left; on one of these rocks there's a rope swing dangling over a good swimming hole. Pass under power lines at 9.1 miles, and a short distance later an intermittent creek slips in on river left. At 10 miles you pass under more power lines and bridge #19. Just downriver of the bridge are a couple of storm sewers on river right. The pace of the river picks up a bit, and you think you are close to the end, but the winding river gives you 2 more miles from that bridge. At 11.8 miles you get your last up-close look at the sandstone, well undercut—perfect for bumping your head on. The takeout is 0.2 mile later, marked with a sign on river left upriver of the WI 82 bridge.

18 La Crosse River

Beginning in a city park just below the dam in Sparta, this intimate little river immediately disappears into a corridor of trees, keeping it sheltered and shaded all the way out of town. Thereafter, it remains lush but open to the sky, offering great birding and other wildlife spotting but also some gentle current with a few easy, small drops along the way.

County: Monroe
Start: Ben Bikin' Park, N43 56.339' / W90 48.523'
End: CR J bridge, N43 54.789' / W90 55.242'
Length: 10.2 miles one-way
Float time: About 3.5 hours
Difficulty rating: Easy
Rapids: A few small Class I drops
River type: Pastoral
Current: Moderate
River gradient: 5.5 feet per mile
River gauge: USGS 05382325 La Crosse River at Sparta; minimum runnable level 100 cfs; avoid at flood stage.
Season: Spring through fall
Land status: Private, with public landings
Fees and permits: State trail daily-use fee if used for bike shuttle
Nearest city/town: Sparta
Maps: USGS Bangor, Sparta; *DeLorme: Wisconsin Atlas & Gazetteer*: Page 41 4A
Boats used: Canoes, kayaks
Organizations: River Alliance of Wisconsin, 147 S. Butler St., Ste. 2, Madison 53703; (608) 257-2424; wisconsinrivers.org
Outfitters: Ellistone Canoe & Kayak Rentals, N 5370 CR J, Rockland 54614; (608) 343-5696 or (608) 487-5114; ellistonecanoerental.com
Local information: La Crosse River State Trail, 111 Milwaukee St., Sparta 54656; (608) 269-4123; lacrosseriverstatetrail.org

Put-in/Takeout Information

To shuttle point/takeout: From Sparta drive west on WI 16 about 5.4 miles. Turn left (south) onto CR J. Drive 0.8 mile, crossing the La Crosse River bridge; the landing is to the right, inside a gravel parking lot. A concrete landing is downriver of the bridge here, on river left. There are no facilities.

Note: A bike shuttle from Rockland to Sparta using the La Crosse River State Trail is a level 7 miles.

To put-in from takeout: From the takeout, go left back onto CR J, backtracking 0.8 mile to WI 16. Go east 5.8 miles to Sparta and turn right onto Dike Road at the park with the large old-fashioned bike and rider statue. Park alongside the park road. There are vending machines, a pavilion, and a portable toilet in season.

River Overview

The La Crosse River stretches just over 60 miles, flowing west to where it joins the Mississippi River at the city of La Crosse. The waters are clear and the bottom sandy.

One of several simple but enjoyable drops on the La Crosse River Preamtip Satasuk

The interstate isn't far off, and a state bike trail runs close, yet this river feels far away from everything once you are on the water. Along the often-grassy banks, wildflowers appear in profusion—coneflowers, nightshade, sunflowers, arrowhead, and so much more. The river is mostly sheltered, almost the entire way, so even on a windy day this should be a pleasant paddle. The corridor of trees provides habitat for a variety of songbirds; shorebirds and waterfowl are also abundant. We've seen eagles and owls here too. Watch for the occasional challenge of sandbars that lie just beneath the surface, sometimes hidden by healthy water foliage. The clear water and its cooler temperature make this a Class 2 trout stream.

Paddle Summary

Put in river right along the grassy bank in the park. The river is a slender 15 feet wide here, and the current creates riffles and a short, easy drop over a couple of ledges before passing under the bike bridge. A heartbeat later you slip under the Water Street bridge and the city seems to disappear as you enter a high-bank wooded section taking you through the west side of Sparta. Ride over an easy 1-foot drop and into some rifles before reaching the Court Street bridge at 0.3 mile. Soon after, the current slows as the river widens to 30 feet. Deadfall is possible but is typically maintained.

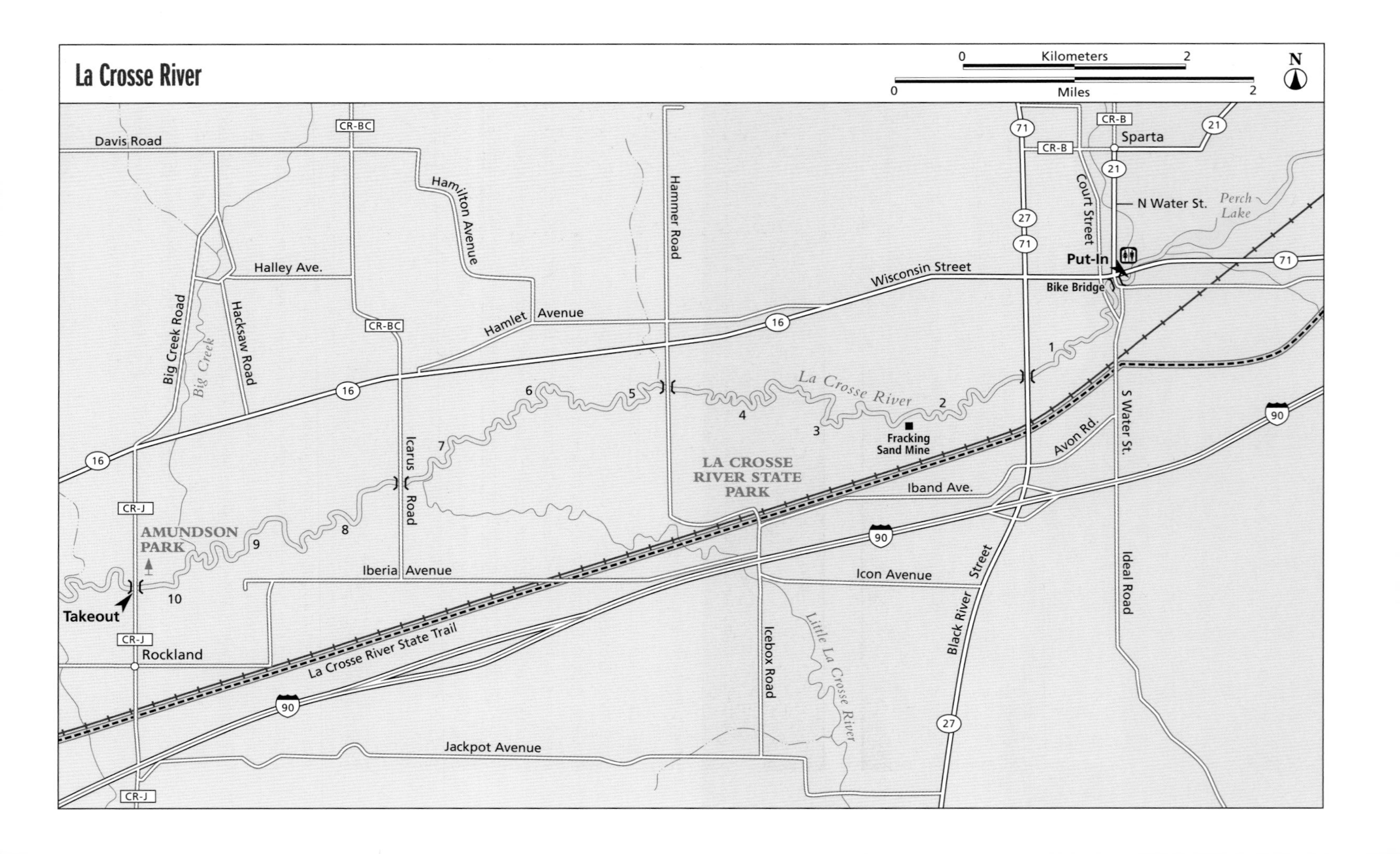
La Crosse River
Kilometers
Miles
N
Davis Road
CR-BC
Hamilton Avenue
Hammer Road
Sparta
CR-B
N Water St.
Perch Lake
Court Street
Put-In
Wisconsin Street
Bike Bridge
Halley Ave.
Hamlet Avenue
Big Creek Road
Big Creek
Hacksaw Road
La Crosse River
Fracking Sand Mine
LA CROSSE RIVER STATE PARK
Avon Rd.
S Water St.
Iband Ave.
Icarus Road
CR-J
AMUNDSON PARK
Iberia Avenue
Icon Avenue
Black River Street
Ideal Road
Takeout
Rockland
La Crosse River State Trail
Icebox Road
Little La Crosse River
Jackpot Avenue

Ben Bikin', at 32 feet in height, is the world's largest bicyclist—located along the La Crosse River in Sparta.

At 1 mile the river widens to 40 feet and passes in front of power lines as it heads into a gentle S-curve. Another 0.1 mile and you pass under the power lines and ride over another short 1-foot drop from rocks lined up straight across the river. Hit another modest drop and pass under the WI 27 bridge at 1.2 miles. A stream feeds in from river right 500 feet later. At 1.6 miles the river curves left in front of a high,

SPARTA: A BIKING MECCA

There's a reason for that giant bicycle rider at the put-in for the La Crosse River: Sparta is the "Bicycling Capital of America." One of the most famous bicycle trails in the state begins here: the Elroy-Sparta National Trail, listed in the Rails-to-Trails Hall of Fame. Just over 32 miles of the old Chicago & North Western Railroad line were converted to a crushed-limestone pathway that's perfect for cyclists. The trail passes over old rail bridges and through three tunnels: The Kendall and Wilton tunnels are each 0.25 mile long; the Norwalk tunnel is 0.75 mile long. Riders need to bring lights to traverse the long, dark passages without walking their bicycles.

The trail passes through three little towns and along prairies, wetlands, farms, and the rolling beauty of the Driftless Area. The Elroy-Sparta Trail connects to the La Crosse River State Trail—a perfect bike-shuttle route for paddlers with just one car.

sandy bank. That sand explains the barbed wire and No Trespassing signs you'll see on river left by the 2-mile mark. Beyond, you may hear the industrial noise of a fracking–sand mining operation. Large piles of sand may be visible in the distance, and you may hear the occasional freight train off to the left as well.

At 3.3 miles you go over another short rock drop. Amundson Park is on the right here. These little drops add a bit of excitement but nothing for beginners to be anxious about. At 3.4 miles you'll come over another row of rocks, the largest of them on this trip, resulting in a short Class I run through a rocky area. Find a tongue, and take the easy ride through.

The river narrows for a bit before opening wide again with grassy banks and taking on a really serpentine course. At 4.8 miles you pass under the Hammer Road bridge. At 5.8 miles the river flirts with power lines but curves away without passing under them, then switches back once more to cross the lines going north and then again as it heads back south 400 feet later. At 7.3 miles the Little La Crosse River, a Class 1 trout stream, joins from river left. A quarter mile later you pass under the Icarus Road bridge. Pass another little stream on the right at 8.9 miles, and at 9.7 miles pass Big Creek, also on the right, possibly with more than one mouth and likely a sandbar. As you come to a bend to the right at 10 miles, you may see a Keep Right sign. Heed it. Deadfall can collect here, pushed against the left bank by the current, and you may need to take the corner short. After the bend the river is a straight shot to the CR J bridge at 10.2 miles. Less than 200 feet past the bridge, on river left, is the concrete ramp of the takeout.

19 Mississippi River–Long Lake Canoe Trail

The Mississippi is mighty and wide, but its smaller channels, backwaters, and marshland make for marvelous paddling. This canoe trail starts in a small lake, skirts along the edge of the larger river, and returns to its starting point through a large marsh and a narrow, intimate channel.

County: La Crosse, Trempealeau
Start/End: Long Lake Landing, N43 59.175' / W91 24.905'
Length: 4.5-mile circle route
Float time: About 3 hours
Difficulty rating: Easy
Rapids: None
River type: Backwater lake, marsh, wide pastoral
Current: Varies from none to moderate
River gradient: Less than 1 foot per mile
River gauge: USGS 05378500 Mississippi River at Winona, Minnesota. Water levels are always sufficient for paddling, but avoid at flood stage.
Season: Spring through fall
Land status: Public
Fees and permits: No fees or permits required
Nearest city/town: Trempealeau
Maps: USGS Pickwick; free maps available at the put-in; DeLorme: Wisconsin Atlas & Gazetteer: Page 48 D1
Boats used: Canoes, kayaks, johnboats
Contacts: Upper Mississippi River National Wildlife & Fish Refuge, 555 Lester Ave., Onalaska 54650; (608) 783-8405; fws.gov/Midwest/UpperMississippiRiver
Outfitters: La Crosse Canoe Outfitters, N5395 Hwy. 108, West Salem 54669; (608) 317-7942; lacrossecanoe.com
Local information: Perrot State Park, W26247 Sullivan Rd., Trempealeau 54661; (608) 534-6409; dnr.wi.gov/topic/parks/name/perrot. Offers camping nearby, and rents canoes but only for within the state park's 3.5-mile canoe trail.

Put-in/Takeout Information

To put-in/takeout: The Great River Road/WI 35 passes through Trempealeau, coming into town from the east as 3rd Street. Turn left (south) onto Fremont Street and continue for 1.5 miles. (It becomes Lake Road after the first 0.2 mile, after crossing the railroad tracks.) At 1.5 miles find the asphalt parking lot for Long Lake on your right. There is a proper ramp and floating dock at the landing, as well as an information board and brochures/maps, but no other facilities.

River Overview

Where the Mississippi passes along the border of Wisconsin, it lives up to the title "Mighty" as it rolls by, muddy and wide, a true force of nature. You might not think of the river as a paddling destination, but abundant narrow passages, backwaters, and sloughs offer beautiful, secluded areas rich in flora and fauna. This particular canoe

DUCKWEED

That bright green covering common in still waters isn't algae or the sign of unclean waters. It is likely duckweed and may actually be a wonder plant. If you look at duckweed closely, you'll see tiny individual plants made up of a very thin single frond. Air pockets within keep it afloat. There are various species, some with a tiny, hairlike rootlet. They reproduce by budding and rather quickly populate still or slow waters. You can find duckweed in most backwaters and small ponds, or even in long bands on a slow-flowing river (e.g., the Bark River) where the current keeps the plants from gathering so conspicuously.

Duckweed contains more protein than soybeans and provides a healthy food source for waterfowl. As it spreads across the surface of the water, it provides shade for the residents below, including frogs and fish. By blocking sunlight, duckweed may also prevent the growth of harmful algae. It also actively cleans the water. The plants grow quickly and take nitrogen and phosphates—commonly problematic substances resulting from agricultural runoff in Wisconsin—out of the water. Duckweed may even control mosquito reproduction and reduce evaporation rates. In parts of Asia, it is even a human food source. And as if that wasn't impressive enough, scientists are considering its feasibility as a source of bio-fuel: It contains more starches than corn, grows rapidly and without fertilizers, and absorbs carbon dioxide. So while it may look as though it is choking off sections of a pond or marsh, duckweed may in fact be a very welcome guest.

trail, within the Upper Mississippi River National Wildlife and Fish Refuge, is a circle tour and so doesn't require a shuttle.

Located just southeast of the city of Trempealeau and Perrot State Park, Long Lake is one of several isolated pockets of water that nevertheless offer narrow channels into the next backwater and, at some points, the wider river itself. Popular with anglers and birders, the counterclockwise canoe trail demands extra time beyond its paddle mileage for lingering and exploring. There are no areas off-limits to paddlers here. Explore at will.

In the brief stretch on the open river, be aware of strong winds, boat traffic, and potential waves or wakes. The backwaters may sound perfectly safe, but high waters on the big river can create a current flowing "backward," and deadfall and strainers could become an issue. River current can push into Big Marsh, especially at the narrow entrance. The listed mileage is approximate; plant life in Big Marsh can get thick in summer, forcing you to paddle a wider path to get through to the return trail. There are other river access points in the area as well. Be sure to wear your personal flotation device.

Paddle Summary

From the put-in, go across the open water and follow the opposite bank south (left) to the narrow Long Lake. The trail is marked with little blue signs with white canoes on them. Straight across from the dock is a tempting channel to explore, though it is not the trail. Along the banks you will find plenty of deadfall, perching herons, and perhaps a few fishing holes. At 0.3 mile a sign points you right (west) and you pass into the next channel, where the trail may curve north a bit but quickly turns south along a narrow channel. The land around you here is heavily forested with large oak, maple, and basswood trees; you could be on a woodland stream in another part of the state. Lily pads are abundant, as is duckweed in summer. The hardwoods bring nice colors in fall.

By about 0.7 mile the channel widens a bit like a small lake, and you can see the exposed rock of a bluff far off in the distance to the south on the Minnesota side of the river. On both sides of this narrow lake you'll see arrows guiding you south-southeast to the next connecting channel. The waters look dark and often smooth, reflecting the sky brilliantly. With closer scrutiny you can see about 2 feet down and observe fish and clams below.

This lake area narrows and appears to come to a dead end until you are right upon the short channel to the left, marked with another sign at 1.1 miles. Take this short,

Wildflowers grow in Big Marsh along the Mississippi. Preamtip Satasuk

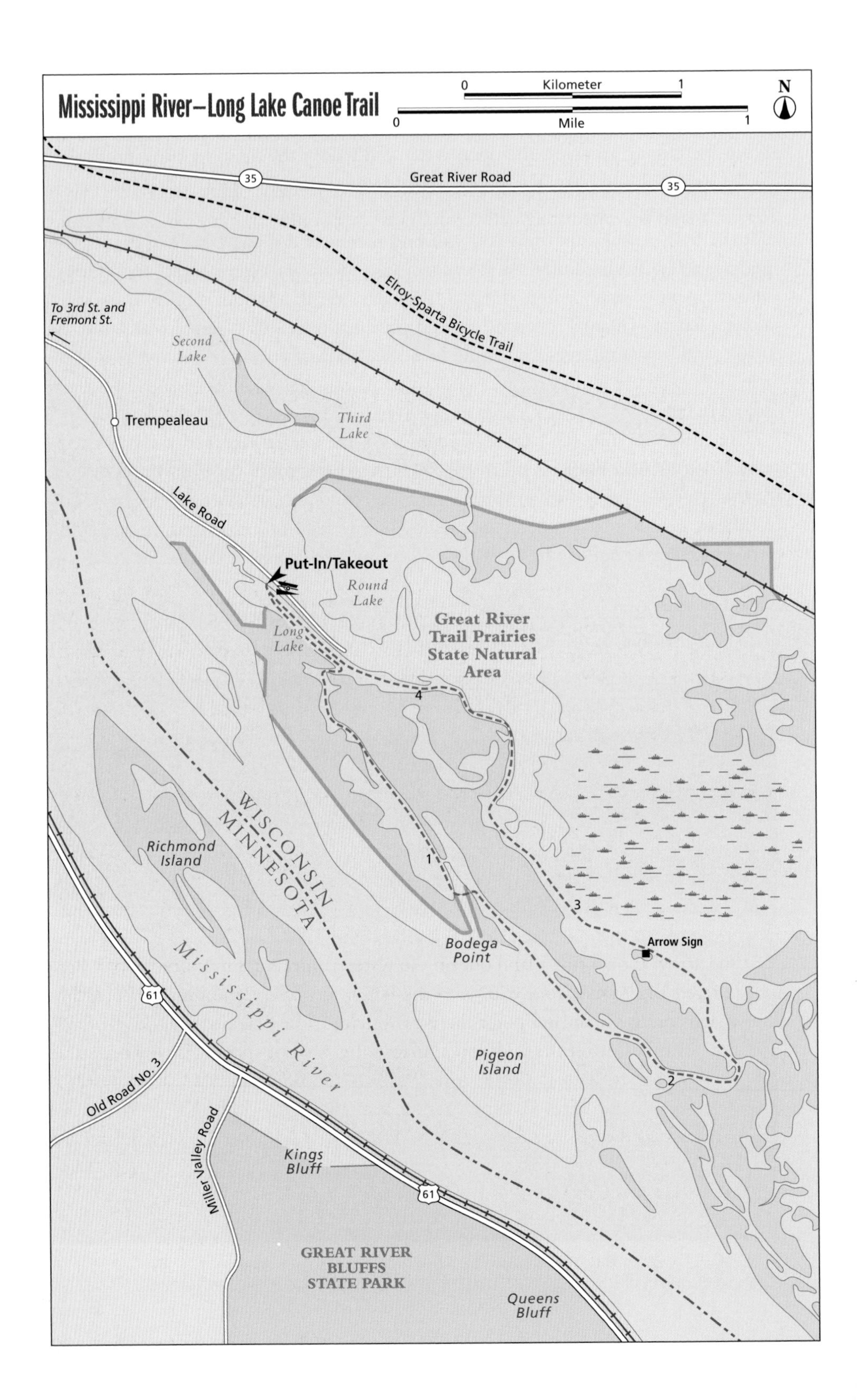

Mississippi River–Long Lake Canoe Trail
0
Kilometer
1
0
Mile
1
N
35
Great River Road
35
Elroy-Sparta Bicycle Trail
To 3rd St. and Fremont St.
Second Lake
Third Lake
Trempealeau
Lake Road
Put-In/Takeout
Round Lake
Long Lake
Great River Trail Prairies State Natural Area
4
1
3
2
Arrow Sign
WISCONSIN
MINNESOTA
Richmond Island
Bodega Point
Mississippi River
Pigeon Island
61
Old Road No. 3
Miller Valley Road
Kings Bluff
61
GREAT RIVER BLUFFS STATE PARK
Queens Bluff

narrow corridor into another wider channel heading right (south), again following the signs. By about 1.4 miles, as you come to Bodega Point on your right, you are likely to see current. The water splits, but you follow an arrow to the left before taking a right turn thereafter, heading out into the open water of the Mississippi River. Pigeon Island is immediately before you. This is a popular camping site, and its sandy beach makes a nice picnic break. Farther upriver is Richmond Island, behind you as you paddle with the river current. Look out over Pigeon to see Kings Bluff to the right and Queens Bluff to the left, on the Minnesota side. Current can be moderate here, but a strong headwind could make this short stretch tough. The main channel of the river follows the state border on the map, coming downriver past Richmond Island on river left but then cutting right around the opposite side of Pigeon, leaving the channel you are using free from the commercial traffic. Smaller craft and fishing boats may still pass through here. Although this is a no-wake zone, stay left to avoid them and to find your reentry into the backwaters after about 0.3 mile on the open river.

At 1.8 miles find the arrows marking your reentry point to the backwaters. Go left, leaving the bluff view behind and entering a channel 80 feet wide. The channel continues southeast on a straight course; with good eyes or binoculars you can see the next trail sign. Just past the 2-mile mark, the trail goes left, and takes a long, slow curve to the east as it begins to head back north. Pass another blue sign at 2.3 miles before entering a huge marshy area—appropriately named Big Marsh—stretching out at least a mile before you. You'll see a farm in the distance and perhaps some cell towers.

You want to continue left (north). The trouble is, when floating vegetation gets thick in summer, that paddle can be pretty strenuous. Before that time, you can just follow along the shoreline on your left. At other times you may need to paddle in a wider arc through open pathways in the lily pads and weeds. Your goal is the mouth of the next narrow segment into the wooded area to the northwest. I've paddled out to the center, and you can still find your way back by watching that shoreline to the west. There are blue signs to reassure you, although one out in the middle of nowhere may mislead you. Stay west of it, closer to the shore on your left.

One arrow is on a tiny island out on the water at about 2.8 miles, north of where you entered Big Marsh. Your path is to the left (west) of that, heading north. Other arrow signs on the mainland point the way. Watch for the channel between the trees at about 3.1 miles. After the wide-open marsh, the 40-foot channel is very quiet and peaceful except for the possible distant call of a train. The channel turns to the right a bit at 3.4 miles and follows a long left-leaning, curving course to the southern end of Long Lake at about 3.9 miles. Follow the left shoreline if you want to avoid the handful of cabin properties on Long Lake's eastern shoreline. Paddle the length of the lake all the way back to Long Lake Landing, which will be on the right.

20 Black River

The paddle begins at the edge of town—well below the dam in Black River Falls—and follows a wide river, mostly through forest and often showing sandbars throughout. It is a slow, relaxing paddle with only a few riffle spots, but the highlight is actually off-river: a riverside canyon toward the end of the journey that is worth getting out of your craft for.

County: Jackson
Start: Bruce Cormican Canoe Landing, N44 17.289' / W90 51.060'
End: David Hansen Memorial Landing in Irving (formerly Irving Landing), N44 11.247' / W90 53.940'
Length: 12.7 miles one-way
Float time: About 5.5 hours
Difficulty rating: Easy
Rapids: Some riffles, one Class I
River type: Wide wooded pastoral with sandbars
Current: Gentle to moderate
River gradient: 1.6 feet per mile
River gauge: USGS 053813595 Black River at Black River Falls; minimum runnable level 200 cfs, maximum 3,000 cfs (see "River Overview")
Season: Spring through fall
Land status: Varied, with public landings
Fees and permits: No fees or permits required
Nearest city/town: Black River Falls
Maps: USGS Black River Falls, Melrose, Shamrock, Stenulson Coulee; *DeLorme: Wisconsin Atlas & Gazetteer*: Page 50 B2
Boats used: Canoes, kayaks
Organizations: Friends of the Black River, PO Box 475, Black River Falls 54615; Facebook.com/friendsoftheblackriverWI; email: info_fbr@yahoo.com
Outfitters: Lost Falls Campground, N2974 E. Sunnyvale Rd., Black River Falls 54615; (715) 284-7133; lostfalls.com. Rents canoes, kayaks, SUPs, and tubes. The takeout point is 2 miles upriver from the campground.

Put-in/Takeout Information

To shuttle point/takeout: From where US 12 and WI 54 meet in downtown Black River Falls, go west on WI 54/Main Street 0.6 mile. Turn left onto 10th Street for 0.1 mile, then take a slight right to remain on WI 54 for another 7.7 miles. Turn left onto John Deere Road. Go 0.1 mile and turn right onto Nichols Road. Cross the bridge and the put-in is at the end of a packed-dirt circle there. Parking is farther south on Nichols Road at the Irving Town Hall, a short walk away. There are no facilities.

To put-in from takeout: From the takeout, backtrack on Nichols Road; go left on John Deere and then turn right (north) onto WI 54, following it 7.7 miles back to town. Turn right onto Pierce Street and drive 0.4 mile. Turn right (south) onto 3rd Street and drive 0.3 mile to the end, where you can see the parking lot for the put-in. Drive up over the bike trail and down the other side to drop off your craft at the landing.

A hidden canyon just off the Black River

River Overview

The 190-mile-long Black River actually joins the Mississippi River—twice. Lock and Dam No. 7 on the larger river creates a 10-mile impoundment, Lake Onalaska, through which the original river passed. From there the original channel of the Black River has its own exit, and it continues about another 6 miles, along the eastern side of French Island, before ending again at the Mississippi just northwest of La Crosse.

The Black River has been referred to as the Mini-Wisconsin—modest and narrow at the beginning; rough waters and broken rock about midway; and then slow, wide, and full of sandbars all the way to the Mississippi. Upriver plant life contributes the tannins for its tea-colored but clear waters. The dam at Lake Arbutus, just north of Black River Falls, is the divider between the rocky and sometimes fast and rough portions and the slow and easy sections of sandbars and sandstone where the river passes into Wisconsin's Driftless Area.

The dam at Black River Falls can give a good indication of what you can expect out on the river. If no gates or just one gate is open, all skill levels are good to go. Two open gates mean the waters are suitable for average-skilled paddlers. Three or more can mean dangerously high water, strong current, and moving deadfall and debris. In dry months and when all gates are closed, the flow can drop well below 200 cfs, which can mean a lot of dragging your canoe or kayak. If water is high enough, you can get around Hawk Island on its left side for a narrow, more intimate stretch of paddling on this otherwise rather wide river. This diversion would add about 1.3 miles to the trip. Because of the region's sandy substrata, high water levels caused by a recent rain can diminish quickly.

Paddle Summary

From the shallow put-in, head right (downstream). Riprap lines the sloping left bank, and houses overlook it. But past that first curve you will see almost nothing but forest and the occasional landing throughout the rest of the trip. At 0.5 mile you pass some large boulders and on the tall left bank see a private put-in with wooden steps to the water. At 1.3 miles there's a landing on river right as the river enters a turn to the left. When water is higher, rocks hide beneath the surface; when the levels go down as summer passes, rocks rise up to meet you and grass grows on shallow islands or in patches of sand among the rocks.

At 2.3 miles Perry Creek comes in from the left; just after that is a concrete state forest boat landing. A long, narrow island stands in the center of the river here, and another with trees and grasses lies another 0.25 mile downriver. At 3 miles the clear Squaw Creek flows in from river right. Another 500 feet later the river slows up. To the left is what appears to be another branch. This left channel is narrow and closed in by trees, and it's not always runnable when water levels are too low. Hawk Island is separated from the mainland by this 2.2-mile diversion; the equivalent distance on the main river is just 0.9 mile to where the two reunite.

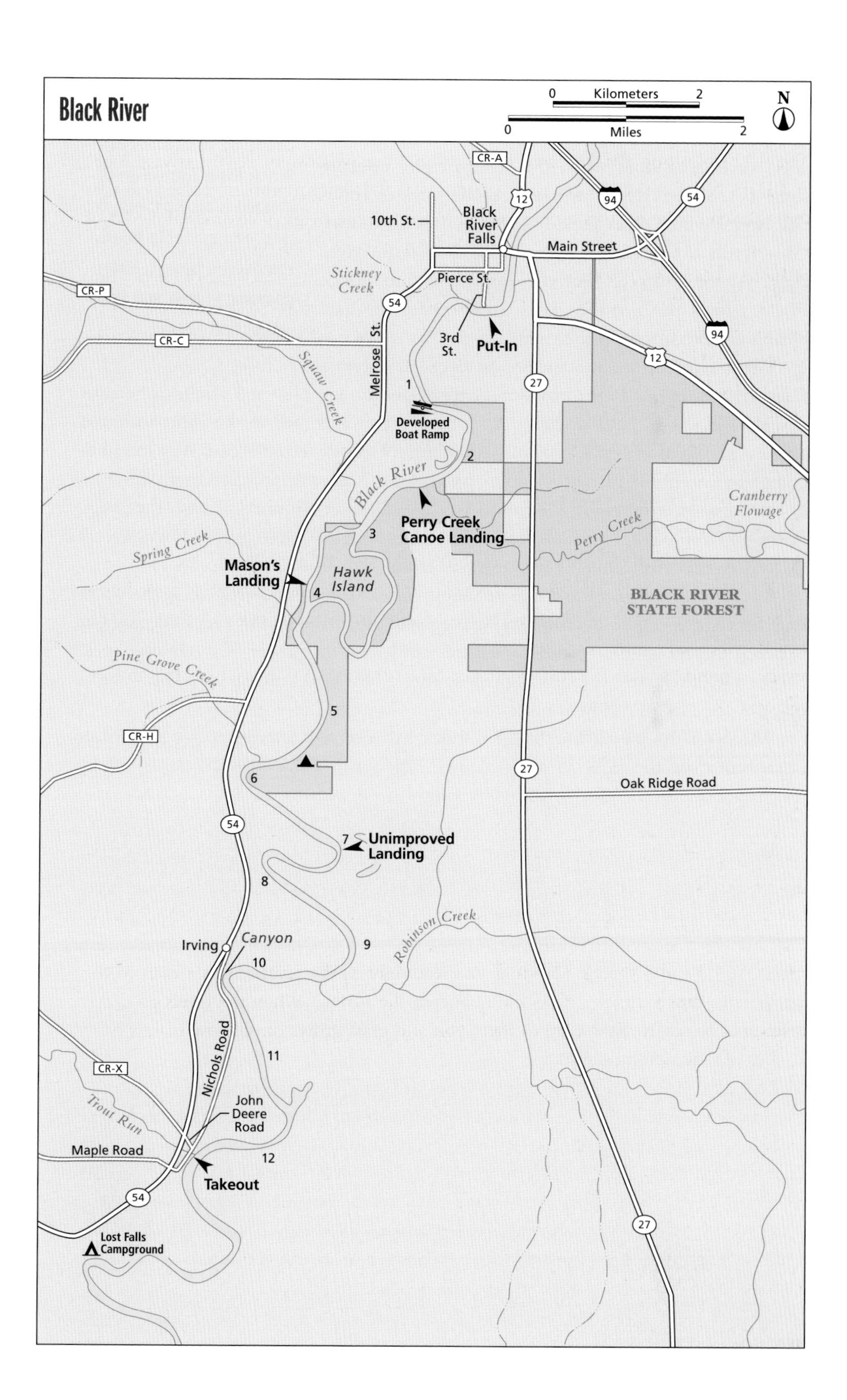
Black River
0 Kilometers 2
0 Miles 2
N
CR-A
12
94
54
10th St.
Black River Falls
Main Street
Stickney Creek
Pierce St.
CR-P
54
3rd St.
Put-In
94
CR-C
Melrose St.
12
Squaw Creek
1
27
Developed Boat Ramp
2
Black River
Perry Creek Canoe Landing
Cranberry Flowage
3
Spring Creek
Perry Creek
Mason's Landing
Hawk Island
4
BLACK RIVER STATE FOREST
Pine Grove Creek
5
CR-H
6
27
Oak Ridge Road
54
7
Unimproved Landing
8
Robinson Creek
Irving
Canyon
9
10
Nichols Road
11
CR-X
Trout Run
John Deere Road
Maple Road
12
Takeout
54
Lost Falls Campground
27

Continuing on the main channel from the beginning of Hawk Island, you come to a slow and deep area—a good swimming hole when the water's right, offering some beach area. Right after that is 0.2 mile of riffles that begins with a short shelf drop and ends with an easy Class I run. At 3.9 miles Mason's Landing is on river right. About 500 feet later the passage behind Hawk Island rejoins the main channel. In another 900 feet, Spring Creek joins from the right.

Go primitive: Two rustic canoe-up campsites in Black River State Forest include a picnic table, fire ring, and portable toilet. You need a permit, but camping is free and first-come, first-served.

The put-in you see at 5.4 miles on river left is a state forest river campsite. Pine Grove Creek flows in from river left at 5.7 miles. The river is wide and can be shallow here. At 7 miles the river bends to the right around a sandy area. On river left is a primitive landing off Hawk Island Road. At a long but complete switchback turn at 7.9 miles, watch for the seeps dripping through the shale of the bank on river right. Robinson Creek widens at its juncture with the Black River on river left at 9.4 miles. A sign here gives the mileage to points downriver all the way to the Mississippi. Your journey to Irving has about 3 more miles.

At 10.4 miles is what looks like just another sandstone bluff overlooking the water on river right. Just past this you may notice a spill of sand and a tiny creek coming out between the two bluffs. Stop here and get out to see the power of water over rock. Follow the little creek; the space opens up into a beautiful little canyon. The water is much colder, and the view is quite lovely.

Watch for the power lines at 12.6 miles. Just 200 feet later a creek called Trout Run joins from the right, creating its own little sandy delta. The takeout is on the downriver side of the creek, marked by a sign.

21 Crystal River

Short and sweet, this section of the Crystal River is a quick paddle with a lot of maneuvering and a historic mill and covered bridge to see along the way. The paddle winds among wooded banks, gradually getting marshier before following a channel from the river to Shadow Lake. The final stretch is the open-water crossing to the takeout point.

County: Waupaca
Start: CR K bridge, N44 19.161' / W89 6.542'
End: South Park Landing, N44 20.814' / W89 5.316'
Length: 4.3 miles one-way
Float time: About 2 hours
Difficulty rating: Easy to moderate due to current and tight maneuvering
Rapids: Riffles
River type: Narrow wooded
Current: Moderate
River gradient: 5 feet per mile
River gauge: No gauge; typically runnable even in dry seasons. Contact an outfitter for current conditions.
Season: Spring through fall
Land status: Private, with public landings
Fees and permits: No fees or permits required
Nearest city/town: Waupaca
Maps: USGS Waupaca; *DeLorme: Wisconsin Atlas & Gazetteer*: Page 53 B8
Boats used: Kayaks, canoes dependent on water levels and good boat control
Organizations: River Alliance of Wisconsin, 147 S. Butler St., Ste. 2, Madison 53703; (608) 257-2424; wisconsinrivers.org
Outfitters: Adventure Outfitters, 106 S. Main St., Waupaca 54981; (715) 258-0775; waupacakayakadventures.com. All trips begin and end at Lower Shelter Area in South Park on Shadow Lake.

Put-in/Takeout Information

To shuttle point/takeout: Several highways converge on Waupaca. From the US 10/WI 49/WI 54 bypass, take the exit for CR K/WI 22. Head north on CR K/Lakeside Parkway for 0.5 mile; the boat landing is in the asphalt parking lot on the right. Facilities are in the next lot down the road, on the right.
To put-in from takeout: From the takeout at South Park, go left (southwest) on Lakeside Parkway/CR K for 1.2 miles, passing under the US 10 overpass along the way. Turn left onto CR K and drive 1.2 miles. After you pass over the river, turn left into the gravel parking lot. This is Nelson Park; put in anywhere along the low grassy banks. There are two pit toilets on-site.

River Overview

The Crystal River earns its name; the waters are clear as a bell. The narrow and often riffly stream is a popular destination near Waupaca for both paddlers and tubers. The stretch here ends with a short lake crossing, keeping the tubing crowd at bay. The river

With its clear waters, the Crystal River earns its name.

winds a bit and passes in and around deadfall maintained by outfitters, but cut out with kayakers in mind. Short kayaks are best; canoes might require some work. While this river is perfectly OK for beginners, a tricky turn or deadfall passage can mean that a paddler with no experience or a moment of inattention gets wet. But the river is shallow and the bottom sandy. This trip stands on its own for a little day's adventure, but it also makes a good combo with the Waupaca River if you are in the area for two days. This stretch passes a couple of historical structures along the way, and the trees and brush are good habitat for wildlife. Birders might hear more than they see. Green herons may outnumber the blue.

Paddle Summary

Set off from the grassy bank on river right in some playful moderate current. At 0.4 mile you come to one of the few landmarks on the river: the Old Red Mill. Now a gift shop and old-world museum, the 1855 structure was originally a gristmill. The water under a footbridge there kicks up a little Class I wave trail; you pass under a covered bridge just beyond at about 0.7 mile. Shadow Road spans the river on a low concrete bridge, and the current picks up a bit underneath.

You'll see a wide variety of trees—oak, birch, pine, maples, basswood, and willows in some spots. On a windy day you'll be sheltered.

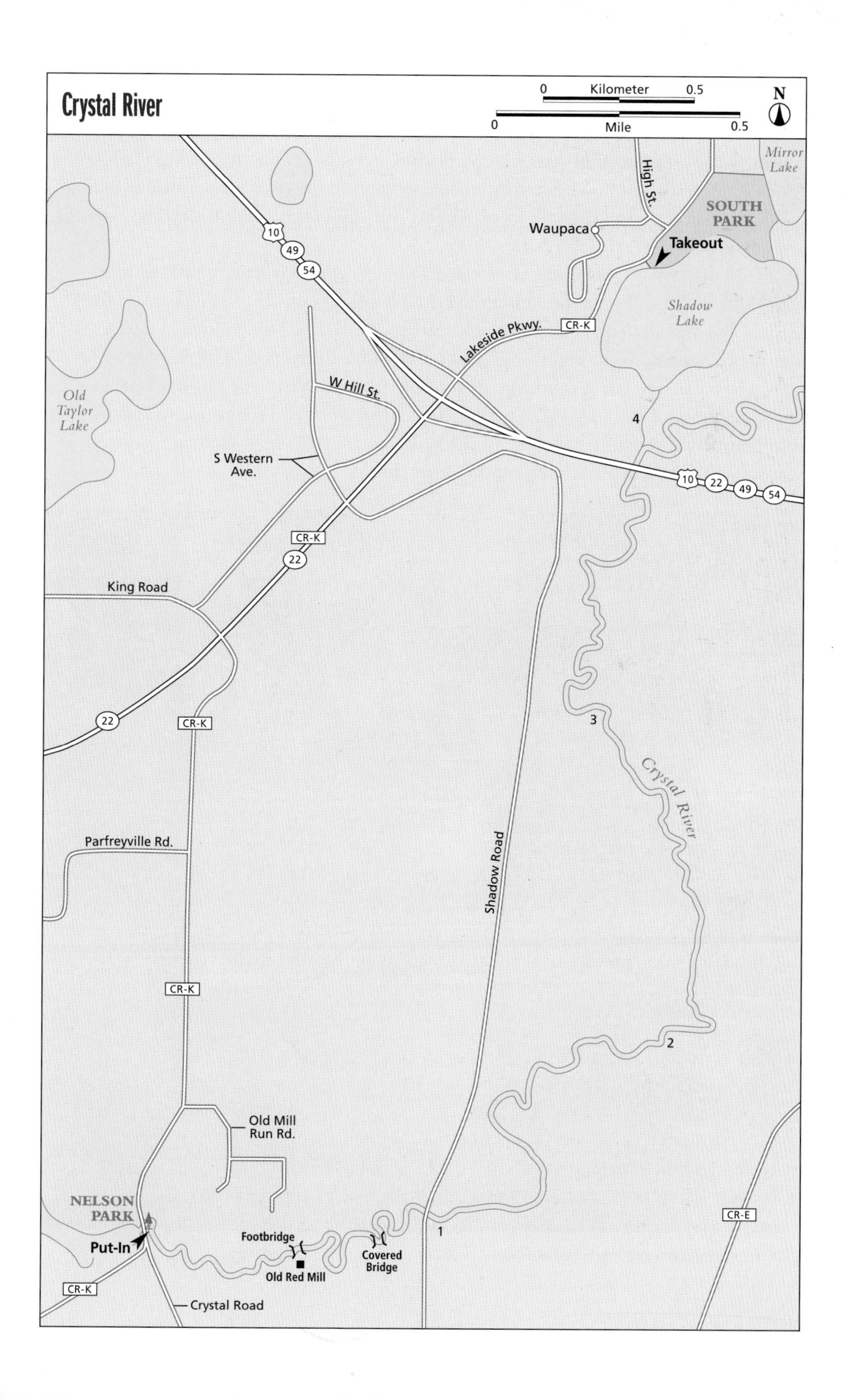

Crystal River
0 Kilometer 0.5
0 Mile 0.5
N
Mirror Lake
High St.
SOUTH PARK
Waupaca
Takeout
Shadow Lake
10
49
54
CR-K
Lakeside Pkwy.
W Hill St.
Old Taylor Lake
4
S Western Ave.
10
22
49
54
CR-K
22
King Road
22
CR-K
3
Crystal River
Parfreyville Rd.
Shadow Road
CR-K
2
Old Mill Run Rd.
NELSON PARK
Put-In
Footbridge
Old Red Mill
Covered Bridge
1
CR-E
CR-K
Crystal Road

Banks are generally low, but a few high places and ridges give root space to bigger trees. The occasional houses and yards appear; some show little docks. At about 2.4 miles, the area becomes a bit marshy. Shrubs and grasses take over along the low banks, and the current slows. You may encounter splits in the river where small islands have emerged, making little side loops. There's one such loop at 2.6 miles. The river widens to 50 to 60 feet along here.

At 3.1 miles you pass under a wooden footbridge. You will start to hear highway traffic and at 3.9 miles pass under the double bridges of US 10. Just beyond the bridges, stay left and you will see the channel to the lake for the takeout. Don't get into the backwater to the right or go right at the fork in the river. The right branch is the Crystal River, but it is not the path to the takeout. When the channel's grown in during summer, this may seem wrong, but there should be a sign there to reassure you. This flatwater path takes you out to the lake, where the boat landing is straight across. Look for the asphalt ramp on the other side.

The covered bridge over the Crystal River

22 Waupaca River

This quick and agile river shows riffles and more not long after the put-in—and it doesn't let up much for the rest of your journey. Small boulder gardens are frequent throughout this wooded paddle, and good boat skills are helpful. As the river works its way from the country into the city of Waupaca, it passes a series of low-grade rapids until it ends in a city park after a short Class I run through boulders.

County: Waupaca
Start: County Q Bridge Landing, N44 22.440' / W89 11.123'
End: Brainards Bridge Park, N44 21.935' / W89 5.922'
Length: 7.8 miles one-way
Float time: About 3 hours
Difficulty rating: Moderate due to navigation and deadfall
Rapids: Several Class I and riffle sections
River type: Pastoral
Current: Moderate
River gradient: 6.2 feet per mile
River gauge: No gauge; typically runnable, but in fall or dry seasons, canoes may find it too low. Contact an outfitter for current conditions.
Season: Spring through fall
Land status: Private, with public landings
Fees and permits: No fees or permits required
Nearest city/town: Waupaca
Maps: USGS King, Scandinavia, Waupaca; *DeLorme: Wisconsin Atlas & Gazetteer*: Page 53 A7
Boats used: Kayaks, canoes with maneuverability
Organizations: River Alliance of Wisconsin, 147 S. Butler St., Ste. 2, Madison 53703; (608) 257-2424; wisconsinrivers.org
Outfitters: Adventure Outfitters, 106 S. Main St., Waupaca 54981; (715) 258-0775; waupacakayakadventures.com. These trips begin and end at Brainards Bridge Park.

Put-in/Takeout Information

To shuttle point/takeout: From US 10 take the exit for WI 49/54 and head east into Waupaca on Fulton Street for 0.8 mile. Turn left onto Hillcrest Drive; go 0.2 mile and turn left onto Morton Street. Take the next left on North Street and then the next right onto Bailey Street. Drive 0.3 mile; the park is on the left, just before you cross the bridge over the river. The takeout is just below the rapids. The park has restrooms and picnic facilities.

To put-in from takeout: From the takeout, turn right onto Bailey Street; go 0.3 mile and turn left onto North Street. Take the first right onto Morton Street, then turn right onto Hillcrest Drive. Go 0.2 mile and turn right onto Fulton Street, taking it 0.8 mile to US 10. Take the ramp heading west toward Stevens Point. Continue 3.9 miles and turn left onto CR Q. Follow CR Q 0.8 mile. Just before the bridge over the Waupaca River, turn right onto Cobbtown Road; the landing is here on the left. Look for a sign that says Waupaca River Fishery Area. There is off-road parking and a gravel loop at the landing area, but no facilities. Launch from either the concrete wall or an opening in the grassy bank.

River Overview

The Waupaca begins where the Tomorrow River and Bear Creek join in Amherst, northwest of Waupaca. But the 44.8 miles of the Waupaca and the 22 miles of the Tomorrow are actually the same river. In fact, the Native American name means "tomorrow." It's a clear and clean river through woodlands, wetlands, and upland grasses; the area near Farmington is a Class 2 trout stream. At the city of Waupaca, the river picks up the waters of the Crystal River and flows on to its confluence with the Wolf River. The portion within Waupaca County is good for paddlers, and the segment described here is quite an exciting challenge. Deadfall is abundant but is maintained with kayaks in mind. With these narrower passages, kayaks may be preferable. But canoeists with good boat control and patience for challenges will really enjoy this if water levels are adequate.

Riffles and low-grade rapids are common throughout. The run of rapids at Brainards Bridge Park is a fun end to a rewarding trip, but in low water they may take some of the color off your craft. Low water makes this more difficult, but in my experience this paddle is still doable even in September with below-average rainfall. Waterfowl, kingfishers, and herons are abundant; if you are lucky, you may even see a river otter.

Paddle Summary

The put-in is on river left just 100 feet upriver from the CR Q bridge. The river is 40 feet wide here, with low grassy banks and sand and cobble along its bed.

At 0.3 mile follow a sharp bend left and then pass under some power lines twice as the river switches back again. Here you'll encounter riffles or Class I rapids through some boulders. You'll see these frequently on this trip. At 0.5 mile you pass under a wire bridge and through a series of little islands. From here to 0.8 mile, you'll zigzag through boulders and some deadfall. The river widens a bit to more than 50 feet and you get some highway noise. At 1.4 miles some navigation is required for a boulder garden, and then you pass under the two bridges of US 10. Expect some Class I rapids under the second bridge. (***Caution:*** On the right passage under the second bridge, there is a metal fence post dangerously sticking up from the middle of the water, just beyond the bridge. It is easily avoided when you can see it.) Pass an old barn on your left through more riffles/Class I rapids.

At 1.7 miles the river goes left below a residence with riprap along the shore and enters a flatwater stretch. The river narrows a bit, and at 2.1 miles the current picks up through some rocks as the river runs parallel to the highway. Pass under a concrete footbridge at 2.4 miles and meet an easy Class I wave train through to the other side. At 2.5 miles a constriction of low rocks gives you a tiny drop and lifts the current a bit; 0.1 mile later you pass under River Drive bridge. After a short narrow spot there, the river widens to 50 feet, with larger trees standing back from the banks. At 3 miles the river bends left past some houses and kicks up riffles for the next 100 feet. Take a sharp right and pass under a metal footbridge. On the other side, an island splits the

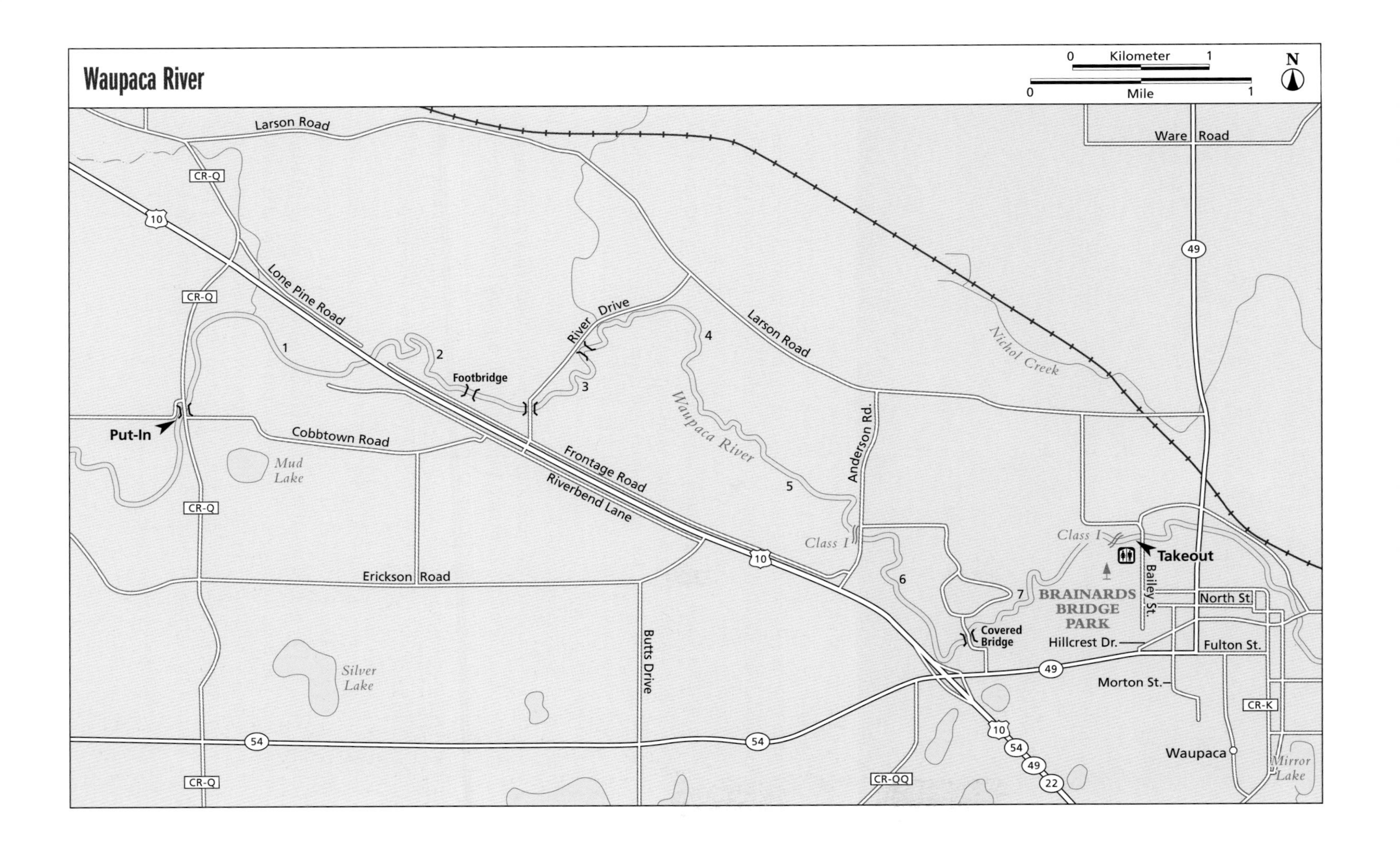
Waupaca River
0 Kilometer 1
0 Mile 1
N
Larson Road
Ware Road
CR-Q
10
49
Lone Pine Road
River Drive
Larson Road
Nichol Creek
1
2
3
4
5
6
7
Footbridge
Put-In
Cobbtown Road
Mud Lake
Waupaca River
Anderson Rd.
Frontage Road
Riverbend Lane
Class I
Takeout
Bailey St.
North St.
BRAINARDS BRIDGE PARK
Covered Bridge
Hillcrest Dr.
Fulton St.
Morton St.
Erickson Road
Butts Drive
Silver Lake
54
CR-K
Waupaca
Mirror Lake
CR-QQ
22

The final run of rapids on the Waupaca River Preamtip Satasuk

river into two narrow channels. Look ahead to make sure deadfall doesn't await you on your chosen route. At 3.6 miles you pass another island, then more power lines at 3.9 miles and again at 4.5 miles. Expect riffles and zigzagging through here. At 4.7 miles is a 40-foot Class I run through some rocks where the river pinches a bit, but by the 5-mile mark, the river is straight, wide, and shallow.

At 5.4 miles you'll find lots of boulders and chutes and spins; with deadfall it's a hassle. At 5.6 miles you'll come to a small drop and Class I rapids under the Anderson Road bridge. By 5.7 miles the more challenging boulder gardens thin out and the banks become grassy. You begin to see the manicured lawns beyond the rocky bank on river right as you enter Waupaca, but the left bank is wooded, low, and marshy. At 6.7 miles you paddle under a covered bridge, which is pretty low for canoes—you'll likely need to duck. After the bridge take a quick left into an S-curve through boulders and riffles. As you come up on 7 miles, you'll start through a boulder garden on Class I rapids, which is much harder when the water is lower. Deadfall can complicate it further.

Pass under power lines at 7.5 miles, and at 7.7 miles begin the final rush with riffles and rapids. About 200 feet in, the river splits; stay right to get to the takeout. The left branch may not be passable, and it runs along the left side of an island that would block you from the takeout. The last hurrah is about 100 feet of Class I rapids, which can be quite bumpy—but still fun—in low water. The takeout is at the end, on river right, before a walking bridge that goes out to the island in the middle of the river. There is also a bridge at the end of the park but no takeout there.

23 Plover River

A surprisingly undeveloped stretch of river runs right into Stevens Point's most popular park. Paddle through hardwood lowlands on the gentle current of a twisting river that makes the city seem a lot farther away than it is.

County: Portage
Start: South Jordan County Park Canoe Landing, N44 34.490' / W89 30.148'
End: Iverson Park Canoe Landing, N44 31.350'/ W89 32.256'
Length: 7.3 miles one-way
Float time: About 3 hours
Difficulty rating: Moderate for boat control and deadfall
Rapids: None
River type: Wooded lowlands
Current: Gentle
River gradient: 3.1 feet per mile
River gauge: No gauge; typically runnable, but in fall or dry seasons, canoes may find it too low. Contact an outfitter for current conditions.
Season: Spring through fall
Land status: Private, with public landings
Fees and permits: No fees or permits required
Nearest city/town: Stevens Point
Maps: USGS Stevens Point; *DeLorme: Wisconsin Atlas & Gazetteer*: Page 64–65 D4
Boats used: Canoes, kayaks
Contacts: River Alliance of Wisconsin, 147 S. Butler St., Ste. 2, Madison 53703; (608) 257-2424; wisconsinrivers.org
Outfitters: Nature's Niche & Nature Treks, Iverson Park, 4201 Main St., Stevens Point, 54482; (715) 254-0247; naturesniche.org

Put-in/Takeout Information

To shuttle point/takeout: From I-39 through Stevens Point take exit 158B and turn west on Main Street. Drive 0.7 mile and turn left into Iverson Park. Park in the first parking lot in front of the outfitter in a stone building. On a direct line 300 feet across mowed grass to the river is a small dock. The park has restrooms and water but farther into the park from here.
To put-in from takeout: The Iverson Park entry on Main Street is one-way. From Iverson Park follow the park road through the southwest corner of the park to the exit; turn right onto Sunrise Avenue and drive 0.3 mile to Main Street. Turn right and continue 0.9 mile, then turn left to take the on-ramp to I-39 North. Drive 1.4 miles to exit 159 for WI 66 and turn right, continuing 3 miles to Jordan County. A sign with an arrow indicates the park is on the left, but turn right, across from Deer Lane on the left, 500 feet before that. Follow the park road through a gate where it turns right and park there. In the parking lot are two pit toilets. Beyond another gate opposite them is a wide grassy trail. Carry your craft 300 feet to the river where there is a wide wooden trail bridge. The bank is low with some large rocks and mud. Put in on river right just above the bridge.

The trail bridge at the put-in on the Plover River

Alternatively, bike shuttles may use part of the Green Circle Trail for most of the route between put-in and takeout.

River Overview

The Plover is a modest, intimate river that originates to the northeast in the Antigo area. The last 30 miles or so make for great paddling, with three dams creating Bentley, Jordan, and McDill Ponds, the latter lying south of Iverson Park, a mile before the Plover flows into the Wisconsin. The segment here begins beneath the Jordan dam and a former hydroelectric plant that operated from 1904 to 1965, and shows almost no development until the bridges at the end. With consistent dam release rates, the water levels are fairly reliable. In periods of drought, however, irrigation in the surrounding potato fields may lower the supply and lead to sandbars and a lot of scraping, if it's navigable at all. The sandy soil of central Wisconsin means that during rainy periods the river level normalizes quickly. If rivers are flooded elsewhere, check here.

The water is clear and the bottom sandy. With the exception of a few holes perhaps, the depth is often 1 to 3 feet unless the water is high. The segment mapped here weaves its way through lowland forest with occasional backwaters and marshy patches, and deadfall is common. The outfitters maintain it well, but don't be surprised by the occasional portage or low pass under a fallen maple; the cuts are often minimal enough that you still need to navigate carefully. That potential for needing good boat control gives this paddle its moderate rating.

Paddle Summary

Slide your craft into the water on the upriver side of the trail bridge; the current quickly puts the dam and boulder garden of the former power plant area—too rocky and low to paddle—behind you. Don't expect even some riffles anywhere, but the

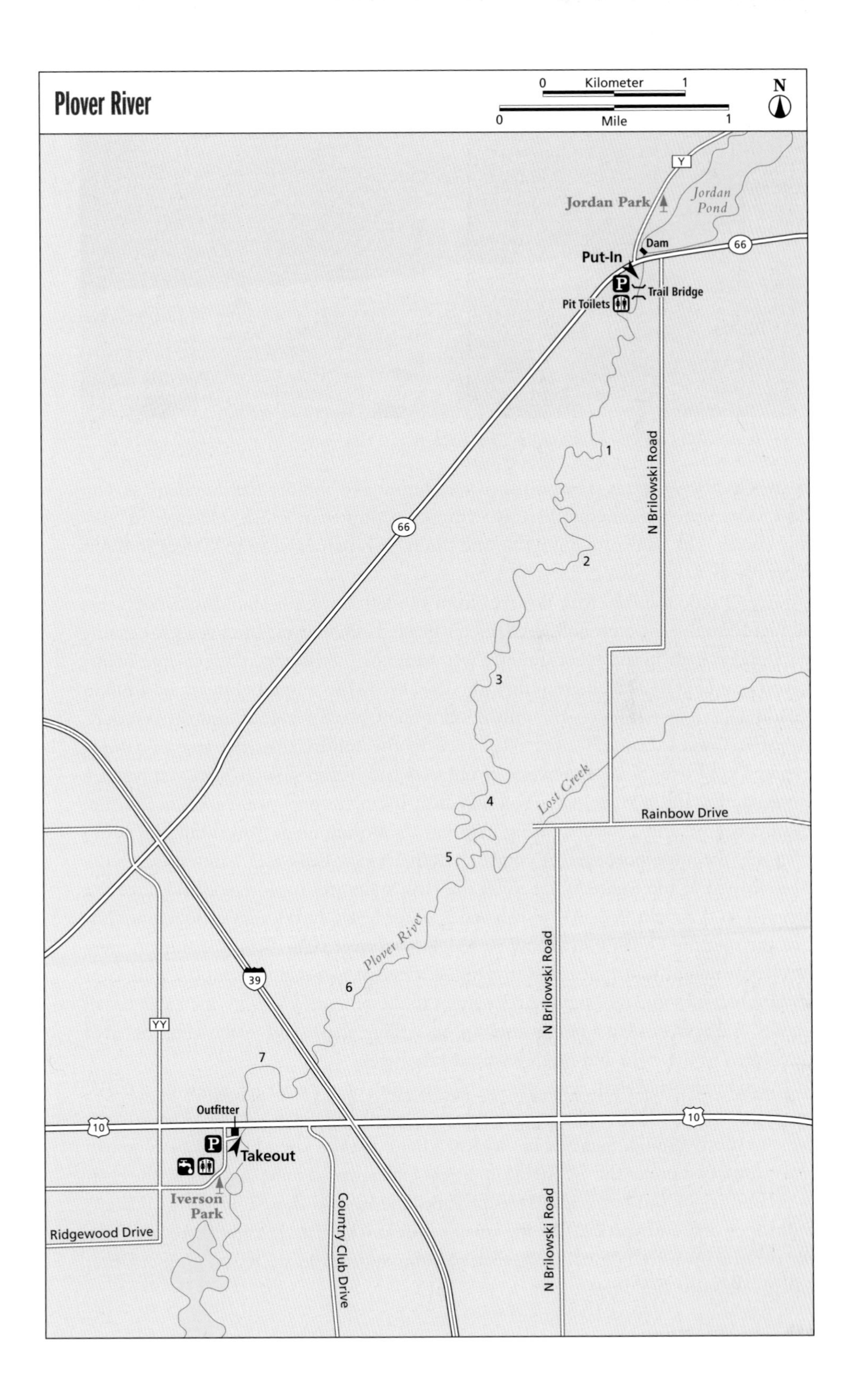

Plover River
0 Kilometer 1
0 Mile 1
N
Y
Jordan Park
Jordan Pond
Dam
66
Put-In
P
Trail Bridge
Pit Toilets
1
N Brilowski Road
66
2
3
Lost Creek
4
Rainbow Drive
5
Plover River
39
6
N Brilowski Road
YY
7
Outfitter
10
10
P
Takeout
Iverson Park
Ridgewood Drive
Country Club Drive
N Brilowski Road

A sandpiper along the low banks of the Plover River

current is always steady. The course is serpentine and the deadfall frequent, so you have to navigate almost continuously without encountering much still water for taking a break. The banks are quite low, and the river is narrow—30 to 40 feet across in most places.

At 0.2 mile a small creek flows in from the left. Look for abundant wildflowers along the banks—swamp milkweed, green-headed coneflower, jewelweed, for example—and cattails in some consistently wet areas. At 0.8 mile you'll see some maintained grass and tree-filled grounds with a gazebo by the water. Behind it, up a hill in the distance, is a residence—the only development you'll see until near the takeout.

At 2.3 miles the river takes a left turn to the south across the face of a high, exposed sand bank with a network of old tires laid out to slow erosion and passes a larger sandy bank 800 feet later. You may hear the occasional plane coming into the nearby airport, and a local sporting club has a shooting range you should be aware of—only for noise purposes, of course. Another sandy bank at 3.7 miles pushes the river around to the right. At 4.1 miles the river splits around a large island. Take the channel to the right (left may also work if water levels and deadfall cooperate). Just past the split the Green Circle Trail passes close to river right. With the thick underbrush, you might not notice it at first unless a cyclist passes, but about 0.2 mile later you should see some trail signs. At 5.4 miles the river comes into an open area of tall grasses, and you can see a few houses up on a ridge ahead and to the left. The river then turns to the right and heads back into the trees.

At 6.3 miles stay right with the current as you enter a clearing, ignoring a backwater to the left. Pass under the double bridge of I-39 at 6.5 miles. The current remains steady though the river has widened here, and the forest briefly opens up to a grassy area. Pass under the US 10/Main Street bridge at 7.2 miles and follow the river as it bends right and heads into Iverson Park. The bank is shored up with landscaping stonework, and you can see the small canoe dock on river right. Take out here; the parking lot is straight back 300 feet, past the outfitter in a Civilian Conservation Corps–era stone building.

24 Wolf River

As soon as you leave the Lieg Avenue put-in point, this river runs wide and slow through forested banks, making it seem farther from civilization that it really is. Abundant bird and animal life make bringing binoculars a good idea. Deadfall is rarely an issue and is easily avoided, and the gentle pace and lack of rapids make this paddle a perfect outing for any skill level.

County: Shawano
Start: Lieg Avenue Landing, N44 46.249' / W88 37.236'
End: Wayside Park Landing, N44 41.756' / W88 34.708'
Length: 7.7 miles one-way
Float time: About 2.5 hours
Difficulty rating: Easy
Rapids: None
River type: Wide pastoral
Current: Gentle
River gradient: 0.8 feet per mile
River gauge: USGS 04077400 Wolf River near Shawano. This section of the Wolf is dam-controlled and consistently runnable; in flood conditions consult an outfitter.
Season: Spring through fall
Land status: Private, with public landings
Fees and permits: Daily vehicle fee, good for both boat landings
Nearest city/town: Shawano
Maps: USGS Lunds, Shawano; *DeLorme: Wisconsin Atlas & Gazetteer*: Page 66 B3
Boats used: Canoes, kayaks, johnboats
Organizations: River Alliance of Wisconsin, 147 S. Butler St., Ste. 2, Madison 53703; (608) 257-2424; wisconsinrivers.org
Outfitters: Mountain Bay Outfitters, 620 S. Main St., Shawano 54166; (715) 526-8823; mountainbayoutfitters.com

Put-in/Takeout Information

To shuttle point/takeout: From Shawano head south on Main Street/WI 22. Pass over WI 29 and take the first left, CR CC. Drive 4.7 miles; turn left onto CR CCC and continue 0.3 mile, turning into the parking lot on the right, just across the bridge over the Wolf River.

To put-in from takeout: From the takeout, backtrack to Shawano on CR CCC and CR CC. Turn right onto WI 22, pass over WI 29 again, and continue 1.1 miles on WI 22. Turn left onto Lieg Avenue and drive 0.6 mile. The park entrance is on the left, just before the bridge over the Wolf. There is a floating dock and asphalt ramp, but no facilities. Pay the daily permit fee and display it in your car window. The permit is good for both takeout and put-in.

River Overview

The Wolf River has a reputation for whitewater. But that is merely one aspect of this 225-mile waterway, which begins deep in the Northwoods and travels about halfway

The sky reflected in the still waters of the Wolf River Preamtip Satasuk

down the state to empty into Lake Buttes des Morts. Along the way it gathers the Red River, the Embarrass, the Little Wolf, and the Waupaca. Along with the St. Croix, the Wolf is one of two National Scenic Rivers in the state. While the rough water farther north is more suitable for rafting, this area, below the dam in Shawano, is perfect for a lazy paddling trip and is especially nice for beginners and families. The river is wide and slow, with nary a riffle. Though never far from farmland or residences, this section of the river is sheltered on either side by abundant trees, and the wildlife will make itself known before you get far from the put-in. An eagle or two typically nests along this stretch each year. Anglers come mostly for the walleyes and white bass, but the most notable fish-related event is the sturgeon coming to spawn.

Paddle Summary

The put-in is just below the dam in Shawano but not in any sort of current. Push off from the asphalt ramp on river left, downriver from the Lieg Avenue bridge. The banks are immediately taken over by trees. At 0.3 mile Rose Brook flows in from river right. You'll see a wide patch of still waters as well as a storm culvert on the right, while the left bank gives glimpses of residences. With few exceptions the woods are thick on either side and the banks are high. If winds are strong from the south,

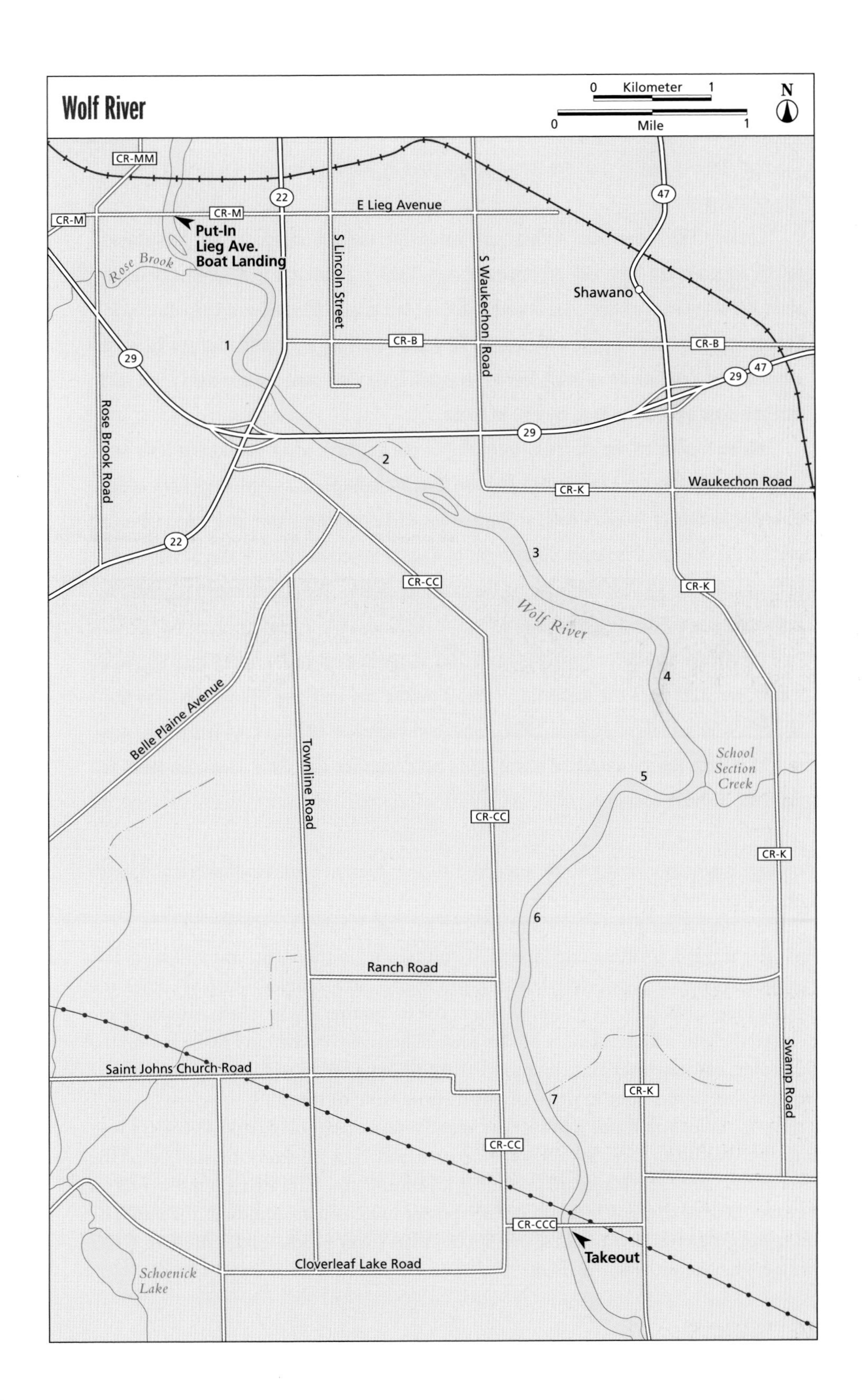
Wolf River
0 Kilometer 1
0 Mile 1
N
CR-MM
CR-M
CR-M
22
E Lieg Avenue
47
Put-In
Lieg Ave.
Boat Landing
Rose Brook
S Lincoln Street
S Waukechon Road
Shawano
1
29
CR-B
CR-B
29
47
Rose Brook Road
29
2
CR-K
Waukechon Road
22
3
CR-CC
CR-K
Wolf River
4
Belle Plaine Avenue
Townline Road
School
Section
Creek
5
CR-CC
CR-K
6
Ranch Road
Swamp Road
Saint Johns Church Road
CR-K
7
CR-CC
CR-CCC
Takeout
Cloverleaf Lake Road
Schoenick
Lake

THE MIGHTY STURGEON

The Wolf River is part of the Lake Winnebago waterway, home to the world's largest population of sturgeon.

Looking like submarines with armor plates, the massive sturgeons are throwbacks to the dinosaur era over 100 million years ago. Their population has dropped drastically since the nineteenth century, due in part to fishing but also to their slow reproductive cycle. Female sturgeon—with a typical lifespan of 50 years—don't lay eggs until they are 20 years old, and then they only do so every four to six years. Even then, odds are less than 1 in 1,000 that the eggs will survive long enough to hatch.

Visitors come to see sturgeon thrashing in the shallows when they spawn from late April into early May after swimming upstream from Winnebago. As sturgeon eggs are valued as highly as that of Russia's beluga sturgeon for caviar, poachers have also taken note. To protect the fish, the Wisconsin Department of Natural Resources uses teams of volunteers to keep watch for 12-hour shifts during the spawning season. The guards report poachers to their head guard, the "sturgeon general."

On average the DNR tags more than 1,200 sturgeon each year. In 2013 they tagged a female over 125 years old, measuring 7 feet 3 inches and weighing 240 pounds. That was minus her 30 pounds of eggs. In 1994 a sturgeon tagged in 1978 in Lake Winnebago was caught in Lake Huron—somehow managing to pass fourteen dams and seventeen locks to make the 850-mile journey.

paddling might not be ideal. Be prepared to see deer, herons, kingfishers, and, with only a bit of luck, an eagle.

Pass under some power lines and then, at 1.3 miles, go under the WI 22/47 bridge. Just after this is a small wooded island. If you pass it on the right, you will see a few riverside residences. Stay river left to avoid them. At 1.7 miles you pass under the twin bridges of WI 29. At 2.4 miles you come to another island. The narrower channel is to the left, with residences up the banks. The river is wider and shallower on the other side, but stay right and close to the island. Watch for trout lilies here in summer. You may see anglers out in their johnboats from time to time.

At 4.7 miles you'll pass a low grassy island and see School Section Creek flowing into the Wolf from river left. Another grass island rises up from the middle of the river at 5.6 miles. The banks are becoming lower, and you can catch glimpses of farms beyond the tree cover. When you can see power lines, you are almost at the end. The lines cross the river at 7.6 miles, and 500 feet later you paddle under the CR CCC bridge; the takeout is on river left.

25 Oconto River

Starting west of Oconto, this wide river is a pleasant paddle through a forested corridor all the way into the city. The current is steady; the bottom is sand and gravel, with occasional boulders. But other than some riffles, there is only one stretch of simple rapids just as you come to Oconto. Fishing is good, and a trout stream joins the Oconto about midway along this section.

County: Oconto
Start: Machickanee Public Boat Landing, N44 51.499' / W88 2.955'
End: Holtwood Park Landing, N44 53.175' / W87 53.178'
Length: 10.5 miles one-way
Float time: About 4 hours
Difficulty rating: Easy
Rapids: Riffles and one Class I run
River type: Pastoral
Current: Gentle to moderate
River gradient: 1.2 feet per mile
River gauge: USGS 04071765 Oconto River near Oconto; minimum runnable level 200 cfs
Season: Spring through fall
Land status: Private, with public landings
Fees and permits: Daily use fee for the boat launch at Holtwood Park
Nearest city/town: Oconto
Maps: USGS Abrams, Oconto West, Pensaukee; *DeLorme: Wisconsin Atlas & Gazetteer*: Page 67 8B
Boats used: Canoes, kayaks, johnboats
Organizations: River Alliance of Wisconsin, 147 S. Butler St., Ste. 2, Madison 53703; (608) 257-2424; wisconsinrivers.org
Contacts: Copper Culture State Park; (715) 757-3979; dnr.wi.gov/topic/parks/name/copperculture

Put-in/Takeout Information

To shuttle point/takeout: From US 41 at Oconto take exit 198 for WI 22/CR Y. Go right at the traffic circle and follow Charles Street as it becomes Main Street. Turn right onto Business US 41 (first Brazeau Avenue, becoming Smith Avenue) and drive 0.5 mile. Turn right onto McDonald Street and take the first right, 0.2 mile later, onto Holtwood Way. Enter the park and turn right after the baseball fields. Drive 0.2 mile to the boat landing, on the west bank of the Oconto River.

To put-in from takeout: From the takeout, backtrack to Business US 41, head back to Main Street, and turn left. This is WI 22; stay on this for 7.5 miles. Turn left to merge onto US 141, heading south toward Green Bay. Drive 2 miles and turn right onto Landing Lane, directly off US 141 and across from Chicken Shack Road to the east. Cross the railroad tracks; the parking lot is the first lane on the right. An asphalt ramp descends to the river. The parking lot has a pit toilet and posted information for anglers.

Note: The Oconto River State Trail, an old rail bed converted to a crushed-limestone bike trail running from Oconto to Stiles, is a decent option for a bike shuttle. At the Stiles terminus you need to cross under US 141 at WI 22 to get to the

The Oconto River Preamtip Satasuk

back roads—Duame and Pioneer Park Roads—that lead south to Stiles, where you can cross the river to the landing using the iron pedestrian bridge. A state trail fee applies (920-834-6995; dnr.wi.gov/topic/parks/name/Oconto).

River Overview

The North and South Branches of the Oconto River pass through the dense forests of northern Wisconsin. Narrow and winding, the branches frequently rewrite themselves on the map over the years, leaving behind isolated pockets of water and former riverbed. The two branches come together near Suring, flow south to about Gillett, and then take an easterly course all the way through Oconto Falls and Oconto on the river's journey to Lake Michigan. The eastbound river gradually becomes much wider and gentler, and its clear waters and rock and gravel bottom are favored by anglers. A dam creates "Stiles Pond," the Machickanee Flowage, just upriver from the put-in point for the listed section here near the town of Stiles. Water levels are thus consistent throughout the seasons—not quite as good as the Peshtigo farther north but still reliable, with limited rock bumping in dry periods. Expect abundant birdlife—herons, waterfowl, kingfishers, and eagles—and great colors in the fall. Fishing is popular, and a trout stream joins the Oconto at just past the 3-mile mark.

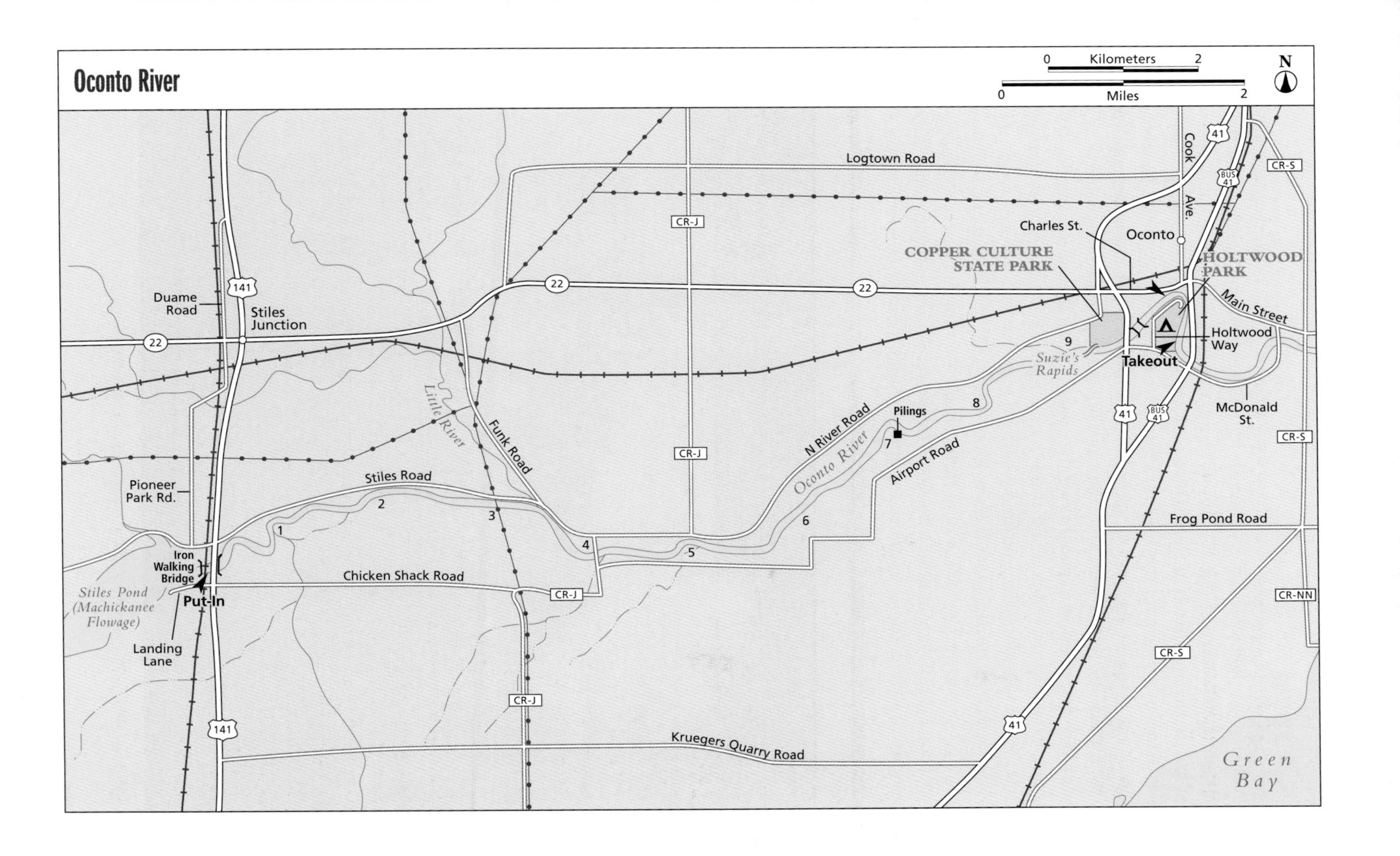

Oconto River
0 Kilometers 2
0 Miles 2
N
Logtown Road
CR-J
Cook Ave.
Oconto
Charles St.
COPPER CULTURE STATE PARK
HOLTWOOD PARK
Main Street
Holtwood Way
Takeout
McDonald St.
CR-S
CR-NN
Frog Pond Road
41
BUS 41
22
141
Duame Road
Stiles Junction
Little River
Funk Road
Stiles Road
Pioneer Park Rd.
N River Road
Oconto River
Pilings
Suzie's Rapids
Airport Road
Iron Walking Bridge
Put-In
Chicken Shack Road
Stiles Pond (Machickanee Flowage)
Landing Lane
Kruegers Quarry Road
Green Bay
1
2
3
4
5
6
7
8
9

Paddle Summary

Paddle to the right toward the highway bridge. Behind you, just upriver of the put-in, is the iron pedestrian bridge. Paddle under the twin bridges of US 141 and come out in a wide, shallow stretch of river, which narrows as you head east until it's about 80 feet across—the norm for this segment of the Oconto. A few houses can be seen, but mostly the banks are sheltered by mixed deciduous forest with a smattering of conifers. Though the river is wide here, the current is steady. At 1.1 miles you pass a little island, the first of many scattered along the course. Go under some power lines at 1.4 miles, and come to another island at the 2-mile mark. Watch the tall trees for eagles. Stiles Road runs along the river to the left, and you may hear the occasional car.

At 3 miles you pass more high-tension wires and, just after them, some more islands. The narrow channels around these islands can sometimes get too shallow or offer some deadfall in an otherwise rather clear riverway. At 3.4 miles Little River, a good trout stream, comes in under a bridge on Stiles Road from river left. Just after

An iron walking bridge over the Oconto River PREAMTIP SATASUK

that is yet another long, narrow island. At 3.7 miles you come to a few more islands strung out in the middle of the river with smaller channels on either side. You can thread a path through them. At 4.1 miles you reach some power lines and the CR J bridge. There is a short rush of riffles under the bridge, but then the river widens again and the current slacks off considerably. Airport Road, on your right, now runs along the river. Come to an island in the middle of the river at 4.3 miles; the current picks up again to a moderate pace at a narrowing point in the river. The bottom is a bit sandier, and after another tiny island, you may see a few more boulders in low water, but they are covered at normal water levels. A seasonal creek comes in from the right at 5 miles; 500 feet later you can see a public boat landing on River Road with a large asphalt ramp and parking lot.

Just after the 6-mile mark, the river becomes wider and channel-like. The thin tree cover on the banks and the open water can create a slow paddle on a day with some wind from the east. Watch for a few pilings in the water on river right at 7.1 miles, all that remains of an old rail bridge. At 8 miles there's a backwater to the right. Stay left, and after 200 feet the river turns right. At 8.9 miles a seasonal stream comes in from river left. Go left around a little island and enter Suzie's Rapids, an S-curve of Class I rapids for about 400 feet. After this you are entering Oconto, with Copper Culture State Park on the left. Pass under the double bridges of US 41 and the adjoining ramp—ascending from river right to left—for the Copper Culture multiuse trail at 9.6 miles. Past the bridges, the river deepens and slows, banks on the left are higher, and straight ahead you can see commercial properties. The river makes a loop around Holtwood Park, passing the park's campground office and canoe landing at 10 miles on river right. Come around the park and past the lines of RVs; the takeout is on river right, just past the campsites.

26 Peshtigo River

Flowing from the town of the same name, the Peshtigo flows wide and slow through forest that gradually gives way to wetlands as the river approaches the waters of Green Bay. Various backwaters mark where the river previously flowed, revealing the evolution of a river. Near the takeout, several paths weave through grassy lowlands and marsh.

County: Marinette
Start: City of Peshtigo East Side Boat Landing, N45 2.796' / W87 44.672'
End: Klingsporn Landing, N44 59.320' / W87 39.948'
Length: 10.2 miles one-way
Float time: About 4 hours
Difficulty rating: Easy
Rapids: None
River type: Wooded pastoral ending in marshland
Current: Moderate
River gradient: 0.7 feet per mile
River gauge: USGS 04069500 Peshtigo River at Peshtigo; minimum runnable level 200 cfs
Season: Spring through fall
Land status: Varied, with public landings
Fees and permits: Boat launch fee at the put-in
Nearest city/town: Peshtigo
Maps: USGS Marinette West, Peshtigo Harbor; *DeLorme: Wisconsin Atlas & Gazetteer.* Page 80 D3
Boats used: Canoes, kayaks, johnboats
Organizations: River Alliance of Wisconsin, 147 S. Butler St., Ste. 2, Madison 53703; (608) 257-2424; wisconsinrivers.org
Local information: Peshtigo Fire Museum, 400 W. Oconto Ave., Peshtigo, WI 54157; (715) 582-3244; peshtigofiremuseum.com

Put-in/Takeout Information

To shuttle point/takeout: From Business US 41 through downtown Peshtigo, turn right (south) onto Front Street just east of the bridge, where US 41 continues on Maple Street. Front Street becomes Pierce Avenue. On Front Street/Pierce Avenue, drive 1.3 miles and turn right onto CR BB. Go 4.9 miles and, in the middle of the curve to the left, take the dirt road on the right 0.2 mile to the unimproved landing. Parking is in a gravel lot; there are no facilities.

To put-in from takeout: From the takeout, backtrack to Peshtigo driving 4.9 miles north on CR BB. Turn left on Pierce Avenue and drive 0.9 mile, then turn left at the entry to the City of Peshtigo East Side Boat Landing. A grooved concrete ramp descends to the water, and a map board contains a box of river trail brochures. The gravel parking lot, a grill, and a picnic table are the only facilities.

River Overview

Famous for its stretch of whitewater in its upper reaches, the 136-mile Peshtigo offers something for every level of paddler. The waters take their dark color from tamarack swamps upriver. This final stretch of the river begins below the dam at Peshtigo, flowing through hardwood forest that gradually gives way to a marshy estuary where the river meets Green Bay on Lake Michigan. The river has a sandy bottom through here, and some of the tall banks also show the sandy nature of the terrain. Anglers catch bass through here, especially smallmouths in summer, but northern pike, walleye, steelhead, and even salmon run here seasonally. The forest and marshland provide a wide range of bird species as well. Hardwoods along the banks are great for fall colors.

The evolving river has left behind various backwaters and dead channels, some of which can be explored, depending on water levels. Be aware that the currents in spring can be rather strong, and strainers and snags can be a danger. While shallow, the river is usually runnable throughout summer and fall, with only a few places where you might scrape a bit. A windy day can make the final couple miles in the wide-open marshes quite a bit of work. This river segment is also the Peshtigo River Trail, which has its own free foldout brochure with an abundance of information, including a map, a birding list, and historical and ecological narratives.

Coming up on some riffles on the Peshtigo River PREAMTIP SATASUK

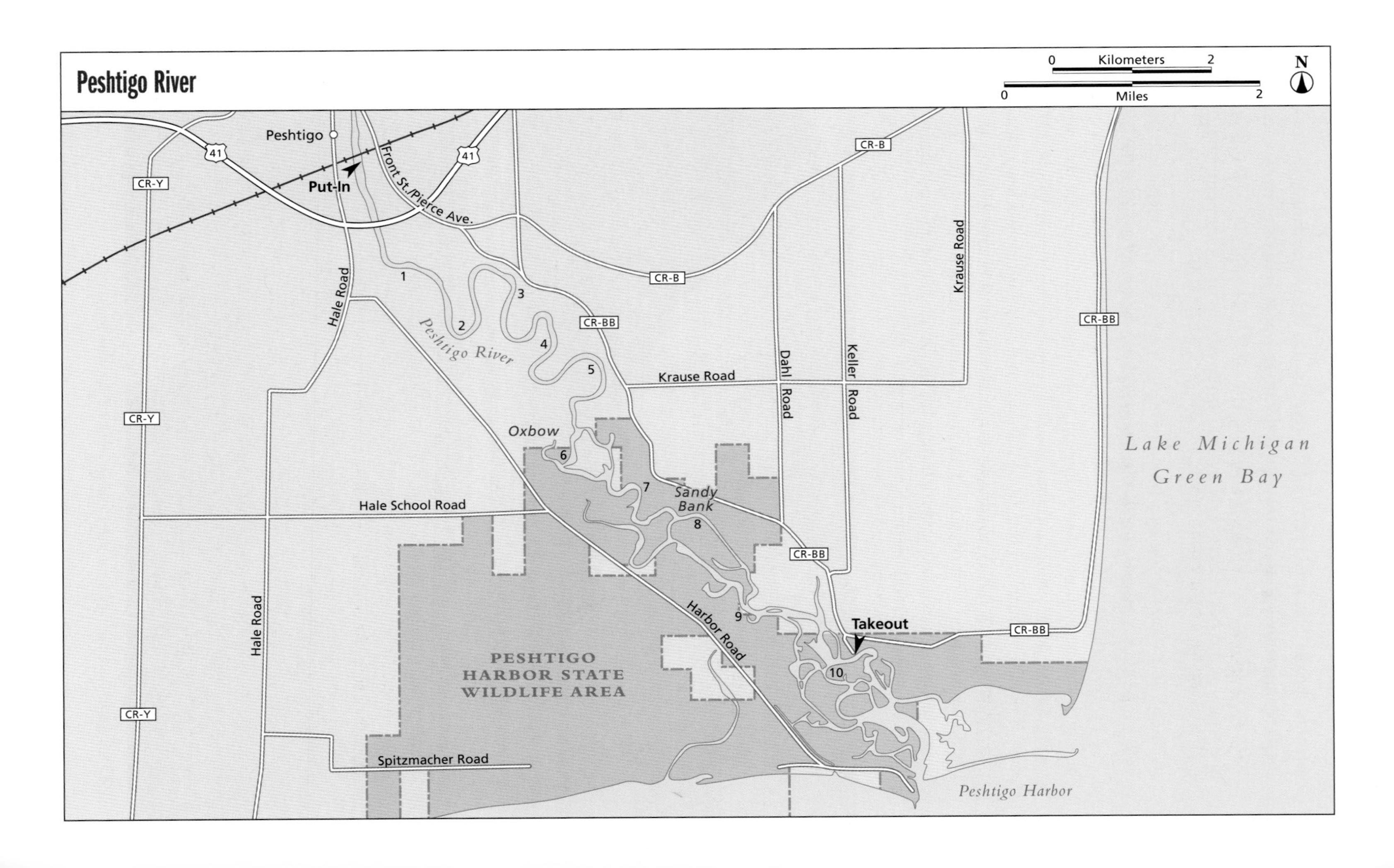

Peshtigo River
0 Kilometers 2
0 Miles 2
N
Peshtigo
41
Put-In
Front St./Pierce Ave.
CR-Y
CR-B
Hale Road
Peshtigo River
1
2
3
4
5
6
7
8
9
10
CR-BB
Krause Road
Dahl Road
Keller Road
Oxbow
Sandy Bank
Hale School Road
Harbor Road
Takeout
Lake Michigan
Green Bay
PESHTIGO HARBOR STATE WILDLIFE AREA
Spitzmacher Road
Peshtigo Harbor

THE PESHTIGO FIRE

The Great Chicago Fire of October 8, 1871, gets a lot more attention than one that occurred on the same night right here in Peshtigo. While the disaster to the south claimed 300 lives and reduced 4 square miles of the city to cinders, the Peshtigo Fire killed at least 1,200 people, perhaps as many as double that. More than 400 square miles burned in a period of 2 hours, and the flames threatened other nearby communities, even killing more than 100 people in Door County across Green Bay. When the wife of the Wisconsin state governor received the news in her husband's absence (he was already in Chicago), she ordered that the train cars full of relief supplies destined for Chicago be shipped to Peshtigo instead.

No one knows for sure what started the fire, but the conditions for its spreading were ideal: vast clear-cut land open to sweeping dry winds, lumberyards, wooden houses, even sawdust in the mattresses. Some residents sought refuge in the river. Father Perrin, a Catholic priest, threw his church's tabernacle—the holy host and chalice locked inside—into the river as well. It was found floating safely days later and today is part of the Peshtigo Fire Museum collection, housed in an old church near the town cemetery, where a mass grave holds the remains of 350 of those who died that night.

Paddle Summary

From the put-in point go left. The railroad bridge crosses behind you upriver. The river is about 100 feet across here, and the current is modest but steady. You immediately pass under some power lines. At 0.5 mile you pass under the double bridges of US 41 and quickly leave the noise behind you. Up until 0.9 mile, the river is a straight shot, with steep, sandy banks and a mixture of pine and aspen.

At 2 miles you'll pass an exposed sandy bank on river right. At 2.7 miles the river takes a long, slow bend to the right, passing some houses on river left. At the 3-mile mark the river pinches just a bit in a shallow gravelly area, possibly kicking up some riffles. At 3.8 miles you come to some more riffles and a tiny island with riffles on either side. At 5.1 miles you'll see more houses on high banks. The river shows increasingly tighter curves, which can cause sandbars that hinder passage in low water late in the season.

A steep, 15-foot sandy bank awaits on river right at 5.6 miles; just beyond that you can see a former river channel, now dried up, also on the right. At 6.2 miles you come to a T-intersection. To the right is the Oxbow, a now-lost river channel turning into an oxbow-shaped backwater. The upper section filled in with sediment and became sealed off. From the juncture take the more recent river channel to the left. You can see another completely silted-in channel on the right at 6.7 miles.

At 7.6 miles the river widens out and shows a long, steep, sandy bank on river left as the river bends to the right. At 7.8 miles you'll see a wide patch of flatwater to the right and a channel leading through it that may or may not be passable. This was once the main channel, and the route you are about to take going left here was once a mere trickle on maps. Now the left channel is the main channel and that wide water to the right is gradually silting in. Maybe. Nature decides.

At 7.9 miles is another steep, sandy bank, bigger than all previous. It continues for 0.25 mile, gradually curving the river to the right. At 8.8 miles head out into a wide-open grassy area. Wind can become an issue here after you've lost the relative shelter of the woods. At 8.9 miles you come to a T in the river. On the right is the other end of the alternative channel you passed back at 7.8 miles. Paddle to the left, passing residences along the right bank.

At about 9.3 miles you pass another backwater on the right. Stay left—in fact, stay primarily left through here to avoid taking any paths out into the middle of the marsh and thus missing the takeout. This is a rather wide area, more than 100 feet across. At a fork at 9.4 miles, stay left again. You can see houses ahead on the left. At 9.9 miles there is an island to the right; stay left once more. This area may change quite a bit from year to year. Pay attention to the silt, and don't get stuck. Watch for some apple trees clumped together in the middle of a grassy/marshy area ahead on the left. Cattails can hide the takeout until you are right on it. Take out at the edge of the gravel of the parking lot. It may be muddy here if the waters are low.

Sand banks along the end of the Peshtigo River

27 Door County–Cave Point

Done as either a one-way paddle or an out-and-back, this trip explores the coastline of Lake Michigan. The journey passes shallow cave formations in the low cliffs on shore, giving paddlers the chance to paddle right up to them, and then follows along one of Door County's finest beaches and the sands of Whitefish Dunes State Park.

County: Door
Start: Schauer Park, N44 56.728' / W87 11.102'
End: Whitefish Bay Ramp, N44 54.342' / W87 12.982'
Length: 4.4 miles one-way
Float time: About 2 hours
Difficulty rating: Easy
Rapids: None
River type: Lake
Current: Varying wave height. Consult the NOAA website for forecasts: forecast.weather.gov/shmrn.php?mz=lmz541.
Season: Spring through fall
Land status: Private and state park with public landings
Fees and permits: No fees or permits required
Nearest city/town: Jacksonport
Maps: USGS Jacksonport; *DeLorme: Wisconsin Atlas & Gazetteer*: Page 69 7A
Boats used: Kayaks; canoes possible
Organizations: Door County Silent Sports Alliance; doorcountysilentsports.com
Contacts: Whitefish Dunes State Park, 3275 Clarks Lake Rd., Sturgeon Bay 54235; (920) 823-2400; dnr.wi.gov/topic/parks/name/whitefish
Outfitters: Bay Shore Outfitters, 2457 S. Bay Shore Dr., Sister Bay 54234; (920) 854-7598; kayakdoorcounty.com
Door County Kayak Tours, 8442 Hwy. 42, Fish Creek 54212; (920) 355-2925; doorcountykayaktours.com

Put-in/Takeout Information

To shuttle point/takeout: From Jacksonport take WI 57 south 6.4 miles (7.4 miles north of Sturgeon Bay) to CR T/Whitefish Bay Road. Turn right (east) and drive 2.4 miles right to the parking lot for the landing. A log and concrete pier are here, but most will just launch from the beach. There's a portable toilet here in season.

To put-in from takeout: From the takeout, drive 0.6 mile west on Whitefish Bay Road and turn right onto Nelson Lane. Go 1.1 miles; turn right onto Clarks Lake Road/CR WD and go 2.6 miles. Take the slight left onto Cave Point Drive and continue 1.2 miles, where you turn right onto Schauer Road. Go 0.2 mile to the large L-shaped dock of concrete and wood. There's a portable toilet here in season.

Note: To avoid a shuttle run, you could simply put in and take out here at Schauer Park.

Lake Overview

The Lake Michigan shoreline along this section of Door County is rather remarkable. What you see on this paddling route is part of the Niagara Escarpment, a far-reaching geological formation that formed over 400 million years ago. At a point along the shore, waves and wind since the last retreat of the glaciers have carved caves out of that rock. Farther south you will pass sand dunes—some exposed, many more grown in with grasses and trees—and white sand beaches stretching off into the distance along Whitefish Bay. The mileage may be short, but the scenery is impressive; plus you have cause to linger in Whitefish Dunes State Park.

It is often—but not always—best to paddle early in the morning. Don't let fog deter you; it can make for a mystical journey as long as you remain in sight of shore. The water can be pretty cold, even at the height of summer. An outfitter once taught me their 100-degree rule: If the water temperature and the air temperature do not add up to at least 100°F, they don't run trips here. Wave height should be given consideration as well, as should wind direction. Winds from the east are going to raise big waves. On those days it is better to watch the waves crash and plume against Cave Point. If you still want to paddle on a day like that, consider doing the Garrett Bay

Paddling in morning mist along Cave Point

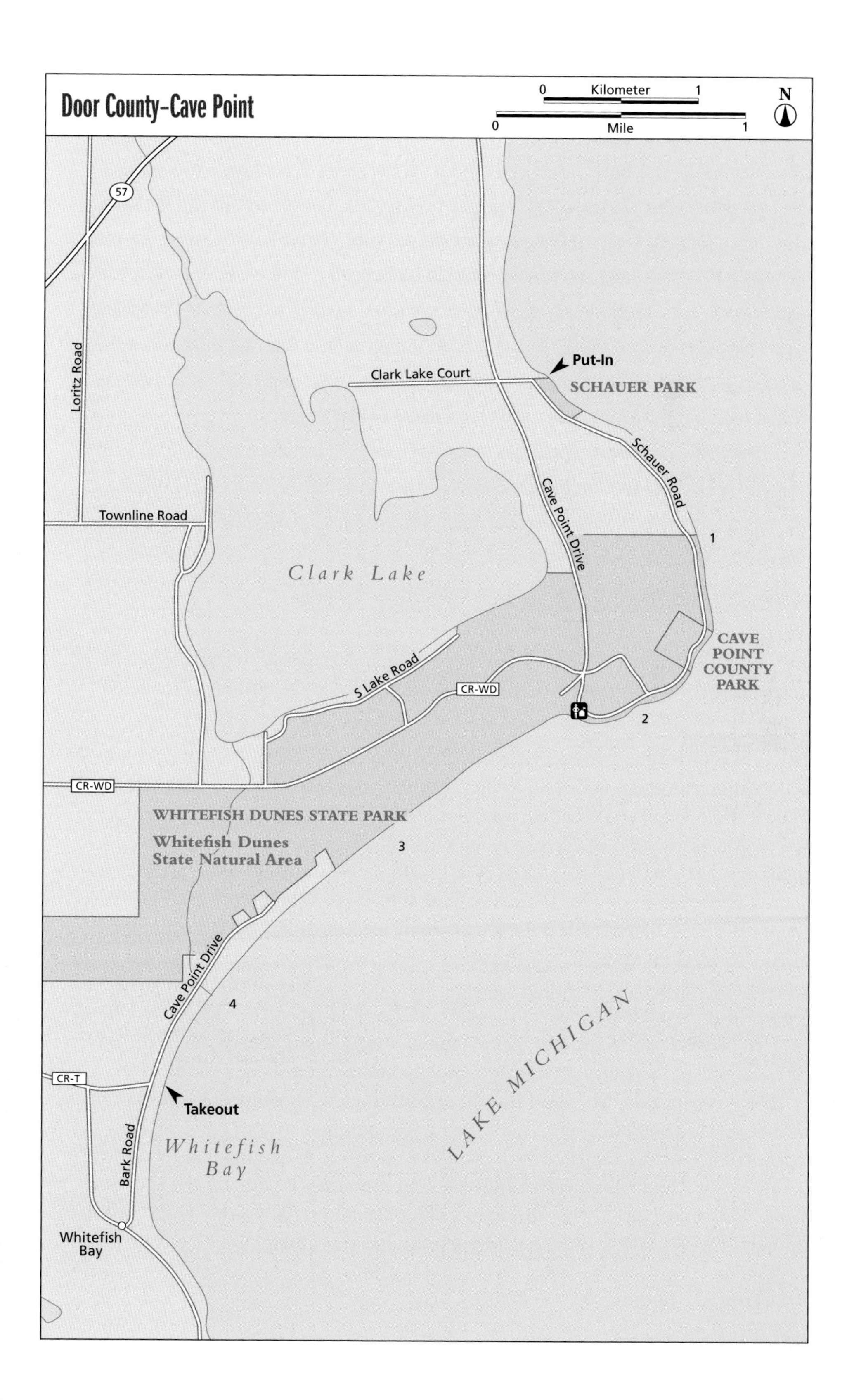

Door County–Cave Point
0 Kilometer 1
0 Mile 1
N
57
Loritz Road
Clark Lake Court
Put-In
SCHAUER PARK
Schauer Road
Cave Point Drive
Townline Road
Clark Lake
1
CAVE POINT COUNTY PARK
S Lake Road
CR-WD
2
CR-WD
WHITEFISH DUNES STATE PARK
Whitefish Dunes State Natural Area
3
Cave Point Drive
4
LAKE MICHIGAN
CR-T
Takeout
Bark Road
Whitefish Bay
Whitefish Bay

THE NIAGARA ESCARPMENT

That cliff that Niagara Falls tumbles over? That's the other edge of a very large layer of rock—an escarpment—that stretches from New York to Wisconsin, through Ontario and Michigan. The rock, a chemical cross between limestone and dolomite referred to as dolostone, started forming 425 million years ago when this region lay beneath a shallow sea. The shells and bones of tiny sea creatures gradually built a couple miles' worth of sediment. By 400 million years ago, the seas had withdrawn and erosion started to wear this rock down. When the glaciers piled their ice across half the continent, grinding as they went, they wore away the softer rocks but also pressed the earth's crust under all that weight.

Since the ice melted, the earth has rebounded about 160 feet and continues to do so at a rate of 0.5 inch per year. The Niagara Escarpment emerged from the ice, its edges still clear. It lies beneath Lakes Michigan, Erie, and Huron and extends down along the eastern side of Wisconsin almost to Chicago. Here in Wisconsin you can see the edge of that rock—those rising cliffs of dolostone—along the shores of the Door Peninsula.

track on the bay-side of the northern tip of the Door Peninsula. If that too is seeing unfavorable conditions, nearby Clark and Kangaroo Lakes are inland and sheltered.

Paddle Summary

Set off from the shore and head straight out into the lake a bit; the water close to shore is shallow, and you may drag over some cobble and limestone sheets there. Once you've gotten just a bit of depth, enough especially for a rudder on a sea kayak, turn right and start paddling south parallel to the shore. You can see some private residences in the forest along the shore, and then, at 0.9 mile, Whitefish Dunes State Park begins. But your first notable sight is Cave Point Park, a county park surrounded on three sides by the state park.

Most travelers visit the park on shore, where you can step up to the edge of the limestone cliffs and look down at the waves crashing in. There are also places where you can climb down to the low rocky shore and walk along the bottom of the rock face. But one of the views you are not going to get from on shore is of the caves.

The waves of Lake Michigan have been battering this shoreline for several thousand years. As you come up on Cave Point, pay attention to waves and currents so that you don't end up too close to the shelflike shoreline. At about 1.3 miles you will be in front of the highest point of the rock face, perhaps 20 feet off the waterline. There you can see directly into the spaces of undercut rock. When the waters are still enough, you can back a kayak right in and use the rebounding waves to hold your position. These caves are not deep, but it is fun to listen to the waves thump while you are in there with them.

From the caves, as you continue paddling, the shoreline bends a bit to the west. You can see where the long beach begins in Whitefish Dunes State Park. The first 100 yards of the beach are plagued by rip currents, and swimming is not allowed. You can see how the waves break differently. If you choose to pull out on the beach and spend some time in the park, climbing dunes, hiking, or visiting the nature center, be sure to pull out to the south of that rip current area.

Continue southwest along the shore and you'll see blowouts of some of the sand dunes emerging from their grassy cover. Beyond them, trees have taken root on ancient dunes. At 3.2 miles you can see where the state park shoreline ends—where the private houses and cabins start to appear. From here it is another 1.2 miles of paddling along the beautiful beach. Take out in the sand near the boat landing.

Paddlers enter the small caves carved by the waves of Lake Michigan.

28 Door County–Garrett Bay

In a bay near the very tip of the Door Peninsula, this out-and-back paddle passes towering limestone cliffs of the Niagara Escarpment and provides some shelter on days of winds from the south. Along the way are some historical rock paintings. Beyond the edge of the bay there are places to go ashore on the rock-strewn, driftwood-laden beach below the high cliff. It makes a nice alternative when conditions on the Lake Michigan side are not suitable for paddling.

County: Door
Start/End: Garrett Bay Boat Ramp, N45 17.151' / W87 3.069'
Length: 4 miles out and back
Float time: About 2.5 hours
Difficulty rating: Easy
Rapids: None
River type: Lake
Current: Varying wave height. Consult the NOAA website for forecasts: forecast.weather.gov/shmrn.php?mz=lmz521.
Season: Spring through fall
Land status: Private, with some public beaches and launch site
Fees and permits: No fees or permits required
Nearest city/town: Ellison Bay
Maps: USGS Ellison Bay; *DeLorme: Wisconsin Atlas & Gazetteer:* Page 81 B8
Boats used: Sea kayaks, kayaks, canoes, johnboats, pleasure craft
Organizations: Door County Silent Sports Alliance; doorcountysilentsports.com
Outfitters: Bay Shore Outfitters, 2457 S. Bay Shore Dr., Sister Bay 54234; (920) 854-7598; kayakdoorcounty.com

Put-in/Takeout Information

To put-in/takeout: Heading north on WI 42 through Ellison Bay, watch for Garrett Bay Road on the left. Take this road 2.4 miles north to the put-in. There is parking along the gravel, a picnic table and grill, and a portable toilet in season. Launch from the cobble-covered shoreline.

Lake Overview

Green Bay the city is probably more famous, but this large inlet between Wisconsin's thumb, the Door Peninsula, and the mainland bears the same name. Depending on wind and wave conditions, the bay does enjoy some shelter from the sometimes temperamental Lake Michigan. Hedgehog Harbor, because of its north-facing direction, has even more to shelter it. This is the northernmost point of the Door Peninsula. Bounded on either side by towering bluffs, the harbor has a sort of W shape, with a low center bulge. To the west of that bulge is Garrett Bay. On a summer day when conditions are not good for water sports on the lake side, the bay side may be just fine—the bluffs add protection from winds coming from the south and west.

Paddle Summary

Set out from the put-in point and then head left along the shore past private property. Look out past the last large dock, at 0.2 mile, to see where public land begins. Washington, Detroit, and Plum Islands are visible off to your right, beyond the tip of the Door Peninsula. Look up at the cliffs; this dolostone is part of the Niagara Escarpment. Look for the high-water mark on the rock; it's where the cliffs are darkened. The lake level has changed over the years, and you can still see where it was so much higher thousands of years ago, when glacial ice blocked Port Huron. Waves at that time made the sea caves high above.

Just past 0.4 mile is a piece of more recent history. Pictographs, likely made with red cedar sap 400 to 600 years ago, can be seen on the rock. These paintings—of canoes, the body of a deer, and an eagle—are listed on the National Historic Register and have been protected from the sun and much of the wind by their placement. If you choose to get out for a photo, do not touch the pictographs.

The rising cliffs beneath Door Bluff County Park

Paddle out to the end of the bay just past the 1-mile mark and continue left along the shore as you enter the wider bay. Eagle's Bluff inside Peninsula State Park and Chambers Island are visible in the distance as you come around the bend. Up above is Door Bluff County Park. The trees along the top of the bluff are primarily cedars. Back when Door County was clear-cut by the logging industry, no one wanted the cedars. Some of these trees are 600 to 800 years old. When biologists took cuttings to determine the trees' age, some years showed a single cell-width of growth.

Along the point here, the rock has slowly been cracking and eroding. The rocky beach is a popular stopping point for paddlers to get out and explore, admire driftwood, and try their hand at building cairns. Paddle as far as you want, even into the next bay, but then make your turnaround and head back toward Garrett Bay. Assuming you turn back at the beginning of the next bay, you will return to Garrett Bay at

DEATH'S DOOR

The whims of the water can make or break a day of paddling. The fast-changing weather of Lake Michigan even has its place in legend and history, once determining a battle between warring tribes. The pictographs at Garrett Bay are believed to record this story.

The Ho-Chunk, often referred to in older texts as the Winnebago, moved north from the modern-day Lake Winnebago area into what is now the Door Peninsula, pushing the Potawatomi tribe out to Washington Island. In retaliation, the Potawatomi planned to attack the Ho-Chunk and sent three scouts to the peninsula to find a safe place for their canoes to land and then light a fire to guide the attacking warriors. The Ho-Chunk captured these scouts. Two allegedly died, while the third gave up the plan. The Ho-Chunk then devised a plan of their own. First they would lure the attackers to a part of the coastline—below the high bluff—where they wouldn't be able to land and could thus be attacked while still in their canoes. At the same time, the Ho-Chunk would set out in their own canoes and attack the undefended Potawatomi villages.

The Potawatomi took to the lake in calm waters. As they were approaching the false beacon, however, the water started getting rough. They fell right into the trap and were caught between the prepared Ho-Chunk warriors above and the angry lake around them. All were lost. But no one was a winner here.

Halfway to the vulnerable island, the Ho-Chunk also found themselves in a stormy lake. All were lost, and the passage between the mainland and Washington Island became known as the "doorway to death." Modern Ho-Chunk dispute the story's veracity, arguing that the Potawatomi were the aggressors. But the name Death's Door lives on, bolstered by a number of shipwrecks that have occurred in that channel.

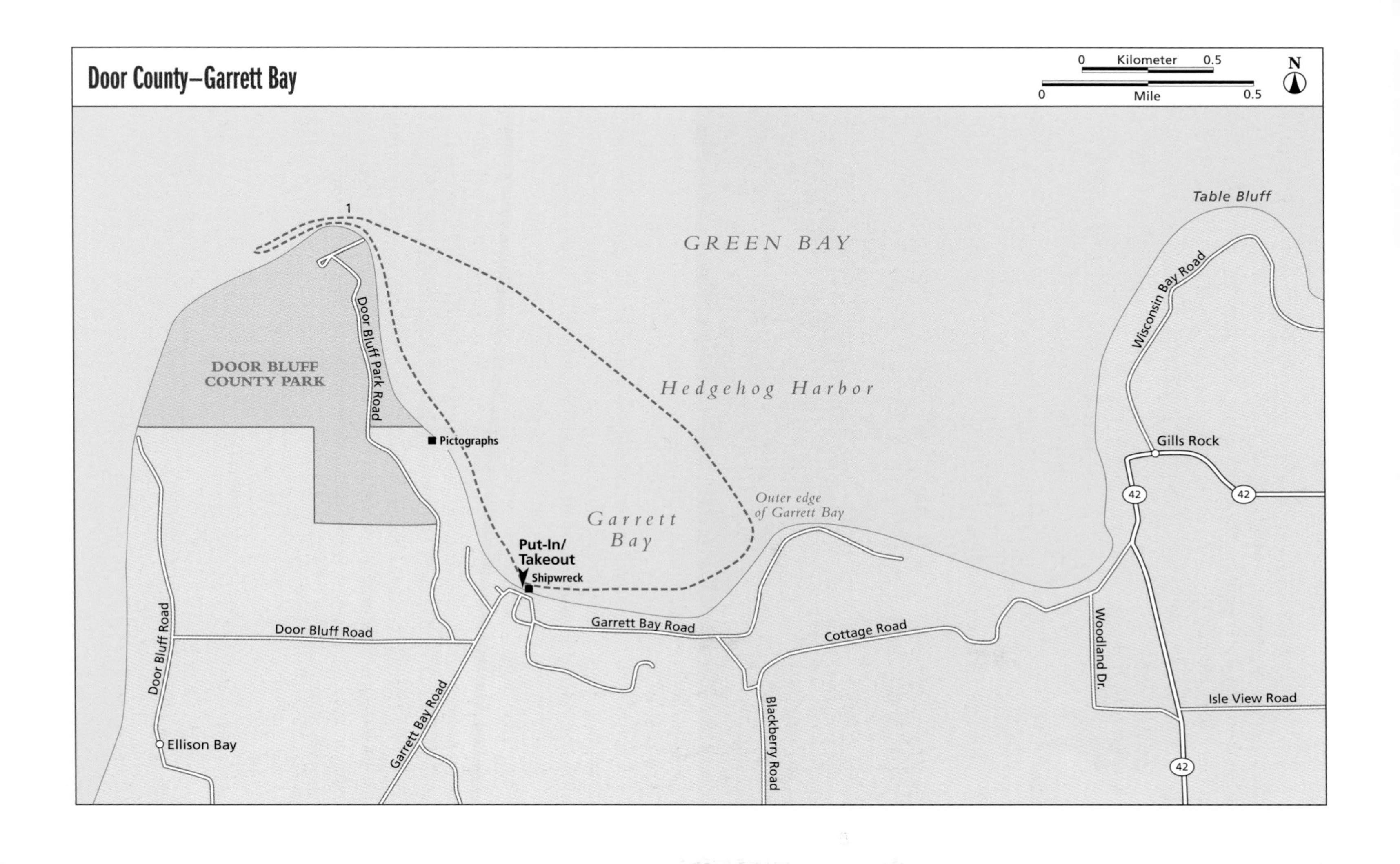
Door County—Garrett Bay
0
Kilometer
0.5
0
Mile
0.5
N
Table Bluff
GREEN BAY
1
DOOR BLUFF
COUNTY PARK
Door Bluff Park Road
Wisconsin Bay Road
Hedgehog Harbor
Pictographs
Gills Rock
42
42
Outer edge
of Garrett Bay
Garrett
Bay
Put-In/
Takeout
Shipwreck
Garrett Bay Road
Door Bluff Road
Cottage Road
Woodland Dr.
Door Bluff Road
Isle View Road
Ellison Bay
Garrett Bay Road
Blackberry Road
42

Paddling out of Garrett Bay to see the cliffs along Green Bay

2.2 miles. Head out into open water, aiming across the bay to a spot on the opposite shore. It's about 1.2 miles across. That puts you at about 3.4 miles on your journey when you reach that shore. Go right along the shoreline back to the takeout point.

Just before you reach the takeout, look for the plastic buoys less than 100 feet from shore. These buoys mark part of the shipwreck of the nineteenth-century schooner Fleetwing. On September 26, 1888, just around dusk, the Fleetwing set sail from Menominee, Michigan, headed for Chicago with a load of lumber. The captain had aimed to pass through Death's Door but mistook a landmark and sailed straight into Garrett Bay, thinking he had cleared the point. At 11 p.m. he received confirmation that he had not. Although the schooner was wrecked, the crew were able to easily swim or wade ashore—just as you will now make the last few paddle strokes to the takeout point.

29 Wisconsin River at Merrill

This central Wisconsin section of the Wisconsin River starts in a city park and flows wide and strong south toward Wausau. The shores are forested on both sides, with very little sign of development. You will pass several islands along the way—often with narrow, more intimate passages behind them—and a collection of small isles with varying paths through them not far after the halfway point and before the interstate bridges. The takeout is in the Wisconsin River Forest Unit, managed by Marathon County.

County: Lincoln, Marathon
Start: Riverside Park in Merrill, N45 10.554' / W89 40.499'
End: Pine Bluff Road Landing, N45 5.360' / W89 38.233'
Length: 8.3 miles one-way
Float time: About 3 hours
Difficulty rating: Easy
Rapids: None
River type: Wide wooded pastoral
Current: Moderate
River gradient: 3.6 feet per mile
River gauge: USGS 05395000 Wisconsin River at Merrill; minimum runnable level 1,000 cfs; avoid at flood stage.
Season: Spring through fall
Land status: Private, with public landings
Fees and permits: No fees or permits required
Nearest city/town: Merrill
Maps: USGS Brokaw, Merrill; *DeLorme: Wisconsin Atlas & Gazetteer*: Page 76 C3
Boats used: Canoes, kayaks, johnboats, small motorized craft
Organizations: River Alliance of Wisconsin, 147 S. Butler St., Ste. 2, Madison 53703; (608) 257-2424; wisconsinrivers.org
Outfitters: Golden Hawk Canoes, 121 N. Valley St., Merrill 54452; (715) 536-4488; goldenhawkcanoes.com
Riverside Canoe & Kayak Rental, 223 Drott St., Schofield 54476; (715) 574-1771; wausaukayakrentals.com

Put-in/Takeout Information

To shuttle point/takeout: From Merrill take Main Street/WI 64 east from downtown out past US 51. Turn right (south) onto CR W and drive 6.4 miles to Pine Bluff Road. Turn right and go 0.6 mile to the gravel loop/parking area at the end of the road. An unimproved spill of sand and gravel leads down to the river. There are no facilities.

To put-in from takeout: From the takeout, head back out on Pine Bluff Road and turn left (north) onto CR W. Drive 6.4 miles and turn left onto WI 64. Follow this 2 miles and turn left onto Center Avenue. Go 0.5 mile and take the first left onto O Day Street. Continue 0.4 mile into the parking area for Riverside Park. There's a dock at the end of the lot. Restrooms and water are on-site.

River Overview

This is one of four Wisconsin River trips featured in this book. At this stage the river is already wide—often at least 200 feet across—having grown considerably since the narrow woodland river up north near the headwaters. But it doesn't quite have the sandbars of the Lower Wisconsin Riverway either. The banks are wooded, heavier with pine than down south, but hardwoods are still abundant, making for some good fall colors. The river still has the ability to narrow up in some places around islands and through shallow stretches that may show some minor riffles. Birdlife is good, with kingfishers, herons, waterfowl, and the occasional eagle to be expected. Fishing is good along here, too; some locals claim the muskies are abundant. Winds can determine your enjoyment of this trip—if the wind is straight out of the south, paddling is going to require some effort. Water levels are good throughout the paddling season, and even when there are low spots, they can be easily avoided. Do not paddle here when the river is at flood stage.

Paddle Summary

Across the river you can see the town hall above the tree line. As you paddle east from the put-in, with Riverside Park on the right, you leave downtown Merrill and the dam behind you. The river is 200 feet across here. Stay left around an island with a shallow and narrow channel to the right. At 0.5 mile, just past the island, the banks on the right are high, sloping up to conifers; on the left they are low and marshy, with hardwoods beyond. Giant boulders are scattered throughout this trip and may lurk just beneath the surface but are not a major nuisance. Highway noise is apparent in the distance, but houses are very few along this route.

At 0.8 mile the river takes the big turn to the south and the banks become low on the right, like on the left. At 1 mile the river comes around to the right, curling back on itself before making a bend to the south through a few islands. At 1.2 miles you pass a low grassy island, taking the left channel. As the channel narrows, you may see some minor riffles; after the island, the larger river bends left.

You can see more than a mile downstream as the river stretches straight toward the south; this is why a southerly wind is not desirable. At 2.8 miles a small perennial creek flows in from the woods on river right. The river takes a turn to the east and passes under some power lines at 3.5 miles, then enters one of the most interesting spots on the river. This is a wide spot on the river, but it is cluttered with several little islands and grassy knolls. Everything you see bends to the left, and you must find your path through these islands to get to the US 51 bridge. There are several ways through here, but in low water you may have to be selective to avoid scraping. At 4 miles, just beyond the collection of islands, pass under the double bridges of the interstate. At 4.5 miles the river makes a long bend to the right to continue south again, and the waters are deep and slow. Along the banks, the forest thickens up a bit. Coming in

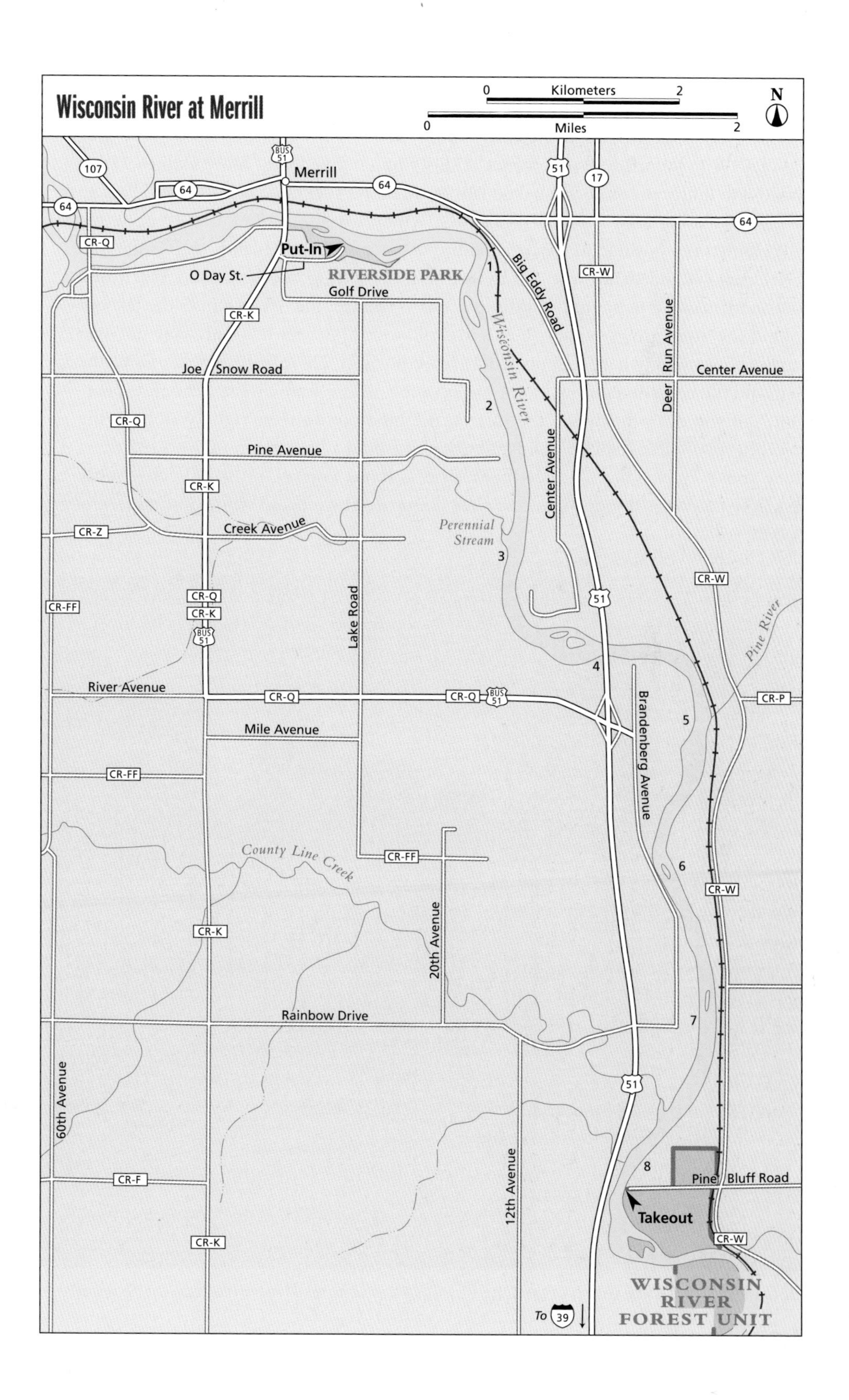
Wisconsin River at Merrill
0 Kilometers 2
0 Miles 2
N
Merrill
Put-In
RIVERSIDE PARK
O Day St.
Golf Drive
Big Eddy Road
Wisconsin River
Joe Snow Road
Center Avenue
Deer Run Avenue
Pine Avenue
Creek Avenue
Perennial Stream
Lake Road
River Avenue
Mile Avenue
Brandenberg Avenue
Pine River
County Line Creek
20th Avenue
Rainbow Drive
60th Avenue
12th Avenue
Pine Bluff Road
Takeout
WISCONSIN RIVER FOREST UNIT
To 39
107
64
17
51
BUS 51
CR-Q
CR-K
CR-W
CR-Z
CR-FF
CR-P
CR-F
1
2
3
4
5
6
7
8

under a railroad bridge on river left at the 5-mile mark is the Pine River. Early in the season, the Pine is fun for whitewater enthusiasts.

The Wisconsin River widens out at this point and becomes more akin to a long lake, with long, narrow tree-covered islands on either side close to the banks. Passage is possible along each—a nice break on a windy day—and the current rises a bit. It is sometimes possible to weave in and out of this series of islands. At 6 miles the river narrows and bends just slightly to the left, meeting another island. You'll find yet another island at 6.9 miles, again passable on either side. As you near the takeout point, the river grows wider again and shallower. The land juts out a bit on river right at 7.7 miles, where County Line Creek flows in. There are a few islands to the left, and the constricted flow might put up a few riffles. Traffic noise becomes apparent, and you can actually see the cars on the highway on river right. Watch for the takeout on the left: a spill of sand and gravel forming a basic ramp up to the parking loop above. The landing is inside the Wisconsin River Forest Unit, a 300-acre county preserve inside the floodplain of the river dominated by red and white pine and some hardwoods.

A rail bridge marks the mouth of the Pine River where it joins the Wisconsin. PREAMTIP SATASUK

30 Eau Claire River

Paddle among high, sandy banks on a wide river east of Eau Claire. The trip starts from a county park and offers some narrowing points of riffles here and there, as well as wide lazy stretches with plenty of sandbars for stops along the way. The final stretch offers one set of basic rapids before the bridge that marks the takeout point.

County: Eau Claire
Start: Harstad County Park, N44 44.388' / W91 9.988'
End: CR K bridge, N44 48.605' / W91 16.976'
Length: 13.8 miles one-way
Float time: About 5 hours
Difficulty rating: Moderate due to sandbars and a few basic rapids
Rapids: Riffles plus one Class I run
River type: Wide pastoral with sandbars
Current: Gentle
River gradient: 2.8 feet per mile
River gauge: USGS 05366500 Eau Claire River near Fall Creek; minimum runnable level 2 feet
Season: Spring, early summer, rainy periods
Land status: Private, with public landings
Fees and permits: Daily vehicle fee at county park
Nearest city/town: Fall Creek
Maps: USGS Augusta West, Lake Eau Claire West, Fall Creek; *DeLorme: Wisconsin Atlas & Gazetteer*: Page 61 C7
Boats used: Canoes, kayaks
Organizations: Pure Water Paddlers Club; purewaterpaddlers.com
Outfitters: Riverside Bike & Skate, 937 Water St, Eau Claire 54703; (715) 835-0088; riversidebikeskate.com

The University of Wisconsin–Eau Claire rents paddle craft/equipment to current students with university IDs and to nonprofit organizations for group outings; (715) 836-3616.

Put-in/Takeout Information

To shuttle point/takeout: From US 12 through Fall Creek, take CR K north 3.3 miles and cross the bridge over the Eau Claire River. The parking lot is an uneven rock and dirt area on the left (west) side of the road. The takeout is a short hike along soft sand trails to the water. It's a bit of a carry from the beach takeout, downriver from the bridge. There are no facilities.

To put-in from takeout: From the takeout, head south on CR K 3.3 miles into Fall Creek. Turn left (east) onto US 12/Lincoln Avenue. Go 4.3 miles and turn left onto CR AF. At 1.6 miles turn left onto CR HHH and drive 0.3 mile to the park entrance on the right. Drive in 0.2 mile, passing the self-pay station, to a sandy parking lot. The put-in is down a short trail and steps to the riverside. Pit toilets are a short walk back up the entry road from the parking lot.

▶ Big Falls, just downriver, is a dangerous Class III waterfall. After this paddle, head to Big Falls County Park and see where the river tumbles over massive rock outcroppings. Facilities include a picnic area and pit toilets. Your daily/annual vehicle entrance pass from the day's paddle will suffice here. Pets are not allowed.

River Overview

There are actually three Eau Claire Rivers in Wisconsin; this one begins as two branches east of the city of the same name. The unified river then flows 40 miles and joins the Chippewa River in downtown Eau Claire. French for "clear water," the river's name is the translation from an Ojibwe name. The water may be clear but is no longer potable, and it has a brown tint to it. As it passes through sandy terrain, the river shows a lot of sandbars; changing water levels can open up narrow side channels and shift those sands so much that it really is a different trip every summer. Two dams control the river, but water levels are nevertheless an issue in mid- to late summer and during dry spells. In low water levels the river can be a dragging nightmare. The river's banks are often high and sandy, and in some areas exposed rocks create some low-level rapids and riffles. Wildlife will often include an eagle or two, plenty of other birds, deer, woodchucks, and more. Lurking in the waters are muskellunge, walleye, and smallmouth bass. Consider a visit (on land) to Big Falls—a 15-foot waterfall just downriver from the takeout—in the county park of the same name. This is not for canoes, and only expert kayakers should attempt this Class III–IV run—and only after carefully reviewing it from the banks.

Paddle Summary

At the bottom of the steps down to the landing, you may have to cross a bit of sandy beach to get to the water, depending on the water levels. The river flows to the left from the put-in and branches around an island. Stay right and take a short run of low Class I rapids just 100 feet from the put-in. It's an auspicious introduction to the river, but just after that you are in flatwater on a river 70 feet across.

The banks are sandy, partly covered with foliage and mixed forest. The river shows a gravel bottom and large swatches of sand with varying depths, but never so deep as a swimming hole. At 1.4 miles the high left bank opens up and becomes sandy, sloping 20 feet down to the water. Pines line up along the grass up top. The river then makes

PURE WATER PADDLERS CLUB

Are you a frequent paddler of the waters of west-central Wisconsin? If you are, you might look up the folks of the Pure Water Paddlers Club (purewaterpaddlers.com). They run a dozen or more trips each summer from places in and around the Eau Claire area to destinations up north such as the Brule or the Apostle Islands. Whether you enjoy kayaks or canoes, whitewater or flatwater, lakes or rivers, the group can connect you with others with the same interests. Membership is available for a modest annual fee for individuals or families and includes discounts at a few regional paddle sport shops. The club keeps a year-round events calendar. Join them in the off-season for instructional classes or workshops and social gatherings.

High sandy banks along the Eau Claire River Preamtip Satasuk

a long bend to the right. At 1.6 miles, passage around an island kicks up some riffles. If you are looking to picnic or lounge in the shallow waters, this is but one of many beach-like areas that would be ideal along this section of the river.

At 1.8 miles Sand Creek flows in on river right. Another 400 feet later you pass the first big rock formation. The river bends to the left. At 3.1 miles Bear Grass Creek flows in from the left and the sandy banks resume. Paddle through some riffles at 3.5 miles. At 5 miles log steps lead down to the water on the left, and at 5.2 miles you pass under some power lines. The river comes up against a tall ridge of exposed sand at 5.4 miles. It slopes down 50 to 60 feet from the top to the water. Erosion is happening here even as you watch. Turtles linger on the deadfall or on sandbars. At 5.6 miles you pass through some minor pinch points in the river, putting up more minor riffles. At 6.4 miles the river makes a tight bend and you can see a collection point for deadfall; you may need to maneuver around some of it, but usually there is plenty of room to pass. At 6.5 miles the river goes under some power lines.

In August the water gets low, and while this final 1.5 miles might be passable in a light kayak, you will need to choose your path carefully. This could mean a lot of dragging. At 8.1 miles you come to the CR D bridge. There is a landing on river left upstream from the bridge. Another 200 feet past the bridge, the river narrows a bit and the current picks up. At 8.8 miles the river bends as it brushes up against CR

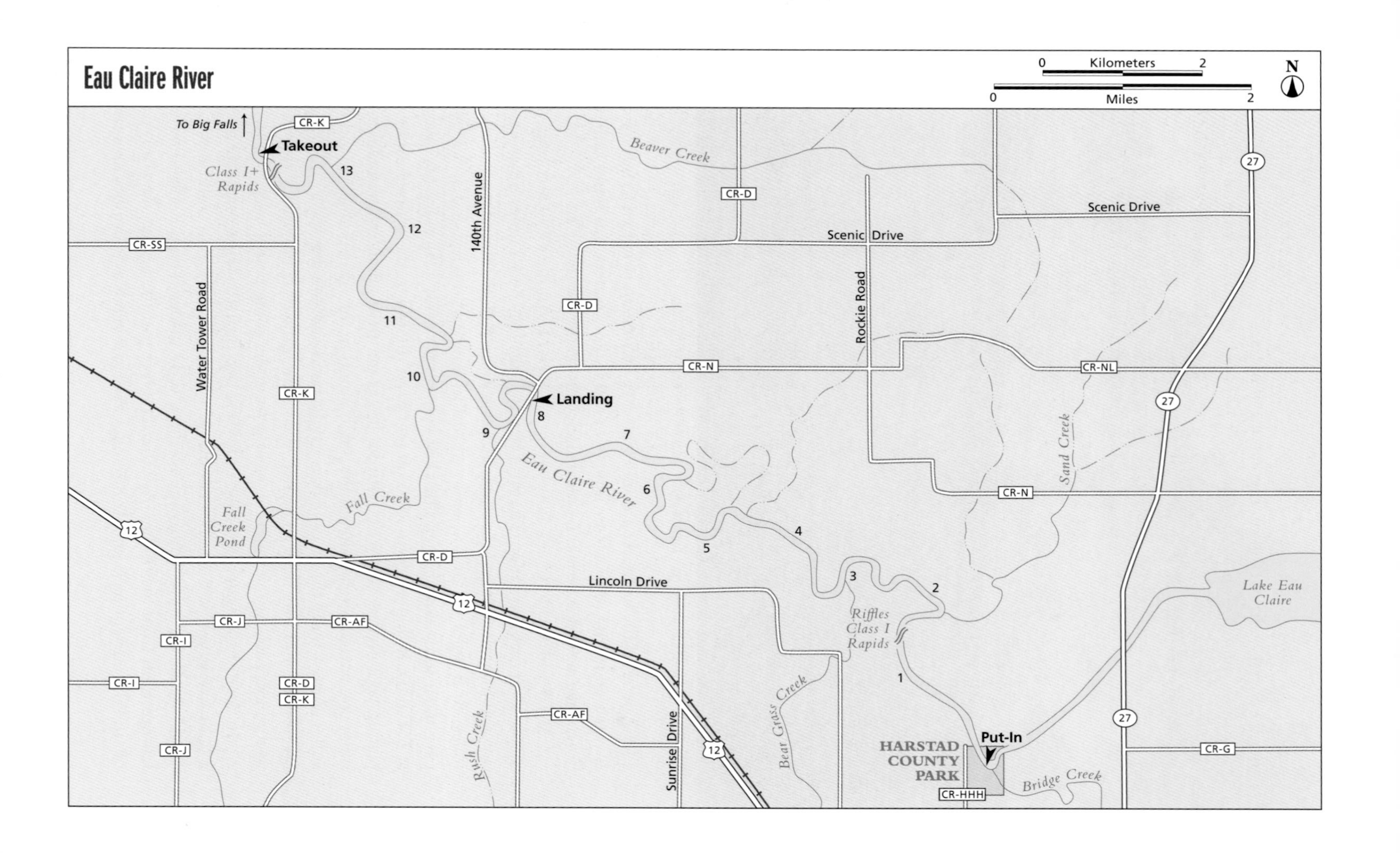

Eau Claire River
Kilometers
Miles
0
2
N
To Big Falls
Takeout
Class I+ Rapids
13
12
11
10
9
8
7
6
5
4
3
2
1
Landing
Eau Claire River
Riffles Class I Rapids
Put-In
HARSTAD COUNTY PARK
Lake Eau Claire
Beaver Creek
Sand Creek
Fall Creek
Fall Creek Pond
Rush Creek
Bear Grass Creek
Bridge Creek
Scenic Drive
Rockie Road
140th Avenue
Water Tower Road
Lincoln Drive
Sunrise Drive
CR-K
CR-D
CR-SS
CR-N
CR-NL
CR-AF
CR-J
CR-I
CR-G
CR-HHH
27
12

D. After another mile the sandy banks return, with swallow homes burrowed inside them. Fall Creek trickles in on the left at 9.9 miles.

Coming in from the right at the 11-mile mark is a rock formation acting almost like a wing dam. Tree-covered and low to the water, the formation forces the current up slightly. Just beyond it, a small creek joins the river on the right. At 12.7 miles Beaver Creek comes in on river right and the river enters one more big S-curve. You come to a rock formation like a wall in front of you. The river breaks through on the right and provides a Class I–II run through some rocks at 13.6 miles. After the rapids you pass under the CR K bridge; take out on the sandy beach to the right, after a small boulder garden without much current. A short walk up sandy paths takes you into an unfinished parking area—just patches of gravel and some large boulders, demanding care with your vehicle so that you don't bottom out on one of them.

Low water requires more navigation on the Eau Claire River. PREAMTIP SATASUK

31 Red Cedar River

As scenic as the companion bike trail that runs along its length, this section of the Red Cedar starts in a city park and flows wide but steady over interesting rock shelves just beneath the surface. Other than some riffles, the paddle is mostly gentle and relaxing while offering only a bit of development along the high forest banks. Along the river's length, small creeks and little cascades trickle in from the trees.

County: Dunn
Start: Riverside Park, Menomonie, N44 52.346' / W91 56.461'
End: Downsville Public Boat Landing/WI 25 bridge, Downsville, N44 46.439' / W91 56.129'
Length: 8.2 miles one-way
Float time: About 3.5 hours
Difficulty rating: Easy
Rapids: Some riffles only
River type: Wide wooded pastoral
Current: Gentle
River gradient: 2.7 feet per mile
River gauge: USGS 05369000 Red Cedar River at Menomonie; flow regulated by power plant; minimum runnable level 500 cfs
Season: Spring through fall
Land status: Varied, with public landings
Fees and permits: No fees or permits required
Nearest city/town: Menomonie
Maps: USGS Menomonie South; *DeLorme: Wisconsin Atlas & Gazetteer*: Page 60 B1
Boats used: Canoes, kayaks, johnboats
Organizations: Red Cedar River Watershed–University of Wisconsin-Extension; fyi.uwex.edu/redcedar
Outfitters: Irvington Campground, E4176 CR D, Menomonie 54751; (715) 235-2267; menomoniecamping.com
Local information: Red Cedar State Trail, 921 Brickyard Rd., Menomonie 54751; (715) 232-1242; dnr.wi.gov/topic/parks/name/redcedar

DEVIL'S PUNCHBOWL

The locals have stories to tell of this beautiful little canyon just west of the Red Cedar River. Some say it's haunted. Others will tell you not to worry, that those ghosts are actually only trolls. Or fairies. Water trickles out from the sandstone walls, rising up from springs or trickling down from the surface. Those who have gathered the water claim it stays cold for days by some ancient magic.

Originally this was called Black's Ravine. Due to its delicate nature, the area is now protected. You can still view it, but you can't go directly inside—unless you are a gnome. If your vehicle doesn't start when you attempt to leave, don't say I didn't warn you.

Follow CR P south along the river and turn left onto Paradise Valley Road. There is a parking lot on the left and a short trail to the canyon.

Put-in/Takeout Information

To shuttle point/takeout: From US 12 through downtown Menomonie, take WI 25 (Broadway Street) south for 7.8 miles. After you cross the bridge over the river, the parking lot for the boat landing is on the left. An asphalt road leads right to the concrete landing, but parking is a short walk from there.

To put-in from takeout: From the takeout, backtrack north on WI 25 for 7.3 miles and turn left onto WI 29 (11th Avenue). Go 0.5 mile, crossing the bridge, and take the first left onto Riverside Park Road. Follow this all the way to the small loop at the southernmost end of Riverside Park and find an unimproved landing along the sandy riverbank. The park has restrooms and water.

Note: The Red Cedar State Trail makes an excellent bike shuttle route, following the river almost exactly from put-in to takeout.

River Overview

The Red Cedar River runs from the dam-made Lake Chetek south through smaller lakes and a few towns to the dam in Menomonie, where it gathers as Lake Menomin. Below the dam it is a wide steady river, mostly amid bluffs until its confluence with the Chippewa River just south of Dunnville. Either side is completely forested right up to the edge of the water. On river left you can see large stretches of flat rock just below the surface of the water; otherwise there is a mix of sand and cobble along the

The sandy put-in on the Red Cedar River PREAMTIP SATASUK

river bottom. This is a lovely area, good for fall colors and a bit of wildlife viewing, but it isn't always the cleanest of rivers.

Warning: Blue-green algae can be a problem on the Red Cedar for a number of reasons: farm runoff, lawn maintenance, heat, and sunlight. Algal blooms occur most commonly from mid-June through September. The algae release powerful neurotoxins, which in large enough amounts can be deadly. Dogs are especially susceptible. Don't swallow the water, don't swim in it, and do not bring your pet along. Contact the Dunn County Health Department (715-232-2388) for current conditions.

Paddle Summary

Just after the put-in you will pass Gilbert Creek coming in from river right, pushing out a small sand delta. Up the creek you can see a bridge; this is the Red Cedar State Trail. Paddle through a short stretch of riffles over a rocky area thereafter. The river is over 100 feet wide here, and already you are looking at forest on either side. If you paddle closer to the left bank, you can see large stretches of flat rock beneath the surface. At 0.6 mile you pass over a nearly imperceptible drop—a tiny riffle may mark it—and then the river bends right. When water is low, keep your eyes open for those rock ledges: They are strong scrape points. Another 0.2 mile later, you may encounter more riffles.

At the 1-mile mark, a tiny creek flows in from the right, one of many you may see along this route. Paddle through another section of riffles, and at 1.6 and 1.8 miles pass two more little creeks on the right. In between are a picnic table and grill. Farther inland here is a county park with a beautiful geologic feature called the Devil's Punchbowl. Also at this point, on the left side of the river, underwater ledges spill the water at an angle from the shore. Look for the little cascade as Birch Creek tumbles in from the hill above.

The riffles end about 0.2 mile later; straight ahead is a large bluff at Irvington, the Accordion Cliffs. The river comes to the bluff and breaks left, passing under the CR D bridge at 2.8 miles. Just before the bridge is a parking lot for the Red Cedar Trail on river right, and just past the structure, Irving Creek flows into the river from the right as well. There is a takeout here under an old railroad trestle, about 300 feet downriver from the bridge; taking out near the highway bridge is prohibited.

Straight out from the trestle, exactly in the center of the river, is a concrete wall, the remains of a previous structure, but it is not an obstruction. Just beyond this are some rocky bits as you come to a bend to the left. Power lines cross high above, and riffles pick up due to the shallow water. The landing for Irvington Campground is on the left at 2.9 miles. This area can get a little shallow in low-water periods. At 3.2 miles the river comes to some power lines and bends gently to the right through about 250 feet of riffles.

At about 3.6 miles you'll pass at least three little streams dribbling in from river left, two of them as tiny cascades. At about 4 miles the river bends to the right and rushes the current a bit. At 4.9 miles, on river right, you can see the bike trail and its

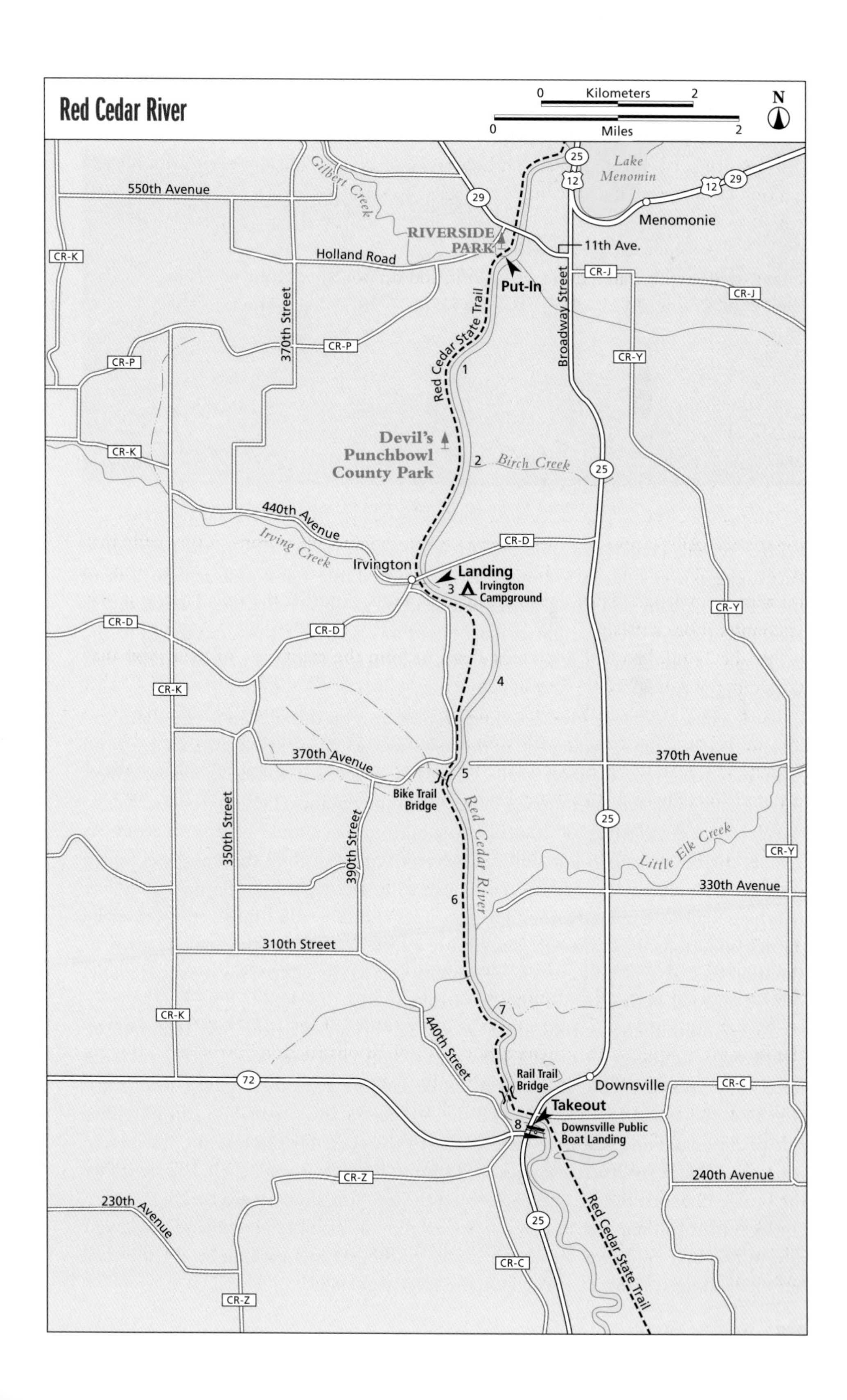
Red Cedar River
0 Kilometers 2
0 Miles 2
N
550th Avenue
Gilbert Creek
29
25
12
Lake Menomin
Menomonie
RIVERSIDE PARK
11th Ave.
CR-K
Holland Road
Put-In
CR-J
370th Street
Red Cedar State Trail
Broadway Street
CR-P
CR-Y
1
Devil's Punchbowl County Park
2
Birch Creek
440th Avenue
Irving Creek
CR-D
Irvington
Landing
3
Irvington Campground
4
370th Avenue
5
Bike Trail Bridge
Red Cedar River
350th Street
390th Street
Little Elk Creek
330th Avenue
6
310th Street
7
440th Street
72
Rail Trail Bridge
Downsville
CR-C
Takeout
8
Downsville Public Boat Landing
240th Avenue
CR-Z
230th Avenue
Red Cedar State Trail

Towering sandy banks along a bend in the Red Cedar River PREAMTIP SATASUK

bridge crossing a creek that spills into the river. Riffles begin around the next curve. Pass under power lines at 5.9 miles. At 6.2 miles Little Elk Creek comes in from the left as a stream, and the river narrows and picks up speed a bit. A creek enters via a storm sewer on the right at 6.5 miles. Now you start to see a change in the landscape—a few more patches of meadow-like features and abundant wildflowers in the summer.

At 6.6 miles, riffles or low Class I rapids pick up a bit through an S-curve and you pass under power lines. At the end of this riffle area, you can expect a small Class I run and a nice wave train in lower water; but at higher levels it will be moderate riffles. A large, sandy cliff face and sloping bank rise in the distance. This guides the river to the right past a collection of deadfall at the bottom that should be easy to avoid. At 7 miles the river channel goes left; the current remains strong through here, but in spring and in high water, islands and a channel to the right become navigable. The river passes along the sandy slope for 0.25 mile and then the banks get lower again, though still sandy. Pass through some more riffles or rapids as the river narrows to about 65 feet. At 7.4 miles you'll see a backwater to the right. This becomes a full-fledged channel of the river in higher water.

At 7.7 miles the river runs under an old rail bridge, now the bike trail. On the right bank, you'll see a lot of sedimentary rock along the waterline. The river widens once more. Paddle around an island at 8 miles, and look for the highway bridge just after that; the takeout is downriver of the bridge, on river right. You can go either side of the island and still have time to get to the right for the takeout. Just before the bridge, more river water comes in from the left over a rock shelf. Paddle under the bridge between the first two pylons on the left. Just after, on river right, is a nice concrete boat landing and, in faster water, an eddy that will catch you and guide you into it. The bike trail goes under the bridge to the left to a parking lot for the trail, but the landing is across the bridge on the river-right side.

32 Kinnickinnic River

The "Kinni" is a delightfully playful stretch of narrow waters threading their rapid and riffly way through some very nice sandstone bluff scenery reminiscent of the Kickapoo. While the rapids are not overwhelming, absolute beginners would likely be frustrated by the demands of boat control. That being said, this is a favorite and a bit of a thrill when water levels are adequate. It is listed as a Class 1 trout stream, which should give a hint to its health and clarity.

County: Pierce
Start: Lake Louise dam at Glen Park, N44 51.041' / W92 38.337'
End: CR F bridge, N44 49.872' / W92 44.008'
Length: 8 miles one-way
Float time: About 3.5 hours
Difficulty rating: Moderate
Rapids: Class I
River type: Narrow, twisting wooded pastoral with rock bluffs
Current: Moderate to swift
River gradient: 13.6 feet per mile
River gauge: USGS 05342000 Kinnickinnic River near River Falls; minimum runnable level 90 cfs
Season: Spring through fall
Land status: Varied, with public landings
Fees and permits: State park vehicle fee at takeout parking lot
Nearest city/town: River Falls
Maps: USGS River Falls West; *DeLorme: Wisconsin Atlas & Gazetteer*: Page 58 B3
Boats used: Canoes, kayaks
Organizations: Kinnickinnic River Land Trust, 265 Mound View Rd., Ste. C, River Falls 54002; (715) 425-5738; kinniriver.org
Outfitters: Kinni Creek Lodge and Outfitters, 545 N. Main St., River Falls 54022; (715) 425-7378; kinnicreek.com

River Guide Kayaks, P.O. Box 292, River Falls 54022; (612) 201-1314; riverguidekayaks.com
Local information: Watch for an annual river clean-up in April. Contact kinniriver.org.

Put-in/Takeout Information

To shuttle point/takeout: From River Falls head south on WI 29/35 and turn right (west) onto CR FF. Continue 5.3 miles and turn right (north) onto CR F. Cross the bridge at 0.4 mile and turn left into the state park parking lot.
To put-in from takeout: From the state park parking lot, go right (south) across the bridge on CR F and take the first left (east) onto CR FF. Go 5.3 miles and turn left (north) onto WI 29/35. Drive 1.5 miles and turn left (west) onto Park Street, following it to the end, where you will find street parking, a short asphalt drop-off-only driveway, and a trail into the woods.

River Overview

The Kinnickinnic—named for an Ojibwe word for a tobacco/plant smoking blend—originates from springs to the east and flows just over 40 miles to empty into the St.

A trout fisherman out with his dogs on the "Kinni" PREAMTIP SATASUK

Croix River. A dam at River Falls creates a lake that separates two types of river: the slower, narrower stream above the dam, and the slightly wider and faster river below. While the upper section of this Class 1 trout stream is colder and supports a lot of small trout, the lower stretch is a bit warmer and has fewer but larger trout, attracting anglers. After River Falls the riverside is undeveloped; there are only two public access points, and after the last at the CR F bridge, the river runs through Kinnickinnic State Park and a large delta as it enters the St. Croix. The only takeout points beyond CR F are far downriver or upriver on the St. Croix. Water height is best early in the season; the float becomes bumpy in August if there is no rainfall, though dragging a couple times may still be worth it.

Paddle Summary

The put-in requires about an 800-foot hike down a packed dirt and gravel trail and some CCC-era railroad tie steps to the river's edge. Be careful to put in well out of the dangerous turbulence during periods of high releases from the dam. The dam is wedged between two sandstone outcrops, indications of the terrain, and the river is about 50 feet across, about as wide as it ever gets from here to the end.

The first riffles come right away, within a couple hundred feet of the put-in, and after a bend to the left in the river, you'll find the first Class I run of rapids. The river alternates frequently between riffles and rapids, with some calm patches in between. Along the banks are abundant wildflowers, and waving in the current in the crystal clear water is abundant and healthy plant life. Power lines cross the river at 0.2 mile, one of the very few signs of development between here and the takeout. At 0.6 mile a rock outcrop forces the river to the right. On the left is the last public exit before that final bridge at CR F. A long, narrow island splits the river into channels roughly 15 feet across, and depending on water levels, you must choose the path of least resistance. The left channel is generally more passable than the one on the right. The river bends right again at 0.7 mile and a stream joins from river left. A string of rapids follows.

WHAT MAKES A GOOD TROUT STREAM?

The Wisconsin Department of Natural Resources lists three classes of trout streams: Class 1 is considered to be completely natural, in that the trout population requires no stocking with fish from a hatchery. Class 2 requires some stocking to maintain the population enough for sportfishing. Class 3 requires stocking every year, as the trout in these rivers do not survive to the next season. Most classified trout streams in Wisconsin are either Class 1 or 2, with 5,400 miles of Class 1 and 5,912 miles of Class 2 together making up 86 percent of all trout streams.

Biologically speaking, a good trout stream requires very high water quality, food, and proper river conditions above and below the water. A good river or stream for trout has crystal clear water, as the fish find their food by sight. The temperature should be cooler, generally in the 55°F to 68°F range for brook and rainbow trout. The cool temperature helps maintain oxygen levels—a must for trout, their eggs, and the insects the fish feed on.

Gravel and rock river bottoms are ideal, while sand or silt can negatively affect the trout's environment, especially for egg laying. Eggs are deposited in fall and winter and must lie protected until spring hatching. Riffles and rapids help maintain a silt-free rocky environment. The adult fish also need places to take cover. Thus you may see indications of human-made pools with rocks arranged to create or protect deeper pockets of water. Natural deadfall, boulders, and rock overhangs are good, as are areas of healthy aquatic plants, which also help oxygenate the water. Tree shade helps keep water temperatures low.

This is a simplistic breakdown of what helps a river support a healthy trout population; the larger equation includes many ecological elements and speaks to the complexity of nature. The Kinnickinnic and Bois Brule are Class 1 trout streams; the Waupaca and Crystal Rivers are Class 2.

***Note:* Trout fishing requires a state fishing license and a special inland and/or Great Lake trout stamp. Go to dnr.wi.gov for more information.**

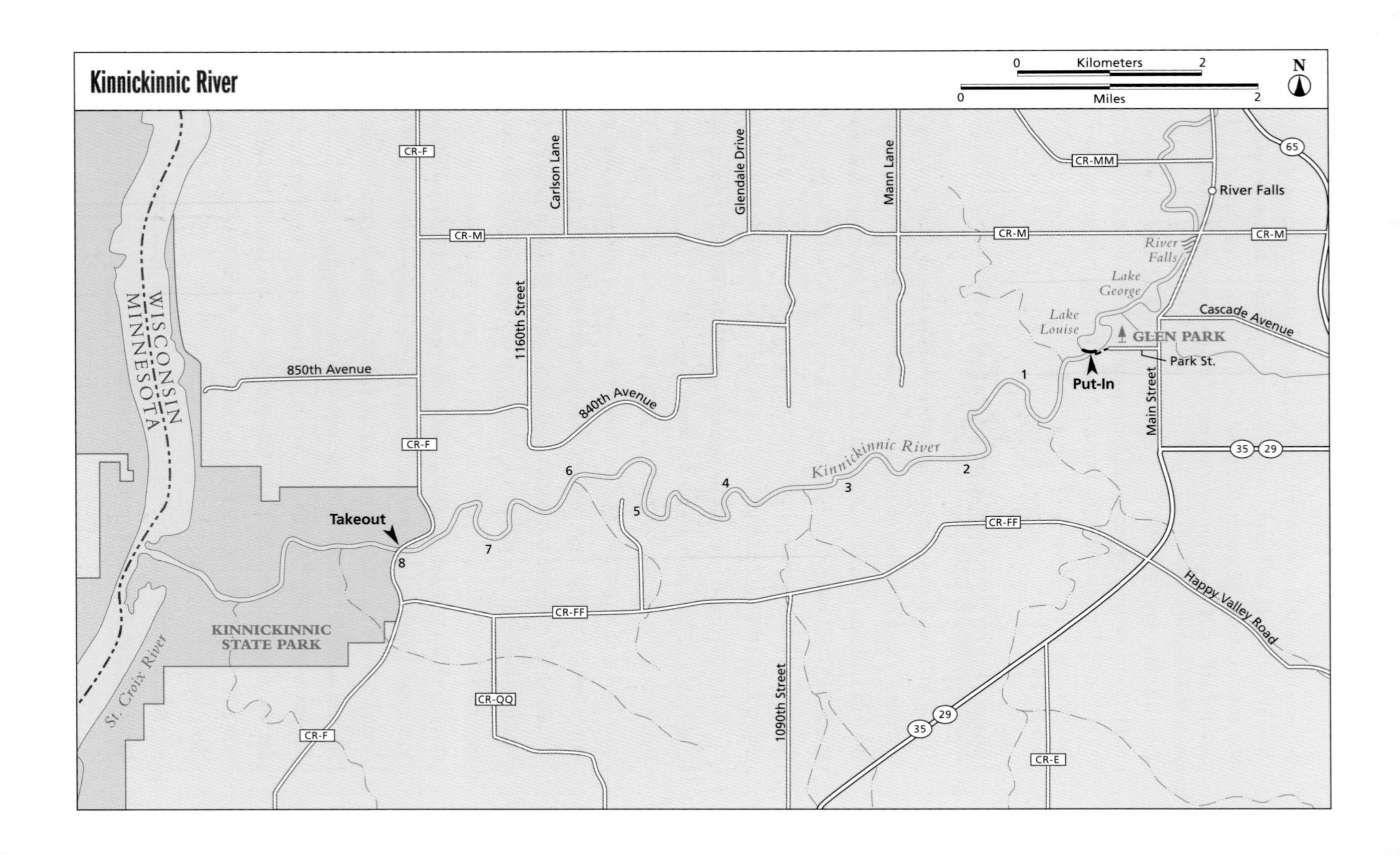
Kinnickinnic River
0
Kilometers
2
0
Miles
2
N
CR-F
Carlson Lane
Glendale Drive
Mann Lane
CR-MM
65
River Falls
CR-M
River Falls
Lake George
Lake Louise
Cascade Avenue
GLEN PARK
Park St.
Put-In
Main Street
WISCONSIN
MINNESOTA
850th Avenue
1160th Street
840th Avenue
Kinnickinnic River
1
2
3
4
5
6
7
8
35
29
Takeout
CR-FF
Happy Valley Road
KINNICKINNIC STATE PARK
St. Croix River
CR-QQ
1090th Street
CR-E

At about 0.9 mile the river tightens up to about 10 feet across. Boat control is very important here; if there is deadfall that hasn't been cleared, you might have issues. At 1.7 miles a seasonal stream comes in, depositing a little delta of sand. At 1.8 miles the river comes up against a rocky ridge covered with foliage. The river takes you to the right through some riffles as you follow the wall for 100 feet. At some of these corners where the river comes to the sandstone walls—and there will be many—the current may force you straight to the stone if you aren't at your paddle. At 2.3 miles you pass under power lines, and at 2.5 miles a wide meadow, full of flowers in summer. This is a popular access point with local fly fishers out looking for trout. After the meadow another ridge forces the river right, and the river is back in between grassy banks and forest.

At 4 miles you paddle another Class I rapids and come to another ridge, forcing the river right again and taking you on to another couple short stretches of rapids. The waters are pretty active through here, offering minimal breaks between the riffles and rapids. At 5.4 miles a little stream cascades in from the right. At the end of the next run, the river widens to 50 feet, showing a sandy bottom and offering a fantastic view of a 100-foot rocky cliff on river right. When the waters are lower, this might be a place to pause and take in the view, though there really isn't a place where the current abates. At the end of the bluff, a spring creek flows in from the right and the river picks up speed again.

At 5.6 miles a Class I run brings you right into another exposed cliff face; be prepared to go right. At 6.3 miles another couple runs of Class I rapids and riffles lead right up to another wall. After you take this right turn, you enter what is literally the coolest part of this river route: The ridge is high on the right; the current is good; and the ferns, trees, and shade make this stretch fresh and chilled even on a summer day. At 6.9 miles you come to a significant Class I rapid on a turn. Coming out of that chute, look for the green-covered rocks to the left, with seeps trickling through them. At 7.2 miles you pass an exposed sandbank, and then the river flows through another scenic channel. Once you are around that corner going left, you still have current, but it is flatwater and you have a moment to truly take it all in. Almost to the end of this section, you'll see an abundance of seeps trickling out of the rock face.

You can find just over half the state's bird species and 40 percent of the plant species in the Kinnickinnic's watershed, including over forty species of endangered, threatened, or rare flora and fauna.

At 7.8 miles you'll encounter some rock vanes, which were put in to make pools to support the trout. These constrict the river a bit and push up some small rapids in places. The final stretch is past a ridge on the left and then through one little stretch of riffles within sight of the bridge. You can take out right after or under the bridge, but in faster current it is best to take out before the bridge on river right. Carry under the bridge in that case; the parking lot is right there, just inside the edge of the state park.

33 Lower St. Croix River

This river trip begins with some lingering: Take time to paddle around the picturesque rock gorge, the Dalles of the St. Croix, before following the slow and wide river south amid bluffs along the border between Minnesota and Wisconsin. The stretch is mostly undeveloped but easily accessible. Pass another rocky constriction and then enjoy an easy paddle to a Minnesota-side takeout across the river at Osceola.

County: Polk
Start: Interstate State Park Landing, N45 23.743' / W92 39.493'
End: National Park Service Osceola Landing, N45 19.289' / W92 42.650'
Length: 6.5 miles one-way, plus Dalles exploration
Float time: About 3 hours
Difficulty rating: Easy
Rapids: None
River type: Wide wooded pastoral
Current: Gentle
River gradient: 0.6 feet per mile
River gauge: USGS 05340500 St. Croix River at St. Croix Falls. Xcel Energy is required to maintain a minimum of 1,600 cfs Apr through Oct, making this consistently runnable; beware of flood stage.
Season: Spring through fall
Land status: Varied, with public landings
Fees and permits: State park vehicle fee at put-in
Nearest city/town: St. Croix Falls
Maps: USGS Osceola, St. Croix Dalles; *DeLorme: Wisconsin Atlas & Gazetteer*: Page 70 B3
Boats used: Canoes, kayaks, johnboats, small motorized craft
Contacts: Interstate State Park, Hwy, 35, St. Croix Falls 54024; (715) 483-3747; dnr.wi.gov/topic/parks/name/interstate

St. Croix National Scenic Riverway, 401 N. Hamilton St., St. Croix Falls 54024; (715) 483-3284; nps.gov/sacn
Outfitters: Riverwood Canoe, 305 River St., Osceola 54020; (715) 222-2288; riverwoodcanoe.com

Put-in/Takeout Information

To shuttle point/takeout: From St. Croix Falls take WI 35 south 7.9 miles to Osceola. Turn right (west) onto Osceola Road and drive 0.5 mile, across the bridge, to the Minnesota side (MN 243). The first left after the bridge is the entrance to a National Park Service boat landing with ample parking, restrooms, water, accessible facilities, and picnic areas.

To put-in from takeout: From the takeout, backtrack across the bridge to Osceola and head back north again on WI 35, but only 7.4 miles. Go left into the Interstate State Park entrance. Follow the park road signs toward the South Campground, but at the entrance to that loop, stay right and head to the boat launch area, where there are facilities and parking.

River Overview

Most of the 169 miles of the St. Croix River are protected as a National Scenic Riverway and managed by the National Park Service. Its major tributary, the Namekagon, enjoys similar protection and is also featured in this book, and there's even a route herein that combines the Namekagon and St. Croix for a multiday trip. The last 130 miles of the St. Croix form the border between Wisconsin and Minnesota before joining the Mississippi at Prescott, Wisconsin, where it widens into a lake. The upper stretches are much narrower and generally swifter; the lower section shows occasional rapids but typically is gentle and wide. Paddle-up campsites are marked throughout its length. After Gordon's Dam, which marks the beginning of the National Scenic Riverway, there is only one other dam—the hydroelectric dam at St. Croix Falls. Just downriver is one of the river's most scenic sites: the Dalles of the St. Croix.

Paddle Summary

From the concrete ramp at the put-in, paddle upstream to the right and explore the impressive cut in the basalt rock. This gorge is known as the Dalles of the St. Croix and is the most scenic thing you'll see all day. The estimated paddle time does not include whatever time you spend here ogling the towering rock cliffs. Look for the Old Man of the Dalles, a rock formation up above.

THE ICE AGE NATIONAL SCENIC TRAIL

One of only eight national scenic trails, the Ice Age Trail lies entirely within the state of Wisconsin, roughly following the edge of the last advance of glaciers in the Wisconsin Glaciation period, over 12,000 years ago. When completed, the trail will run over 1,000 miles through some of the most scenic areas of the state, especially through terrain that shows the dramatic effects of a continental glacier. Over 600 miles of trail sections have already been completed, offering very rustic trails through the woods; connecting sections may use country roads or pass through small towns. One segment includes a free ferry ride across the Wisconsin River.

The westernmost point of the Ice Age Trail is in Interstate State Park. The park is quite a remarkable place to begin, with the St. Croix River running through a basalt gorge, carved by a torrent of glacial meltwater, and glacial potholes–holes drilled by swirling rocks and boulders caught in the massive eddies from glacial runoff. The trail meanders through the state as far south as Janesville and up through Kettle Moraine State Forest before ending in Door County.

A complete trail guide and atlas are available from the Ice Age Trail Alliance, 2110 Main St., Cross Plains 53528; (800) 227-0046; iceagetrail.org.

Impressive rock formations along the Lower St Croix River PREAMTIP SATASUK

As you paddle south from the put-in point on river left, the river is more than 200 feet across, wide and slow. At 0.1 mile is Folsom Island, actually on the Minnesota side of the border, which runs right down the river. Either side is typically passable. Due to the proximity of the highway on the Minnesota side, traffic noise is steady at the beginning of the trip, but the cars are generally invisible in this green corridor through tall bluffs. At 1.2 miles you'll see a seasonal stream from the left and a small island on river right. This attaches to the mainland in low water. On the Wisconsin side the banks are 12 feet high, with stratified sand and mud, and topped with tall grasses. Across in Minnesota, the banks are lower to the water.

After the first 1.5 miles, the highway noise disappears and the river becomes peaceful as it also narrows a bit. At 2.1 miles you pass a rocky island in the middle. The river has cut a channel in the rock, and you can see cliff faces rising up 60 feet or more on either side. On the rock face to the left is a large white X once used to guide steamboats. Sunburst lichen (*Xanthoria elegans*) and moss can be seen in many places along the rock. In the center of the river is a little rocky island, often with a sandbar trailing downstream—a nice place to make a stop.

At 2.3 miles the cliff faces end and rock formations are lower to the water. Recreational pontoon boats are docked at a few private residences on the Minnesota side. The river widens a bit again, showing low banks, green and grassy, and the occasional

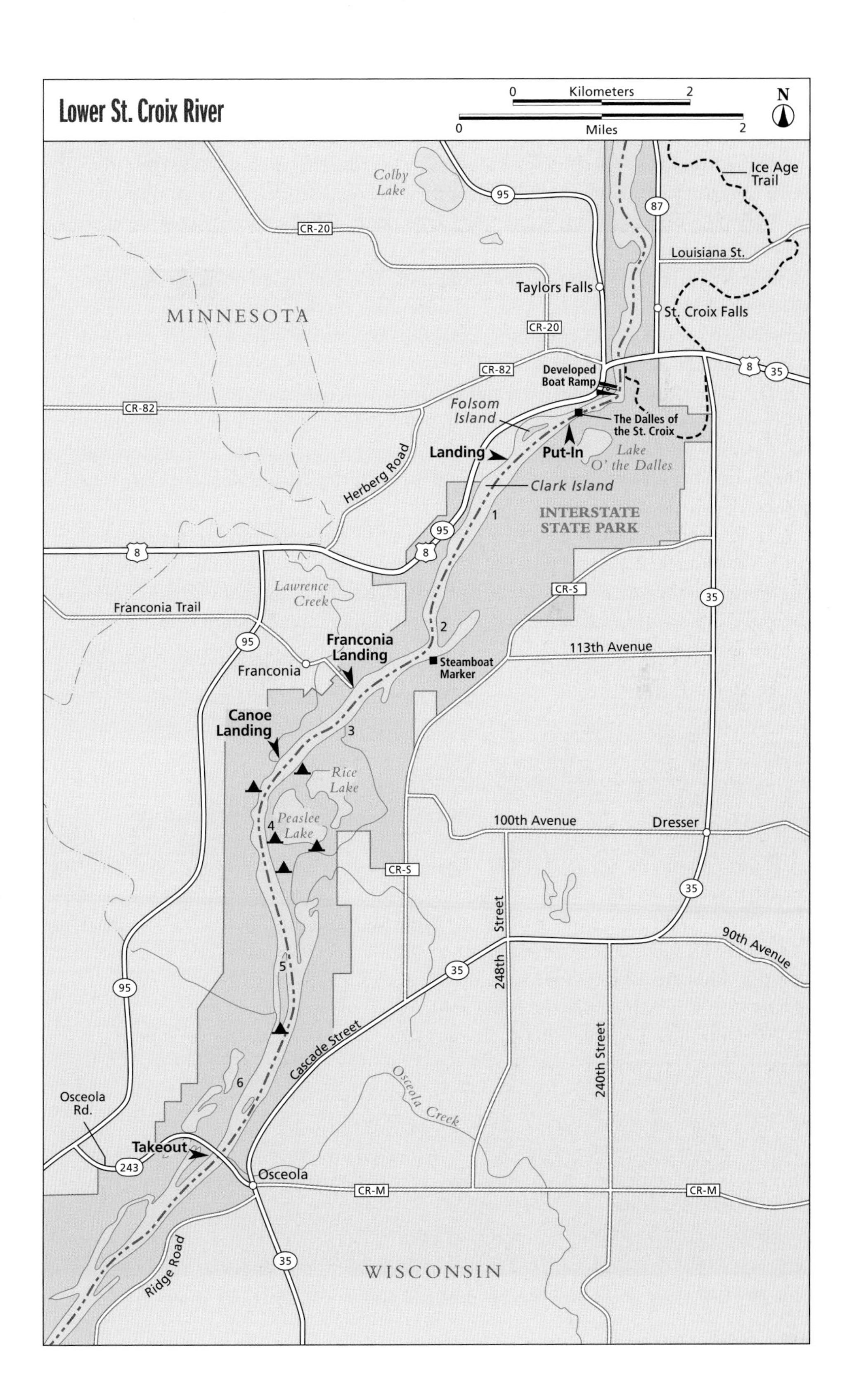

Lower St. Croix River
0
Kilometers
2
0
Miles
2
N
Colby Lake
95
87
Ice Age Trail
CR-20
Louisiana St.
Taylors Falls
MINNESOTA
St. Croix Falls
CR-20
CR-82
Developed Boat Ramp
8
35
CR-82
Folsom Island
The Dalles of the St. Croix
Landing
Put-In
Lake O' the Dalles
Herberg Road
Clark Island
1
INTERSTATE STATE PARK
95
8
8
Lawrence Creek
CR-S
35
Franconia Trail
2
95
Franconia Landing
113th Avenue
Steamboat Marker
Franconia
Canoe Landing
3
Rice Lake
Peaslee Lake
4
100th Avenue
Dresser
CR-S
35
Street
248th
90th Avenue
5
35
95
Cascade Street
240th Street
Osceola Creek
6
Osceola Rd.
Takeout
243
Osceola
CR-M
CR-M
Ridge Road
35
WISCONSIN

rock formation. Pass the Franconia landing at 2.7 miles. The river gets riffles in low-water periods as it bends left just past the landing.

At 3.4 miles pass a campsite on river left and a creek that spills into the river from Rice Lake, a small lake set back from the banks on river left. On river right is another sandy sloping canoe landing at the same mile mark, and Lawrence Creek flows in near there. Just after that, at 3.7 miles, there's a campsite on the Minnesota side and another at 4.1 miles on river left, with some wooden steps up the bank. Beyond it to the east and just south of Rice Lake is Peaslee Lake, another trapped bit of the river turned lake. At 4.3 miles is one more campsite on river left, with wooden steps and some erosion protection.

The taller bluffs are now gone, and just some low hills mark the skyline. At 4.9 miles you'll come to a long island—just over 0.5 mile long—with a navigable channel on either side and a campsite at its southernmost point. Take the left channel and you can explore a backwater to the left and back. During high waters, the river runs through the backwater as well.

At 5.7 miles you come around a gentle bend to the right and can see the steel bridge at your takeout in the distance. The Osceola water tower and the large bluff it sits on rise on the left, beyond the bridge. Stay right, being mindful of strainers. The takeout is just downstream of the bridge on river right, at a sandy beach with a couple of concrete boat ramps.

A rocky island with a sandy beach near the steamboat marker on the St. Croix River

34 Namekagon River

Similar to the upper stretches of the St. Croix River, the Namekagon—also part of the St. Croix National Scenic Riverway—offers a relaxed paddle through a wooded corridor roughly following the same course as US 63 but far enough off to avoid most traffic noise. The clear waters run gently except for a few easy passes of riffles, and wildlife is abundant. The park service offers free campsites along the route, and the last stretch is popular for tubing up to the takeout, right across the highway from the National Park Service visitor center.

County: Washburn
Start: Springbrook Landing, N45 57.225' / W91 41.178'
End: Namekagon River Visitor Center Landing, N45 54.326' / W91 48.980'
Length: 12.9 miles one-way
Float time: About 4 hours
Difficulty rating: Easy
Rapids: One Class I run
River type: Wooded pastoral
Current: Gentle to moderate
River gradient: 1.6 feet per mile
River gauge: USGS 05331833 at Leonards Bridge; minimum runnable level 100 cfs. Check the national park website for water levels specific for paddling each river section: nps.gov/sacn/planyourvisit/riverlevels.htm.
Season: Spring through fall
Land status: Public
Fees and permits: No fees or permits required
Nearest city/town: Trego
Maps: USGS Springbrook, Trego; *DeLorme: Wisconsin Atlas & Gazetteer*: Page 84 A3
Boats used: Canoes, kayaks
Contacts: Namekagon River Visitor Center, W5483 Hwy. 63, Trego 54888; (715) 635-8346; nps.gov/sacn
St. Croix National Scenic Riverway, 401 N. Hamilton St., St. Croix Falls 54024; (715) 483-3284; nps.gov/sacn
Outfitters: Jack's Canoe & Tube Rental, N7504 Wagon Bridge Rd., Trego 54888; (715) 635-3300; jackscanoerental.com

Put-in/Takeout Information

To shuttle point/takeout: From where US 63 joins US 53 in Trego, go east 0.6 mile on US 63 North and turn left onto Lakeside Road. The parking lot for the landing is immediately on the left.
To put-in from takeout: From the takeout landing on Lakeside Road, go left (east) on US 63 for 7.2 miles. Take a left onto the angling Legion Lane and drive 0.4 mile to the end, where there is a gravel parking lot at the landing.

River Overview

The Namekagon is a lovely, clear river that starts from a lake of the same name north of Hayward and flows 101 miles to feed into the St. Croix River. The name is from the Ojibwe people and means "river at the place abundant with sturgeons."

The takeout on the Namekagon trip lies across the highway from the National Scenic Riverway's visitor center. Preamtip Satasuk

It is narrow and full of riffles in some stretches along its upper sections, but because it is shallow, low water can make it inconsistent in late summer or during dry periods. After it passes Hayward, the river gradually gets wider and often slower, passing through some marshy patches but mostly thick forest.

Paddle Summary

Putting in from the bottom of the steps may be trickier than simply using the ledge above the water to the right of them. Push off from the calm water at the put-in and immediately head into some riffles and Class I rapids as the current splits around a small island. The river narrows along here but widens out again within the first 0.25 mile. At 0.4 mile Hay Creek flows in from the right; another 200 yards later a seasonal branch of the river comes in on the left. Past here you can see the sandy bottom and the river becomes flatwater. At 1.3 miles Spring Creek joins from the right. At 1.6 miles—marked by a sign as 48.3 miles on the larger river—you encounter a campsite on river right. For the first 3 miles, the trees stand off from the grassy banks; in some areas there are no banks at all, just marshy areas. At 3.5 miles Gull Creek flows in on river right. Just 0.2 mile past here is another right-bank campsite, this one at 46.3 on the river map. Bean Brook joins from the left over a sandy bottom at 4 miles.

RIVER CAMPING

The Namekagon, like the St. Croix, has a number of rustic campsites throughout its length, all managed by the National Park Service. Individual sites allow up to three tents and a maximum of eight people; the group sites accept six tents and sixteen people. Sites include fire rings and throne-style pit toilets (i.e., an outhouse without the house part). There is no fee to camp, and all sites are first-come, first-served. Pack out whatever you pack in, and don't bring any glass on the river.

***Caution:* This is bear country. Don't keep food in your tent, and be sure to hang your supplies from a tree where a bear can't get to them.**

At 4.2 miles a ridge covered with a pine plantation rises up on the left, pushing the river right and leading you to a campsite on the left at 45.7 miles on the river map. After this site, any wind will affect the paddling through this section, as the river is wider than 100 feet across and unsheltered. At 5 miles you'll see some steps up to

One of several riverside campsites along the Namekagon River PREAMTIP SATASUK

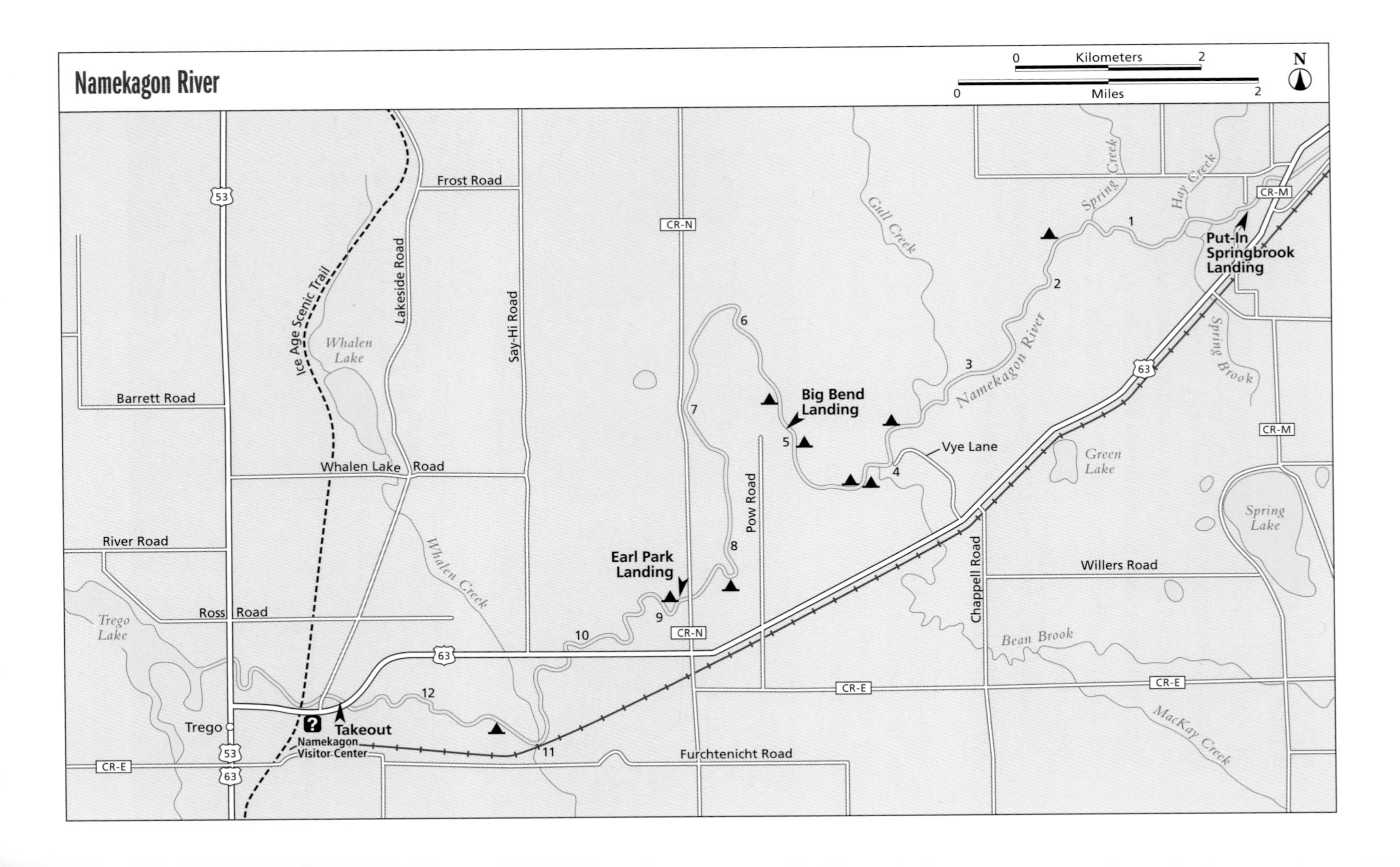
Namekagon River
0 Kilometers 2
0 Miles 2
N
Frost Road
Lakeside Road
Say-Hi Road
Ice Age Scenic Trail
Whalen Lake
Barrett Road
Whalen Lake Road
River Road
Ross Road
Trego Lake
Trego
Whalen Creek
Takeout
Namekagon Visitor Center
Furchtenicht Road
CR-E
CR-N
CR-M
53
63
Earl Park Landing
Big Bend Landing
Pow Road
Vye Lane
Chappell Road
Willers Road
Bean Brook
MacKay Creek
Gull Creek
Namekagon River
Spring Creek
Hay Creek
Put-In Springbrook Landing
Spring Brook
Green Lake
Spring Lake
1
2
3
4
5
6
7
8
9
10
11
12

another campsite on river right. Just past that on the left is Big Bend Landing. Paddle on to 5.3 miles and pass another campsite on the left. Waterfowl lurk through here, and you'll see plenty of turtles out sunning themselves on the deadfall, plopping into the water as you near. Snapping turtles are a common sight, and the water is clear enough for you to see them swim off. At 6 miles the river bends right, creating a collection point for a lot of deadfall along that bank.

Pass under power lines at 7.2 miles, and 0.5 mile later come to a long island. A high left bank pushes the river to the right. As you come around a curve at 8.3 miles, there is a campsite on river left. The river passes under the North Avenue bridge at 8.8 miles; just beyond it on river right is Earl Park Landing. Another 500 feet later you can see a campsite on the Earl Park side. Tubers use this landing, so on summer days—weekends especially—you may be sharing the rest of this journey with a few inner tubes.

The current picks up a bit, showing some riffles in higher water. At 9.5 miles you head south into an oxbow and come back up at 9.7 miles, where the river bends left into some riffles over a shallow area. At 10.1 miles the river goes under US 63 through some riffles, which may grow to Class I waves in high water. A power line and more riffles are on the other side of the bridge. At 10.6 miles the river passes through an area of small islands clustered together. Narrow and often shallow passages crisscross through what may have been one island at one time. The current is pretty clear to follow.

With the creation of the Wild and Scenic Rivers Act in 1968, the St. Croix National Scenic Riverway was born, joining seven other US rivers as the first to receive this designation. As a major tributary of the St. Croix, the Namekagon was included as part of the protected riverway.

At 11 miles the river splits, with a narrow and sometimes impassable channel to the right—where Whalen Creek flows in from the north about 150 feet in—and a wider channel to the left. The two branches come together again 300 yards downstream, where the river comes up against a railroad embankment that forces the flow to curve to the right. At 11.3 miles the river does another short split around an island, again with the left channel wider. There's a campsite marked at 38.8 on the river map on the left bank. Just past there, the bank is high on the right. The river bends left and bounces back between a couple ridges as it flows. At 12.6 miles pass under the US 63 bridge and the river bends gently to the left and in another 700 feet you pass under the Lakeside Road bridge. The takeout is another 400 feet from here, some log steps up the steep left bank.

35 Namekagon to St. Croix River

Starting below the Trego Dam to avoid portages, this longer paddling segment along the St. Croix National Scenic Riverway offers short day trips but is an excellent multiday trip with riverside camping when taken as a whole. The Namekagon is modestly wide but pristine, with hardly any sign of development in the 31 miles before it merges into the wider, but no less wild, St. Croix.

County: Burnett and Washburn
Start: CR K Landing, N43 8.955' / W90 42.916'
End: Nelsons Landing, N45 54.325' / W92 40.606'
Length: 65.5 miles one-way (dividable)
Float time: About 4 days
Difficulty rating: Easy to moderate
Rapids: Class I riffles with some Class I-II on the St. Croix
River type: Wooded
Current: Moderate
River gradient: 3.5 feet per mile, falling to 2 past Mile 18 (Namekagon); 1.5 feet per mile (St. Croix)
River gauge: USGS 05333500 St. Croix River at Danbury. The Namekagon is typically runnable due to minimum flow rates from the dam; under 950 cfs is not good for paddling; avoid flood stage. Paddling conditions are posted daily on the national park website, or call the Namekagon River Visitor Center to speak with a ranger: (715) 483-2274.
Season: Spring through fall
Land status: Public landings, Wisconsin DNR, some private
Fees and permits: No fees or permits required
Nearest city/town: Trego
Maps: The National Park Service has excellent maps and downloadable PDFs, including river mile markers for all landings and campsites; USGS Dunn Lake, Horseshoe Lake, Frog Lake, Webb Lake, Danbury East, Danbury West, Yellow Lake, Monson Lake, Lake Clayton; *DeLorme: Wisconsin Atlas & Gazetteer*: Page 84 A1
Boats used: Canoes, kayaks, johnboats; motorized craft on the St. Croix
Contacts: Namekagon River Visitor Center, W5483 Hwy. 63, Trego 54888; (715) 635-8346; nps.gov/sacn

St. Croix National Scenic Riverway, 401 N. Hamilton St., St. Croix Falls 54024; (715) 483-3284; nps.gov/sacn
Outfitters: Jack's Canoe & Tube Rental, N7504 Wagon Bridge Rd., Trego 54888; (715) 635-3300; jackscanoerental.com

Put-in/Takeout Information

To shuttle point/takeout: From Grantsburg on WI 70, take CR F north for 8.7 miles. At a long curve to the right, turn left onto Nelsons Landing Road and continue 0.7 mile to the landing. There are restrooms, parking, and a small camping area here.
To put-in from takeout: From Nelsons Landing, exit to CR F and turn left (east); drive 20.7 miles to Danbury. Turn right on WI 77 (Main Street here) and stay on it through turns for 24.3 miles. Turn right (south) on CR K and drive 7.1 miles. Cross the bridge over the river; the entry to the boat landing is on the right. There are restrooms and a parking lot here.

River Overview

This extended route starts on the last 31 miles of the Namekagon, below the dam at Trego Flowage. The river character is very similar to the upper Namekagon River trip in this book: occasionally riffly and gently switching back and forth through a wooded corridor, but with far less potential for road noise in the distance. The first 20 miles show more frequent stretches of riffles, and then the river widens as it gets closer to its juncture with the St. Croix, which is even wider and fuller, but no less scenic and wild. This two-river combo segment, part of the St. Croix National Scenic Riverway, ends where the St. Croix River Marshlands paddle in this book begins, which offers yet another excellent day of paddling to what is already a multiday trip. Free campsites are numbered by river mile throughout and are first-come, first-served.

Paddle Summary

Plan your trip based on how many miles you want to paddle in a day. A park official or two suggested 10 miles per day. I've done days of even 20. I'd recommend something in between. Quit with plenty of daylight (which is actually pretty late in midsummer). Campsites are typically not hard to come by, but because you can't reserve them, it is better to take the one at hand than to paddle until dusk only to find your intended site occupied. The park service maps are quite detailed with mile markers for all campsites and landings.

Push off from the CR K Landing, a shallow beach entry just west of the bridge. The river shows a good current from the get-go and begins its serpentine course. If arriving late in the day, don't worry: The first three campsites are at 0.5, 1, and 1.5 miles. Right away you meet some riffles or Class I rapids. You should easily be at the first campsite in 15 minutes. After that auspicious welcome the river is smooth, but a nice mild current still moves you along. At 8.7 miles pass Stuntz Brook on river right and then head into a hairpin curve that brings you into a short stretch of Class I rapids. At 9.9 miles Whispering Pines Landing is on the right with pit toilets. This segment makes a good day-trip option.

Pass another campsite on the right, then the river makes a quick bend back toward the south, passing Casey Creek at 11.7 miles and McKenzie Creek 0.2 mile later, both on river left. The pines are tall through here; watch for eagles in the tallest of them. Though you encounter at most riffles here, the current is steady, giving you 3 mph just coasting. At 14 miles West Howell Landing is on the left and Howell Landing is opposite. Both have campsites, but the latter also has drinking water. At 16.5 miles you'll see your first bridge on this trip as you pass under WI 77. Fritz Landing, with toilets, is another 0.5 mile along on the left. The next bridge marks 19.6 miles, and McDowell Bridge Landing on the right just past it offers more toilets. From this point on, the campsites are more numerous and closer together. The Totagatic River adds its water from the right at 24.6 miles, and by now the river has widened noticeably.

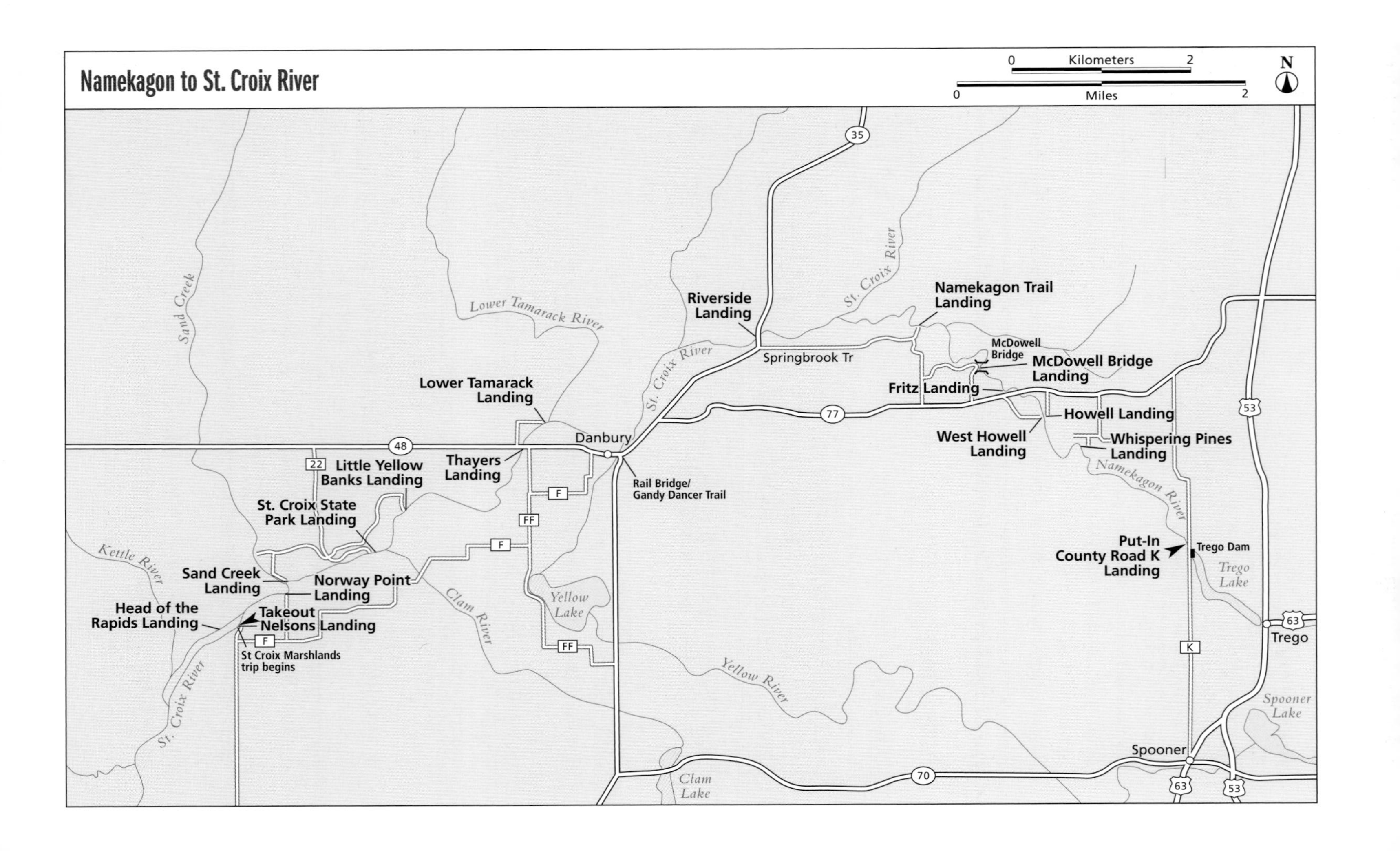
Namekagon to St. Croix River
0 Kilometers 2
0 Miles 2
N
Sand Creek
Lower Tamarack River
St. Croix River
Riverside Landing
Namekagon Trail Landing
Springbrook Tr
McDowell Bridge
McDowell Bridge Landing
Fritz Landing
Lower Tamarack Landing
Howell Landing
West Howell Landing
Whispering Pines Landing
Danbury
Rail Bridge/ Gandy Dancer Trail
Thayers Landing
Little Yellow Banks Landing
St. Croix State Park Landing
Kettle River
Sand Creek Landing
Norway Point Landing
Head of the Rapids Landing
Takeout Nelsons Landing
St Croix Marshlands trip begins
Clam River
Yellow Lake
Yellow River
Namekagon River
Put-In County Road K Landing
Trego Dam
Trego Lake
Trego
Spooner Lake
Spooner
Clam Lake
35
77
48
22
F
FF
K
53
63
70

First night's camp on the Namekagon

Some current remains, of course, but expect to paddle more. With the longer, less-winding passage, wind can become a factor.

The next bridge, at 25.8 miles, alerts you to Namekagon Trail Landing on river left just past it. This is the last landing on the Namekagon before it joins the St. Croix, putting the next landing nearly 9 miles ahead. The last Namekagon campsites are at miles 29.4 and 29.6, both on the left. After that the Namekagon is riffles and Class I until you see a similarly wide river enter from the right—the St. Croix. After 1.5 miles from this juncture, the waters pick up a series of Class I rapids, and the first of three campsites appears on river right. More camping and toilets await at Riverside Landing at 34.5 miles, but still no drinking water. Pass under the WI 35 bridge, and after a mile you encounter a few small islands. At 36.7 miles a large island offers a fun Class I run on the right. At the upstream end of that same island is a great campsite.

At 43.5 miles pass under an old Soo Line Railroad bridge; this is the Gandy Dancer State Trail, a converted rail bed. Of the next two landings—Lower Tamarack Landing on river right at 47 miles and Thayers Landing on river left at 48.5 miles—only the latter offers toilets. Neither has water nor camping, though a site lies between on river right. Be careful when you see the WI 77 bridge before Thayers Landing: Upriver from the bridge is a ledge drop spanning the river. Stay left.

At 55.7 miles on the Minnesota side (river right) is an island. At the head lies Little Yellow Banks Landing with water and toilets. Otherwise stay left of the island for sufficient water to paddle in. All along the right is Minnesota's St. Croix State Park, with a landing and access to all the park's amenities at 58.2 miles. It does require a fee. At 59.5 miles paddle another stretch of riffles and Class I rapids, and at 61.4 stay left around a large island. At 62.4 miles Sand Creek Landing lies on river right, with water and toilets. At 63 miles Norway Point Landing on the left has toilets and camping. For the last 2.5 miles you'll pass several small islands and one last campsite on river right at 64.7 miles. Then 1.3 miles later watch for Nelsons Landing on river left, with a proper boat landing as well as camping and toilets. Looking to extend this trip? Continue from here with the St. Croix River Marshlands trip.

36 St. Croix River Marshlands

This rather remote stretch of the St. Croix River runs between Wisconsin and Minnesota. It shows rapids and riffles, an uncommon sight along the lower section of this National Scenic Riverway. An optional narrow channel, passable only with sufficient water, offers more experienced paddlers some extra excitement for a portion of this paddle, while the main channel of this wide river provides a bit of advanced beginner–friendly riffles and rapids.

County: Burnett
Start: Nelsons Landing, N45 54.325' / W92 40.606'
End: WI 70 Landing, N45 46.442' / W92 46.782'
Length: 11.9 miles one-way
Float time: About 4 hours
Difficulty rating: Moderate
Rapids: Class I-II
River type: Wide wooded pastoral
Current: Gentle to moderate
River gradient: 4.6 feet per mile
River gauge: USACE gauge St. Croix River at Grantsburg; minimum runnable level 3 feet (at least 4 feet for the Kettle River Slough); above 8 feet produces Class III waves and is not recommended. The physical gauge at WI 70 reads 1 foot lower, so minimum level is 2 feet here, 3 feet for the slough; at 7 feet the flow becomes dangerous. Levels are posted daily at the outfitter's and national park's websites.
Season: Spring through fall
Land status: Varied, with public landings
Fees and permits: No fees or permits required
Nearest city/town: Grantsburg
Maps: USGS Bass Creek, Grantsburg, Lake Clayton; *DeLorme: Wisconsin Atlas & Gazetteer*: Page 82 A3
Boats used: Canoes, kayaks
Contacts: St. Croix National Scenic Riverway, 401 N. Hamilton St., St. Croix Falls 54024; (715) 483-3284; nps.gov/sacn
Outfitters: Wild River Outfitters, 15177 Hwy. 70, Grantsburg 54840; (715) 463-2254; wildriverpaddling.com

Put-in/Takeout Information

To shuttle point/takeout: From Grantsburg take WI 70 west about 2.9 miles. Just before the bridge over the river, turn right into the landing area. The asphalt goes all the way to the water, upstream of the bridge on river left. A parking lot is nearby.

To put-in from takeout: From the takeout, turn left onto WI 70, heading east for 4.6 miles. Turn left (north) onto CR F (Pine Street) and follow it as it weaves north through Grantsburg. At the final turn to the north on Pine Street/CR F, continue 7.6 miles and take the soft left off the curve onto Nelsons Landing Road. Go 0.7 mile to the landing. Pit toilets and a picnic area here are managed by the National Park Service.

▶ Add another 1.5 to 2 hours to your paddling trip by starting a bit farther upriver at Norway Point Landing, which is just off CR F, another 1.9 miles past Nelsons Landing Road.

River Overview

The Upper St. Croix River is narrower and shows more twists and faster water, while the Lower St. Croix gets wide and slow—a sort of smaller-scale version of what the Mississippi is like farther downstream. This section of the National Scenic Riverway is known as the Marshlands and offers a sort of transition between the two—wider perhaps than upriver, but with a few sections of good rapids unlike the waters to the south. The Kettle River Slough is an option in higher waters, when the narrow channel becomes navigable and shows more rapids than the main channel. Take the channel to the right of Head of the Rapids Island to access it, but be sure the water levels are adequate. The river has a rocky bottom and dark waters, and this stretch shows no signs of development other than a few nice landings. You can expect lots of wildlife: eagles, ospreys, deer, and even a black bear from time to time.

Paddle Summary

From the put-in the river is nearly 200 feet across. Straight out and to the right is a small island. Head downstream, and at 0.5 mile pass a river campsite on the right. The river channel splits around two islands. Here are the riffles of Pike Rapids, which can get up to Class I with enough water, as you pass the islands on the left. The other channels are passable in higher water. At 0.7 mile there's another campsite on the right. Just beyond is the opening to the channel that takes you into Kettle River

MINING FOR PAINT

Native Americans used a pigment, likely for body paint, and once dug it up from an area where the Kettle River joins the St. Croix. Back in the 1890s, when David Caneday came to the area in search of copper, he also found the clay-like substance. While his shafts turned up no ore, one of them proved to be rich with the pigment, which turned out to be a pretty good ingredient for paint. The Copper Paint Company set up shop on the spot, with a tall building and a dammed creek to provide waterwheel power.

The pigment was dried first in the sun, then broken up and sifted until it was just a powder. Then, with the addition of linseed oil, paint was produced. The company sold twelve colors, ranging from red and yellow to lavender and green, and the paint was said to last well over twenty years once applied. In fact, when the paint dried, it was so hard that a knife could be sharpened on a board with a coat or two of it on the surface.

Ironically, the high quality of its product led to the company's demise. Partly due to the lack of repeat customers, the company faded away–unlike its paint–in the early 1930s. You can still see part of the waterwheel here.

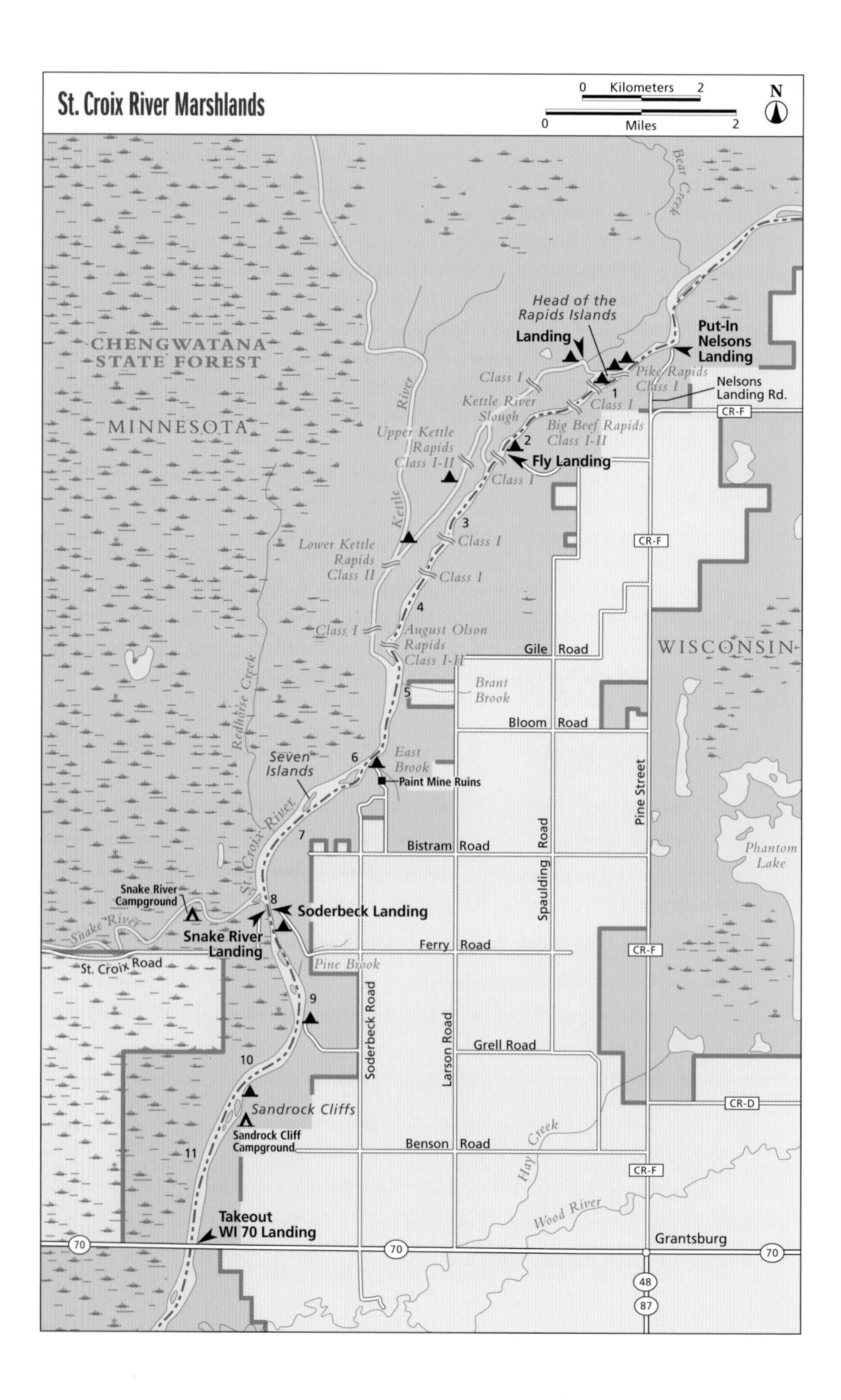
St. Croix River Marshlands
0 Kilometers 2
0 Miles 2
N
CHENGWATANA STATE FOREST
MINNESOTA
WISCONSIN
Bear Creek
Head of the Rapids Islands
Landing
Put-In Nelsons Landing
Pike Rapids Class I
Nelsons Landing Rd.
Class I
Kettle River Slough
Class I
Big Beef Rapids Class I-II
Upper Kettle Rapids Class I-II
Fly Landing
Class I
Kettle River
Lower Kettle Rapids Class II
Class I
Class I
Class I
August Olson Rapids Class I-II
Gile Road
Brant Brook
Bloom Road
Redhorse Creek
Seven Islands
East Brook
Paint Mine Ruins
St. Croix River
Bistram Road
Spaulding Road
Pine Street
Phantom Lake
Snake River Campground
Snake River
Soderbeck Landing
Snake River Landing
Ferry Road
St. Croix Road
Pine Brook
Soderbeck Road
Larson Road
Grell Road
Sandrock Cliffs
Sandrock Cliff Campground
Benson Road
Hay Creek
Wood River
Takeout WI 70 Landing
Grantsburg
CR-F
CR-D
70
48
87
1
2
3
4
5
6
7
8
9
10
11

Slough. Be sure water levels are adequate for passage or you will have a devil of a time with bumping, dragging, and deadfall. The rapids along this stretch aren't much greater than in the main channel, but the rarity of its being passable makes it desirable to many paddlers.

Staying left of the Kettle River Slough entrance, in the main channel of the St. Croix, you pass Head of the Rapids Island, with a campsite on its point. At 0.8 mile, on the island's left side, pass through 100 feet of riffles to Class I rapids. At 1 mile you pass the island and paddle through riffles thereafter. This is easier to do in when the water is a good foot off the minimum level; in lower water you can pass with minimal bumping, but it will require some good navigation and river reading. At 1.1 miles you enter Big Beef Rapids, several hundred yards of Class I–II rapids, depending on water flow. Beyond here the river widens a bit and the current remains steady, with occasional rocks in low water but a nice clear ride when the river is even just 6 inches above the minimum. At 2.1 miles is a campsite on the left. You'll find a lot of cobble and some long stretches of sand and sandbars in lower water. Just past the campsite, also on the left, are Fox Landing and its gravel ramp. The river narrows up, and the rocky bottom and swift current kick up riffles and some Class I rapids in higher water.

At 2.8 miles you catch some riffles just before an island. The river is 200 feet across here, its widest point thus far. At 3.3 miles and again at 3.6 miles are two long stretches of low-grade rapids. At 4 miles the river widens out and grows shallow; this is a scraping point at the lowest water level but easily passable with just 6 inches more. Riffles begin again as the river narrows thereafter. At 4.4 miles is another island. The channel goes around it to the right, but with enough water you can pass along the left side of the island where August Olson Rapids can put up Class I–II waves; this route is impassable in low water.

At 4.7 miles more rapids begin. At 4.9 miles the combined waters of the Kettle River and its slough join from the right, raising more riffles or low-grade rapids where they come together, and Brant Brook flows in from the left. At 5.8 miles you pass East Brook, flowing in on the left, as well as another campsite there. A hike into the woods here takes you to the ruins of an old paint mine. At another island at 6.2 miles, stay left for another short stretch of rapids. This is the Seven Islands area, which may or may not add up to the name before the islands end at 6.8 miles. After this the river widens like a lake, more than 300 feet across. On a windy day, you don't want winds from the south.

One of the outlets of the Snake River joins from the right at 7.8 miles; another enters a short distance farther on. The "lake" area narrows to a third of what it was. You are between two landings: Snake River Landing on the right in Minnesota and Soderbeck Landing on river left in Wisconsin. Both have concrete bar ramps into the water, pit toilets, camping, and picnic areas. At 8.3 miles you pass another campsite on river left. Then you enter another collection of fragmented islands, showing some riffles as you pass. Pass another campsite on river left at 9.2 miles; the river gradually becomes wide and lakelike again.

Watch for a campsite on the left bank at 10.2 miles; 50 feet past that, a channel to the left is navigable in high enough water. Otherwise it's a 200-foot hike to Sandrock Cliffs, a sandstone cliff with a stand of red pine above it. Up the steps is a campsite with pit toilets.

Continuing downriver you will soon see the WI 70 bridge in the distance. At 11.3 miles you pass a few more little islands; on the left bank are some rock ledges. Keep to the left as you approach the bridge; the takeout is on river left, just upstream from the bridge.

A hidden canyon on river left at the end of the Marshlands segment requires sufficient water levels to paddle.

37 Bois Brule River

The famed "River of Presidents" and a Class 1 trout stream, the Bois Brule is an ideal paddle along a crystal clear river through the Brule River State Forest. The trip begins narrow and intimate, passing through a cedar bog, before widening out into two long lakes. The transitions show some exciting rapids, and then it is back into the woods for the final serpentine stretch to the takeout point. Midway along the journey you'll pass Cedar Island and its estate, where three of five presidents who have visited the Brule have stayed.

County: Douglas
Start: Stone's Bridge Landing, N46 26.058' / W91 40.481'
End: Winneboujou Landing, N46 31.002' / W91 36.162'
Length: 9 miles one-way
Float time: About 3.5 hours
Difficulty rating: Moderate due to rocky bits of rapids
Rapids: Class I
River type: Narrow wooded pastoral trout stream
Current: Gentle to moderate
River gradient: 4.1 feet per mile
River gauge: USGS 04025500 Bois Brule River at Brule; spring-fed and consistently runnable
Season: Spring through fall
Land status: State forest and private, but with public landings
Fees and permits: No fees or permits required
Nearest city/town: Brule
Maps: USGS Brule, Island Lake, Lake Minnesuing; *DeLorme: Wisconsin Atlas & Gazetteer*: Page 93 A7
Boats used: Canoes, kayaks
Organizations: Brule River Preservation, PO Box 15, Brule 54820; bruleriverpreservation.org
Outfitters: Brule River Canoe Rental, 13869 US 2, Brule 54820; (715) 372-4983; brulerivercanoerental.com
Local information: Brule River State Forest, 6250 S. Ranger Rd., Brule 54820; (715) 372-5678; dnr.wi.gov/topic/stateforests/bruleriver

White Winter Winery, 68323 Lea St. #A, Iron River 54847; (715) 372-5656; whitewinter.com

Put-in/Takeout Information

To shuttle point/takeout: From US 2 in Brule, head south on WI 27 for 3 miles. Where WI 27 takes a hard turn to the south, CR B goes straight off WI 27. Stay on CR B for 0.1 mile; the entry to the parking area is on the left. A pit toilet and an artesian well are on-site.

To put-in from takeout: From the takeout parking lot, turn left (west) and follow CR B for 3.6 miles. Turn left (south) onto CR S and continue 6 miles. The put-in is on the left, just before a bridge over the Bois Brule. Facilities here include pit toilets, grills, tables, and an artesian well.

River Overview

Often pronounced as a French-English hybrid—"bwah brool"—or just referred to as the Brule, this river is not to be confused with the Brule that runs along the border with Michigan's Upper Peninsula. The whole 44-mile length of the Bois Brule River runs through a 47,000-acre state forest. The river is mostly spring-fed, ensuring that water levels are consistent throughout the season, and the water is clear and cold. The high water quality, rocky bottom, and natural cover make this a Class 1 trout stream. It flows north to Lake Superior from a glacially impacted divide between the Brule and the nearby headwaters of the St. Croix River, which flows south and west to the Mississippi. The northern half of this river, above US 2, offers more rapids suitable for more confident paddlers, but much of the rest of the river is gentle and perfect for beginners. Brown, rainbow, and brook trout flourish in the waters, and coho and chinook salmon come up the river from Lake Superior each year. No motorized boats are allowed, guaranteeing peace for the silent sports. Landings are clearly marked and nicely maintained.

The Bois Brule widens into a couple of small lakes along the way. PREAMTIP SATASUK

Paddle Summary

From the crushed rock put-in, the river flows left. Measuring about 35 feet across, the crystal waters flow over sand and gravel as they pass through a bog environment. Rock vanes create pools for the trout, and the river widens a bit in a few areas. The river is maintained, but recent deadfall may require some navigation. At 1.9 miles the waters of McDougal Springs flow in from the right and the river widens, offering less shelter. At 2 miles a sign warns you that the next 10 miles are private land—a slight exaggeration, but at least true until the takeout about 7 miles from here.

Due to the dark rocks of the riverbed, the Brule can look black despite its clarity and often acts as a mirror for some stunning photos. Some stretches have abundant river grass, and the glassy water reflecting the blue sky becomes almost dreamlike, as though you are floating over a meadow. At 2.8 miles you reach Rainbow Bend; the river seems to split around an island, but stay left, as that rightward channel does not go through. At 3.4 miles the river almost seems to come to a dead end, but ahead to the right you'll find a pile of rocks; the river narrows to about 30 feet and picks up its pace.

At 3.7 miles the river comes to a small wooded island, passable on either side. Past the island is a large private boathouse on river left—part of Cedar Island Estate, a private residence where three of five visiting US presidents have stayed. Pass the

OF VOYAGEURS AND PRESIDENTS

Native Americans had been using the Bois Brule River for travel long before the Europeans arrived, but the name we use today was given by the early French explorers. In 1680 French soldier and explorer Daniel Greysolon, Sieur du Lhut–from whom Duluth gets its name–was the first European to record the existence of a trail from the Brule to the St. Croix, thus making a Lake Superior–Mississippi River passage possible with a portage of less than 2 miles. Other notables followed: Pierre Charles le Sueur in 1693, Jonathan Carver in 1767, Jean Baptiste Cadotte in 1819, and Henry Schoolcraft in 1832.

In the 1880s Henry Clay Pierce, who made his vast fortune in oil, purchased over 4,000 acres on the river with a couple partners and built an estate he dubbed Cedar Island. Five US presidents–Ulysses Grant, Grover Cleveland, Calvin Coolidge, Herbert Hoover, and Dwight Eisenhower–have been here, taking advantage of the peace and solitude, as well as the trout fishing. Pierce eventually became sole owner after his two partners lost it by not visiting at least once per year to hold their claims (as their agreement stated).

Pierce, whose Waters-Pierce Oil Co. was notably fined for antitrust violations to the tune of $1.7 million, died in 1927, leaving the property to become delinquent on taxes. Jack and Charlotte Ordway purchased Cedar Island in 1947, and the estate remains in the Ordway family.

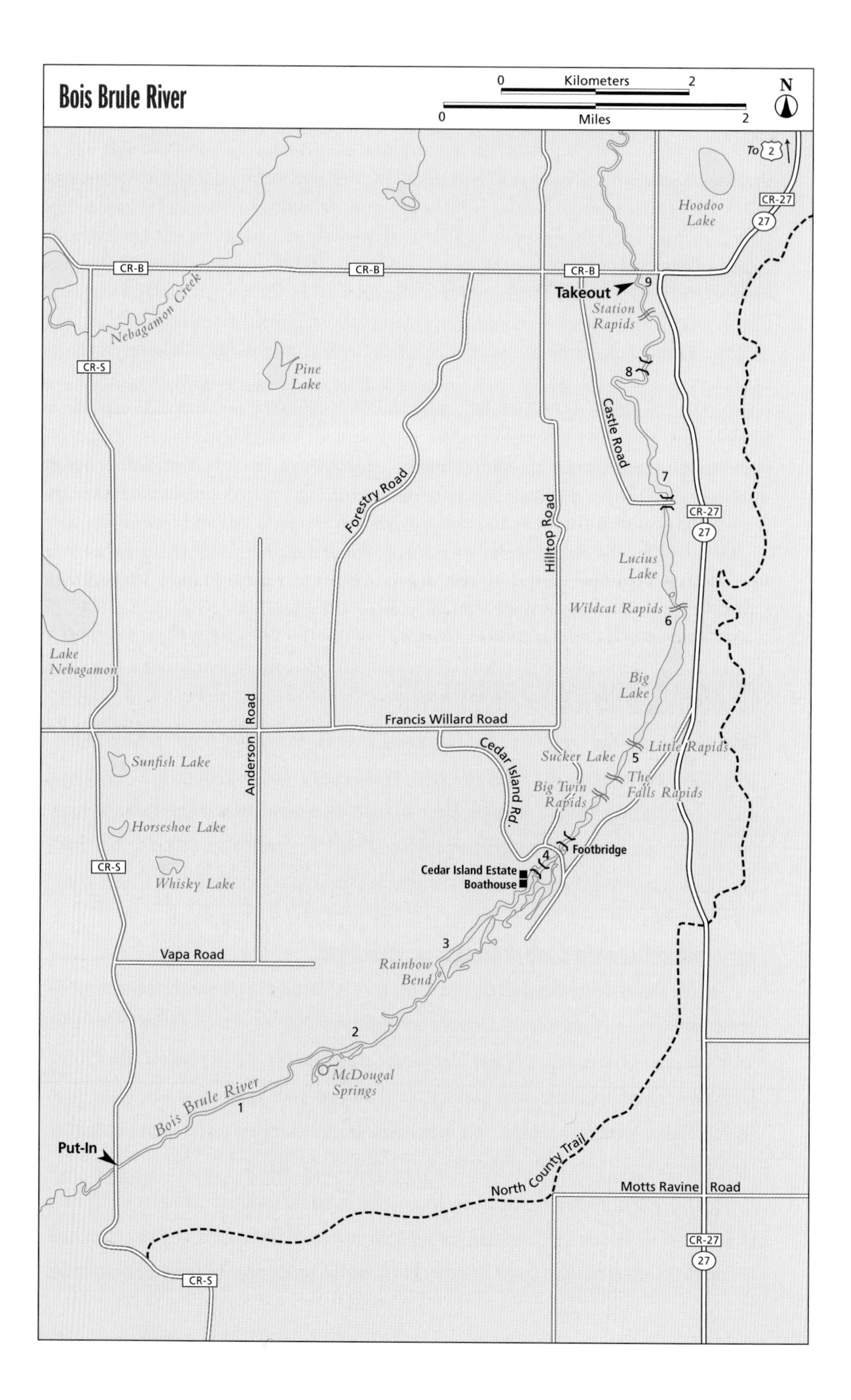
Bois Brule River
0 Kilometers 2
0 Miles 2
N
To 2
CR-27
27
Hoodoo Lake
CR-B
CR-B
CR-B
Takeout
9
Station Rapids
Nebagamon Creek
CR-S
Pine Lake
8
Castle Road
Forestry Road
7
CR-27
27
Hilltop Road
Lucius Lake
Wildcat Rapids
6
Lake Nebagamon
Big Lake
Anderson Road
Francis Willard Road
Cedar Island Rd.
Sucker Lake
Little Rapids
5
Sunfish Lake
The Falls Rapids
Big Twin Rapids
Horseshoe Lake
Footbridge
4
CR-S
Cedar Island Estate
Boathouse
Whisky Lake
3
Vapa Road
Rainbow Bend
2
McDougal Springs
Bois Brule River
1
Put-In
North County Trail
Motts Ravine Road
CR-27
27
CR-S

Clear waters reflect the sky on the Bois Brule, an excellent trout stream. PREAMTIP SATASUK

island and its cabins on either side, going under wooden walking bridges. After the island the river widens, and you can look downstream and see power lines crossing. A few hundred feet later the banks close in, raising the current; you pass under a bridge and through some riffles here and there as the river takes a gentle curve to the left. At 4.2 miles the river hits another split. Go left and around a wider river or enter a short, narrow channel—about 10 feet across and 30 feet long—under a footbridge with riffles and then into a wide stretch again.

At 4.7 miles you come to another narrow passage, Big Twin Rapids, about 200 feet of Class I with some possible bumping along the rocks, then pass under a bridge—watch your head—and pass a similar run of riffles and rapids. Finally, slip through a Class I chute, The Falls Rapids, and into the still waters of the diminutive Sucker Lake, really a widening of the river. It narrows at 5 miles and puts up some riffles, though they are named Little Rapids, and then takes you into the wide and rather long Big Lake. Now you've got some paddling to do, almost a mile, with no perceptible current; a strong headwind can make it tiresome. Big Lake narrows at a point just about a third of the way across but widens again until the end, at the 6-mile mark.

Pass a private boathouse on the right, and the narrow channel passes through woods into Lucius Lake via the Class I Wildcat Rapids. Go around a grassy, cattail-covered island and paddle the 0.75-mile length of the lake. At 6.9 miles pass a wooden walking bridge as the "lake" gradually returns to a river look before reaching its end at about 7.2 miles. Pass under a power line at 7.3 miles and another wooden bridge at 8.2 miles. At 8.5 miles you come around a bend and the river shows riffles to low Class I for much of the next half mile of the paddle, zigzagging all the way to the takeout, where current drops off enough to allow an easy takeout on river left. Carry your boat up the path to where there's a circle of gravel where you can pull up your vehicle and load your craft and gear. The parking area is a short walk past that.

You can extend this trip and try a short bit of Class II rapids by staying on the river for about another 45 minutes and hitting Little Joe Rapids just before taking out at the Bois Brule canoe landing. While parts of the river north of US 2 are beginner friendly, there is an 8-mile stretch from Pine Tree Landing to US 13 that is almost entirely Class I, with two series of four-drop ledges that rate Class II or a bit more.

38 White River

Far upstream from the dam in Ashland, even farther west of the Bibon Swamp, the White River is a narrow Class 1 trout stream with an intimacy like no other in this book. The current of this spring-fed beauty doesn't rush but is always apparent, and the narrow passages and serpentine course require decent boat control. You might not see another soul out here, but you may see plenty of fish and birdlife.

County: Bayfield
Start: Pike River Road Bridge, N46 27.409' / W91 14.421'
End: Mason Delta Road Bridge, N46 26.173' / W91 10.579'
Length: 6.9 miles one-way
Float time: About 3 hours
Difficulty rating: Moderate
Rapids: None
River type: Narrow pastoral trout stream
Current: Moderate
River gradient: 2 feet per mile
River gauge: USGS 04027080 White River near Mason; spring-fed and always runnable
Season: Spring through fall
Land status: Private, with public put-in
Fees and permits: No fees or permits required
Nearest city/town: Ashland
Maps: USGS Grandview NW; *DeLorme: Wisconsin Atlas & Gazetteer*: Page 94 A3
Boats used: Canoes, kayaks
Organizations: River Alliance of Wisconsin, 147 S. Butler St., Ste. 2, Madison 53703; (608) 257-2424; wisconsinrivers.org
Outfitters: Bear Country Sporting Goods, 52150 Wisconsin Ave., Drummond 54832; (715) 739-6645; northcountryvacationrentals .net. Rents canoes and kayaks but does not run shuttles on the White River, only the upper Namekagon.
Local information: Delta Diner, 14385 CR H, Delta 54856; (715) 372-6666; deltadiner .com. Fantastic diner food, coffee, pie, and even a few beers in a 1940 Silk City aluminum diner. Not to be missed.

Put-in/Takeout Information

To shuttle point/takeout: From Ashland take US 13, going west for about 8 miles. Turn left (south) onto US 63 and drive 7.1 miles. Turn right onto CR E, go 1 mile, and take the slight left onto Sutherland Road. Go another 5.1 miles and turn left onto Mason Delta Road. The boat landing is 500 feet from the turn, past the bridge and on your right; it is a simple mud-and-grass bank. Parking is OK on the grass here. There are no facilities or fees, but a simple tip in the jar is a nice thank-you for the locals who keep this area mowed all summer. When you park, leave room for trucks with trailers to move in and out. Parking is allowed on the grass across the road as well.

To put-in from takeout: From the takeout, turn left (south) onto Mason Delta Road, crossing the bridge over the river, and drive 0.5 mile. Turn right onto Sutherland Road and drive 4 miles. At the fork bear right for Pike River Road and go 0.5 mile to the put-in on the left, just before you cross the river again. There are no facilities at this unimproved landing, but there is room to park.

Narrow and intimate, the White River is also a good fishing spot. PREAMTIP SATASUK

River Overview

Rising up from springs, this little river winds as a narrow trout stream through some pristine woods, eventually entering Bibon Swamp—a large wetland area that was once the basin of a glacial lake. The river passes through the swamp with a river mile distance of about double what a crow would fly. Beyond that the river picks up speed and shows riffles and rapids almost all the way to the flowage behind the dam on WI 112. It continues on to the south of Ashland, heading east and north until it joins the Bad River and flows into Lake Superior through the Bad River Reservation. The section of the river described here is upriver of the swamp, where the fishing is good, the current is ample, and any development is nearly unseen. While there are no rapids, the current and course demand navigation lest you spend time tangling in the brush on either side of the river. This is as secluded as they come.

Paddle Summary

Put in upstream river right and pass under the bridge on Pike River Road. The current is steady and the water clear. Spring-fed, it is cold and shaded enough to make for a Class 1 trout ranking. The river is 20 feet wide or less. Much of this is private property. You pass a house on the left at 0.2 mile, but from there on expect complete seclusion. The current, narrow turns, and occasional deadfall mean you need to control the boat. Complicating this are the banks, full of bushes reaching out over the water; your passage between the branches might be just wide enough for your craft at times. That said, the current is gentle enough and the water shallow enough that you have nothing to fear here.

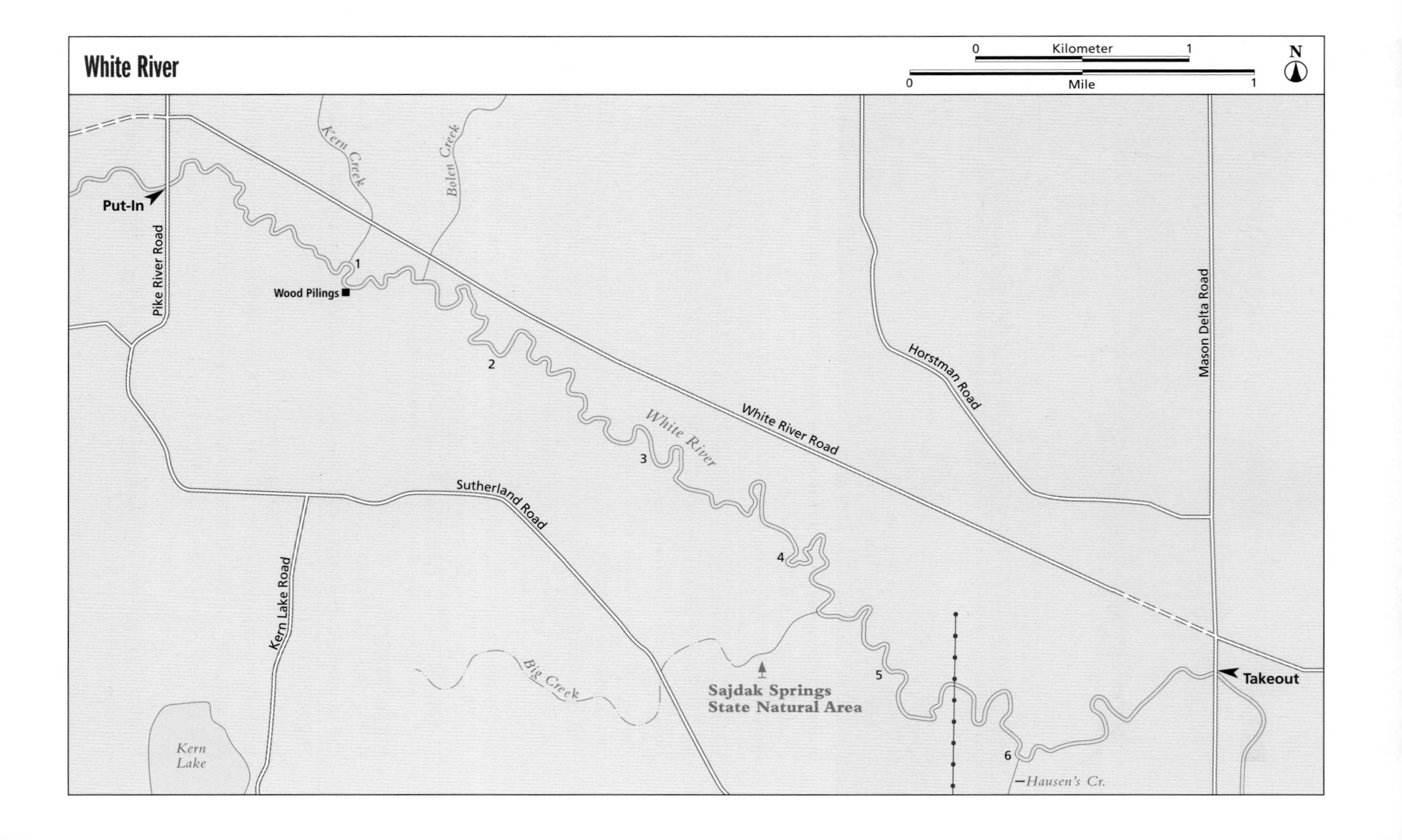
White River
0
Kilometer
1
0
Mile
1
N
Put-In
Pike River Road
Kern Creek
Bolen Creek
1
Wood Pilings
2
White River
3
White River Road
Horstman Road
Mason Delta Road
Sutherland Road
4
Kern Lake Road
Big Creek
Sajdak Springs
State Natural Area
5
6
Hausen's Cr.
Takeout
Kern
Lake

The final bridge before the takeout on the White River PREAMTIP SATASUK

Just before 1 mile, Kern Creek flows in from the left. The river is incredibly serpentine, and the banks—when you can see them—are 2 to 3 feet tall. Cedars get close at times, but mostly the cover is shrubs. Just after the 1-mile mark, around the next bend, you pass through some old wooden pilings standing in the water, remains of an old rail bridge. At 1.6 miles the river bends right at a pine plantation, and a couple power lines pass on the left side of the river. Plant life creates little underwater islands of sand, like coral heads, protected from erosion around them. Fish life is notably abundant. Pass near some power lines at 2 miles, and see a house on river left at 2.2 miles. At 3.3 miles another stream comes in from the right. At 3.6 miles you enter a little hairpin turn where the river is starting to split. On the right the flow is working its way through the bank—by the time you read this, it may be the main channel, leaving the left channel a narrow hairpin section of the river to slowly be filled in again by plant life.

At 4 miles the terrain really begins to become more marsh-like, a hint at the conditions of the areas downriver, but the current remains strong. There's not a lot of deadfall in this stretch of the river due to lack of trees, and any that makes its way down the river would likely be cleared out by anglers and paddlers. At 4.5 miles Big Creek flows in from the right, rising up from Sajdak Springs State Natural Area. At 5.4 miles you paddle under a couple power lines. Hansen's Creek joins from the right at 6 miles, seemingly wider than the river you're on but actually a smaller creek originating at Kern Lake.

These last couple miles of the paddle show more marsh features, especially cattails. Wildflowers—arrowhead, bittersweet nightshade, even coneflowers—show throughout here. Birds are abundant, and cedar waxwings are common, swooping and hovering to check you out. For the last mile listen for occasional little streams or cascades hiding among the brush, tumbling into the river. When you see the Mason Delta Road bridge, you are near the end. Pass under the bridge; the muddy takeout is to the left.

39 Chippewa River

What was once a working highway for the lumber industry is now a recreational paddler's delight. A lively river of riffles and some low-grade rapids, the Chippewa starts wide and passes through large boulders and a scattering of islands in a secluded forest setting. A few narrower passes go around wooded islands, and the current rarely wavers. Pass under a high railway bridge, one of the few signs of civilization through here. The waters are clear but reflect the sky—beautiful but sometimes hiding a bump or two over a boulder. Fun for all skill levels, except in high water, the trip ends at a highway bridge similar to the one at the put-in.

County: Rusk, Sawyer
Start: CR D bridge, N45 40.268' / W91 10.862'
End: CR A bridge, N45 33.148' / W91 13.711'
Length: 10.8 miles one-way
Float time: About 4 hours
Difficulty rating: Easy
Rapids: Class I
River type: Wooded pastoral
Current: Moderate
River gradient: 6.4 feet per mile
River gauge: USGS 05356500 Chippewa River near Bruce; dam-controlled in Arpin and always minimally runnable. Beware of high waters in May and rainy periods.
Season: Spring through fall
Land status: Private, with public landings
Fees and permits: No fees or permits required
Nearest city/town: Ladysmith
Maps: USGS Crane, Exeland; *DeLorme: Wisconsin Atlas & Gazetteer*: Page 85 C7
Boats used: Canoes, kayaks
Organizations: River Alliance of Wisconsin, 147 S. Butler St., Ste. 2, Madison 53703; (608) 257-2424; wisconsinrivers.org
Outfitters: Flater's Resort, N270 CR E, Holcombe 54745; (715) 312-0821; flatersresort.com; located at the confluence of the Flambeau and Chippewa Rivers. Rents craft but usually doesn't do shuttles for this particular trip.

Put-in/Takeout Information

To shuttle point/takeout: From Ladysmith head north on WI 27 for about 3 miles and turn left (west) onto CR A. Drive 8.5 miles and park on the roadside just before the bridge over the Chippewa. The unimproved landing is on river left, upstream of the bridge, reachable by a path down from a wide crushed-rock shoulder suitable for parking.

To put-in from takeout: From the takeout on CR A, continue across the bridge and turn right (north) onto WI 40. Go 8.3 miles and turn right onto CR D. Drive 1.7 miles and cross the bridge. There is a shoulder area for parking on the right side of the road and a path down to the unimproved gravel landing.

River Overview

The Chippewa River runs 183 miles on its course from northern Wisconsin southwest to the Mississippi River. It begins at Lake Chippewa, a dam-made reservoir where the East and West Forks of the Chippewa come together. The lower stretches, closer to urban areas such as Eau Claire and Chippewa Falls, are wider and slower and are popular with recreational paddlers. But farther north the river is a bit livelier, showing rapids in many places and passing through undeveloped land. The water is clear, running over a gravel and sand bottom with occasional boulders and steady current. This section offers consistent water levels, thanks to dam control. Even in dry periods it should be runnable. But high river levels in spring from melting snow, as well as from major rainstorms and dam releases at other times of the year, can raise all the noted riffles and rapid class levels up a notch, demanding caution—especially for inexperienced paddlers, who should avoid getting on the river at all in these cases. Outside of those conditions, the river is good for most skill levels. Anglers fish for northern pike, walleye, musky, panfish, and some smallmouth bass.

Paddle Summary

Put in at the gravel landing on river left, downstream of the bridge. The river is 150 feet wide here. Just 200 feet downstream you can already see riffles and boulders. Pass through 150 feet of riffles to Class I rapids, and then off you go. The banks are low and grassy here, and the river is deeper and slower just after this initial run of riffles. At 0.5 mile you'll find another 300 feet of them. You will see huge boulders scattered throughout the river, on the shores, below the surface, and some rising above the water. These are not typically a navigation issue but can be an occasional surprise when you come up quick on one just under the reflected sky.

At 1.6 miles come around a bend to the left and paddle through some riffles, boils, and lurking boulders in low water levels. At 1.7 miles you come to a long island with passable channels on either side. After the island the river bends to the right and then back again to the left into a narrower rocky area of riffles. At 2.4 miles you pass another island, with a narrow channel behind it along the shore. White Birch Creek flows in on the left at 3.2 miles. At 3.5 miles the river comes to about 200 feet of Class I rapids; Nail Creek slips in nearly unnoticed from river left. Then the river widens and slows just before another section of riffles. At 4 miles you paddle another couple hundred feet of riffles, again at 4.6 miles. Here you find some small islands and oddly shaped rocks standing up in the center of the river. The riffles can get up to Class I rapids with enough water.

At 4.9 miles take a riffled ride through some rough-looking rocks, then come to 300 feet of riffles and Class I rapids at 5.3 miles. Another 0.2 mile after that, the river narrows as rocks pinch it from either side, and you begin to pass lots of little islands. There are some houses on the right bank here, one of the few signs of development you'll see. Highway noise is not an issue, but you may hear the occasional train rolling

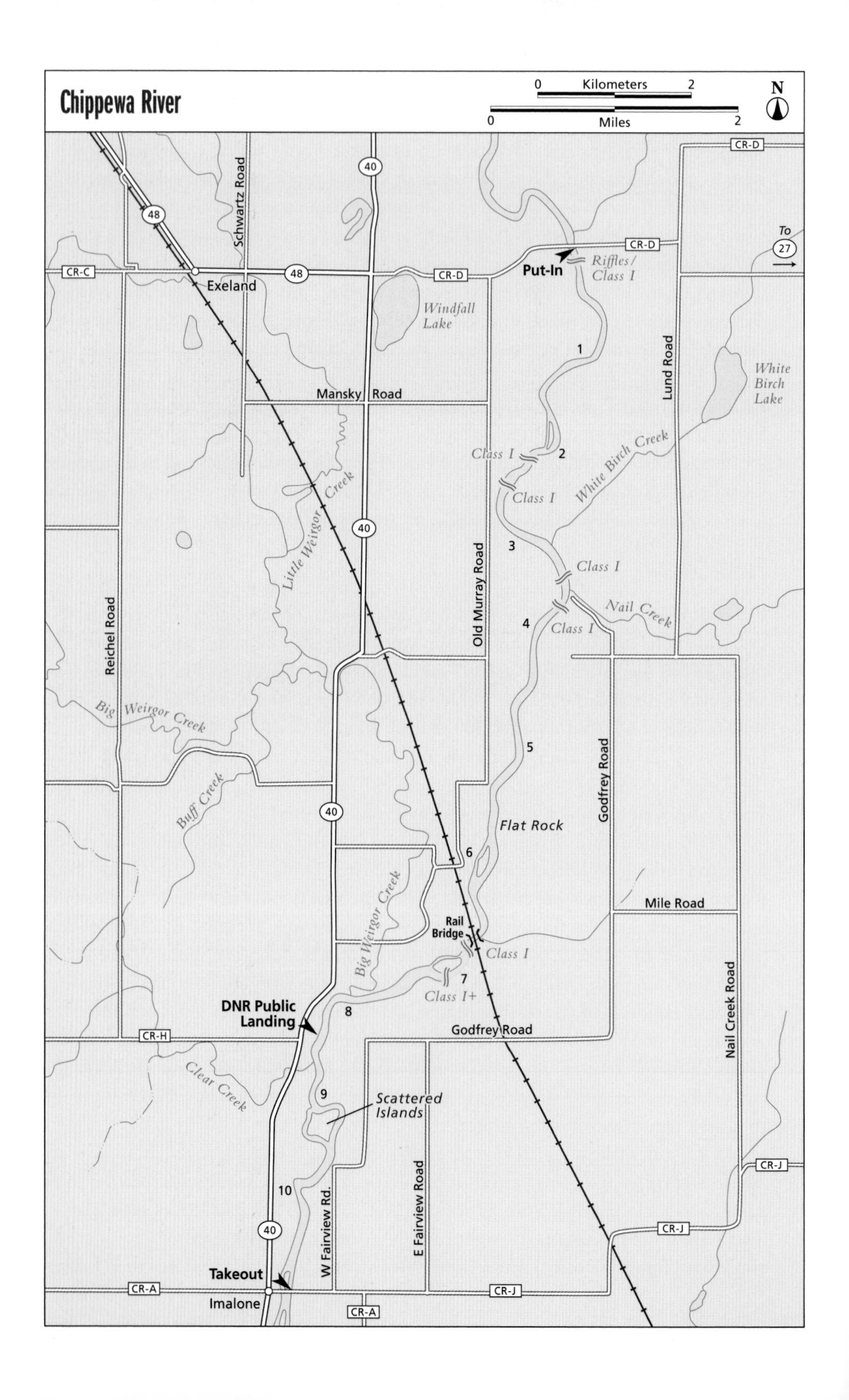
Chippewa River
0 Kilometers 2
0 Miles 2
N
CR-D
To
27
CR-C
48
Exeland
Schwartz Road
40
CR-D
Put-In
Riffles/
Class I
Windfall
Lake
1
Lund Road
White
Birch
Lake
Mansky Road
Class I
2
White Birch Creek
Class I
Little Weirgor Creek
3
Old Murray Road
Class I
Nail Creek
4
Class I
Reichel Road
Big Weirgor Creek
Buff Creek
5
Godfrey Road
Flat Rock
6
Big Weirgor Creek
Mile Road
Rail
Bridge
Class I
7
Class I+
Nail Creek Road
DNR Public
Landing
8
Godfrey Road
CR-H
Clear Creek
9
Scattered
Islands
CR-J
10
W Fairview Rd.
E Fairview Road
CR-J
Takeout
CR-A
Imalone
CR-J
CR-A

Passing under the rail bridge on the Chippewa River

through nearby. At 5.6 miles there's a nice expanse of flat rock on river left, a picnic point if the water level allows.

Another 400 feet later is an island in the middle of the river with trees on it and clear channels on either side. At 5.8 miles is another island; the channel to the right shows a bit of rapids. The left channel is milder, and the channels rejoin at the end of the island at 6.1 miles.

At 6.4 miles is another stretch of riffles that ends with a Class I rapid. The river narrows past some flat rock on the right bank and then bends to the right. You may notice a stream coming in on river left at 6.6 miles. At 6.7 miles the river passes under a high steel railroad bridge. There are large rocks on the left side and riffles or Class I right under the bridge, with a wave train in one area toward the left.

At 6.8 miles, after the bubbly run past the bridge, come up to a wall of rock that forces the river to the left and around an island behind it. At 7.1 miles you paddle through more rapids and a chute that is Class I+ with no obstructions. The river is broken up by a collection of little islands, with passable channels weaving among them at 7.4 miles. By 7.8 miles, however, the river is wide and slow again. Big Weirgor Creek joins the river from the right at the 8-mile mark.

By 8.3 miles the current is back up to riffles as you pass under power lines and, another 0.1 mile farther on, pass a boat landing with a gravel ramp and asphalt parking lot on river right. The banks and the terrain are lower here, and it feels more open. Trees are smaller and scattered, standing back from the river. Pass another tree-covered island at 8.8 miles; the current moves nicely past here. At just shy of 9 miles, you are faced with many options as you pass through yet more little islands. Some potential deadfall may lie in the shaded channels, but the zigzagging navigation through the islands is fun. At 9.7 miles the river starts to look just like it did at the beginning. At 10 miles the river takes a hard left to the south. Now it's just a straightaway to the bridge in the distance. An island lies at 10.6 miles; go left. The takeout is on river left, upstream from the bridge; the end of the island is almost under the bridge.

40 Flambeau River–North Fork

Set off through the Flambeau State Forest on this remote-feeling section of the river. Occasional islands and a few stray boulders are all you need to paddle around, and the wildlife is undisturbed. Several campsites lie along this path, including Camp 41, just past the takeout point. The trip ends at the Camp 41 landing, just 4 miles from the confluence with the South Branch.

County: Sawyer
Start: CR W Landing, N45 46.061' / W90 45.668'
End: Camp 41 Landing, N45 41.528' / W90 48.796'
Length: 8.2 miles one-way
Float time: About 3.5 hours
Difficulty rating: Easy
Rapids: One series of Class I
River type: Wide wooded pastoral
Current: Moderate
River gradient: 3.2 feet
River gauge: USGS 05358500 Flambeau River at Babbs Island; consistently runnable due to dam releases
Season: Spring through fall
Fees and permits: No fees or permits required
Land status: Mostly state forest with public landings
Maps: USGS Babbs Island, Ingram NE; *DeLorme: Wisconsin Atlas & Gazetteer*: Page 86 B2
Nearest city/town: Phillips
Boats used: Canoes, kayaks
Contacts: Flambeau River State Forest, W1613 CR W, Winter 54896; (715) 332-5271, ext. 105; dnr.wi.gov/topic/stateforests/flambeauriver
Outfitters: Big Bear Recreational Rentals, W1614 CR W, Winter 54896; (715) 332-5544; bigbearrecreationalrentals.com. Rents craft and runs shuttles on both the North and South Branches of the Flambeau.
Note: Glass containers are prohibited within the Flambeau River State Forest or within craft on the Flambeau River.

Put-in/Takeout Information

To shuttle point/takeout: From US 13 passing through Phillips, turn west onto CR W (Beebe Street); take the first right at Flambeau Avenue to stay on CR W. Drive 21.5 miles, crossing the bridge over the river and then taking the next left onto West Lane. Stay on this mostly gravel road for 6.8 miles to the Camp 41 landing entrance on the left. Drive in about 800 feet to find the landing, with parking, a pit toilet, and a water pump.
To put-in from takeout: From the takeout, backtrack to CR W and turn right toward Phillips again. Cross the bridge over the Flambeau and the landing is immediately on the right. A short asphalt lane leads to the short steps to the water. The large parking lot has a pit toilet and water pump.

Note: A bike shuttle is doable, but West Lane is a gravel road, often with washboard patches, so even with a mountain bike it is not ideal.

River Overview

If you never chose another river for the summer, you'd still have plenty of canoeing to do on the two branches of the Flambeau. Both the North and the South Forks rise up in north-central Wisconsin and flow south and west until they join and empty into the Chippewa, eventually connecting out to the Mississippi. The North Fork begins just above the Turtle-Flambeau Flowage, where the Bear and Manitowish Rivers come together before flowing into the vast impoundment. The Turtle River comes in from the north, and below their joint flowage, the North Fork passes through four more dams, which help give it the more dependable water levels of the two forks. The section described here passes through state forest and has that wonderful remote feeling. It runs wide but strong, with occasional riffles and a three-stage stretch of very modest rapids.

Entering into riffles near Horseshoe Rapids on the Flambeau River

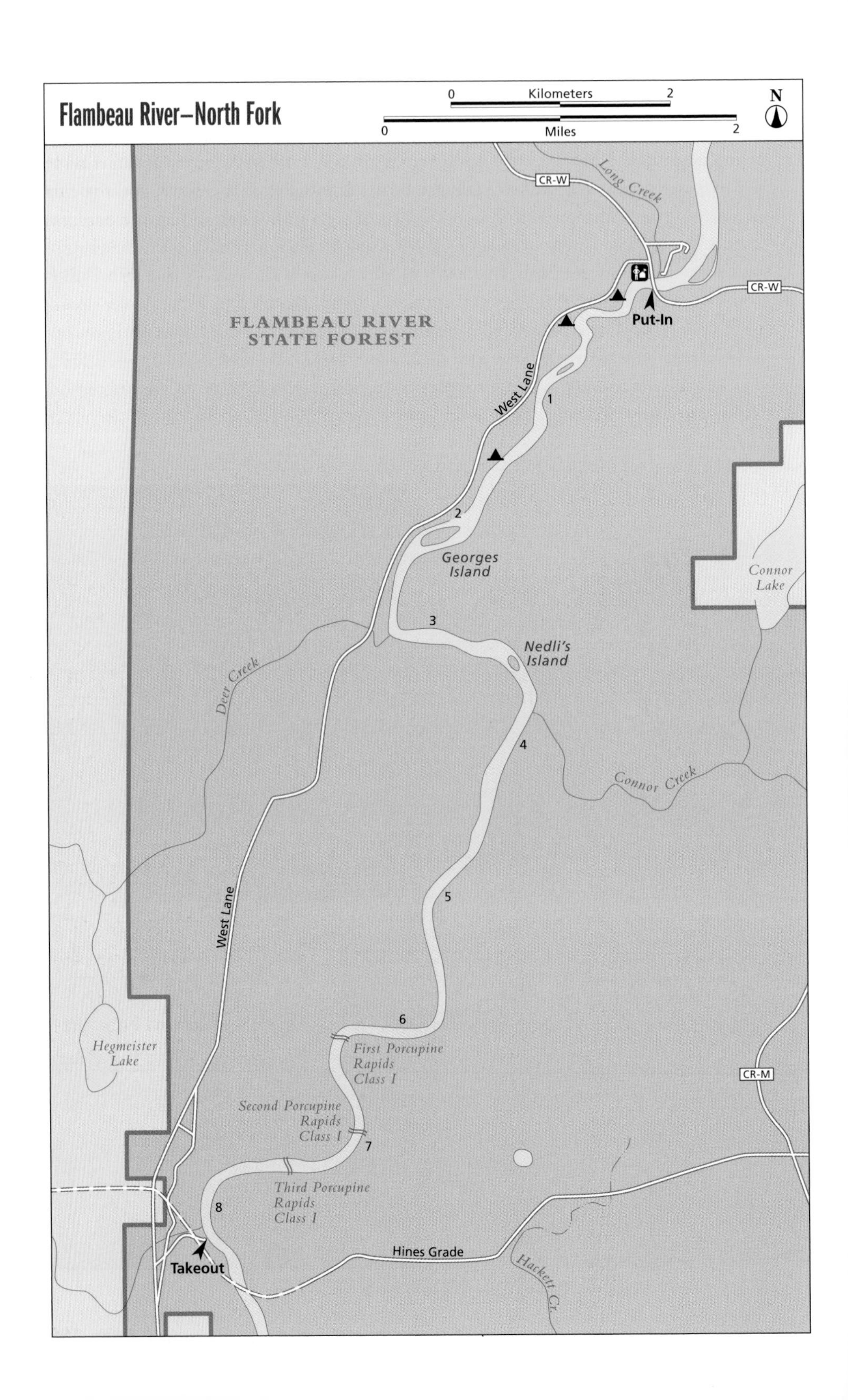

Flambeau River—North Fork
0
Kilometers
2
0
Miles
2
N
CR-W
Long Creek
CR-W
Put-In
FLAMBEAU RIVER
STATE FOREST
West Lane
1
2
Georges
Island
Connor
Lake
3
Nedli's
Island
Deer Creek
4
Connor Creek
5
West Lane
6
First Porcupine
Rapids
Class I
Hegmeister
Lake
CR-M
Second Porcupine
Rapids
Class I
7
Third Porcupine
Rapids
Class I
8
Hines Grade
Takeout
Hackett Cr.

Paddle Summary

From the put-in, head away from the bridge. Straight across the river, 150 feet wide at this point, is the state forest office. A canoe landing there marks where the first set of three rustic campsites are on river right. At 0.5 mile steps lead up the bank on river right to a cluster of three more campsites; the river bends left then right, with some riffles around the corners. At 0.8 mile you reach a forested island. Deadfall is easily avoided on either side. At 1.5 miles stone steps on the right mark another set of campsites. You'll see the sign for Georges Island Campsite on the right at 1.6 miles.

The first of three long, narrow forested islands begins just after that site; the third and largest is Georges Island, ending at about the 2.3-mile mark. Just downstream are some residences with maintained lawns, and docks appear on river right. Then, at 2.8 miles, the river bends left where Deer Creek meanders in from river right, and the pace of the Flambeau increases. The river takes a turn to the south at 3.4 miles as you come up on tiny Nedli's Island, with a small gathering of trees in its center. Just past it, on river left, Connor Creek flows in.

At 4.5 miles you pass through about 100 feet of boulder garden, but with mere riffles. At 6.3 miles you'll encounter riffles again as the river bends left. This is the first of the three runs of the Porcupine Rapids. The second set is the biggest of the three, running about 0.3 mile—a nice series of riffles to Class I, which can get up to Class II in higher water. The third run is mostly riffles, starting at 7.3 miles and running just over 400 yards. Then the river takes a gentle turn to the south; the takeout is river right—a landing of sloping, crushed rock with a short trail up to the vehicle drop-off point.

MORE RIVER CAMPING

All along the river are clearly marked campsites, typically showing three sites clustered together, either for separate campers or as a group site. Camping is free but is allowed only at designated sites, only for paddlers, and with a one-night limit. All sites have fire rings, water pumps, and pit toilets, but no trash containers: Carry out all your garbage, and remember, no glass allowed. Use only deadfall for fires. Caution: Do not pack in wood from more than 10 miles away from any state park or state-managed property due to the potential for spreading the emerald ash borer throughout the state.

41 Turtle-Flambeau Flowage

Consider this the book's free-form paddle excursion. This is Wisconsin's smaller, more accessible version of the Boundary Waters. Totaling nearly 19,000 acres of water plus almost double that in protected land, this dam-controlled lake offers paddlers short out-and-back routes and longer, overnight expeditions through the wilderness with free rustic camping. There are even a couple of portages if you want. Wildlife is abundant, making this a popular destination for birders as well as anglers. This is Wisconsin wilderness at its paddling best. Multiple landings also make a point-to-point trip possible.

County: Iron
Start/End: Murray's Landing, N46 4.912' / W90 4.789'
Springstead Landing, N46 4.404' / W90 10.429'
Length: Varies; 8 miles one-way from Murray's Landing to Springstead Landing
Float time: Varies; about 4 hours between the two landings; overnight camping an option
Difficulty rating: Moderate due to navigation and potential wind
Rapids: None
River type: Lake
Current: Only some very gentle current in the Flambeau River where it meets the still waters of the flowage
Season: Spring through fall
Land status: Public, with some private
Fees and permits: No fees or permits required, not even for camping
Nearest city/town: Mercer
Maps: USGS Turtle Flambeau Flowage, Wilson Lake; *DeLorme: Wisconsin Atlas & Gazetteer*: Page 96 D4
Boats used: Canoes, kayaks, johnboats, small motorized craft
Contacts: Turtle-Flambeau Scenic Waters Area, Department of Natural Resources, 5291 N. Statehouse Circle, Mercer 54547; (715) 476-7846; dnr.wi.gov/topic/lands/turtleflambeau
Outfitters: Hawk's Nest Canoe Outfitters, 263 Hwy. 51 N., Manitowish Waters 54545; (715) 543-8585 (summer only); hawksnestcanoe.com
Local information: John Bates, Trails North, Mercer; (715) 476-2828; manitowish.com. Hire a former naturalist from the DNR for full- or half-day paddles or hikes.

Put-in/Takeout Information

To Murray's Landing: From Mercer head south on US 51 for 3 miles. Turn right onto Murray's Landing Road and continue 5.5 miles to the unimproved gravel landing on the right. A pit toilet is on-site.
To Springstead Landing: From Mercer take US 51 south for 3.5 miles and turn right onto WI 47/182. Go 3.8 miles and turn right onto WI 182. Continue 10.8 miles; turn right onto Flowage Road and drive 3.7 more miles. Turn left onto Flowage Landing Road and enter the parking lot. The landing has a proper dock and asphalt ramp for boaters, plus restrooms and water.

Lake Overview

To the east of this flowage, the Bear and Manitowish Rivers come together to form the Flambeau River. But the Turtle Dam, built in 1926 on the Flambeau at what is now the western end of the flowage, flooded all the lowland terrain between here and there, creating these 19,000 acres of still water while erasing sixteen smaller lakes from the map. The purpose was hydroelectric power and flood control downstream, but the bonus was a fantastic natural destination. The Turtle River once flowed into the Flambeau River, but now its mouth is on the northern edge of the flowage. In addition, there are 35,500 acres of undeveloped public land, combining with the water to create 212 miles of shoreline. While the entire flowage is generally secluded and wild, with the only boat traffic being the occasional anglers either crossing the wider stretches of open water or puttering slowly through narrow channels, there is still a designated section devoted to those who come here for the silence and solitude: The eastern fifth of the flowage is a voluntary quiet area. Scattered throughout the flowage, mostly on the many islands and often separated by great distances, are sixty-six rustic campsites. Of the six boat landings, Springstead, Murray's, and Fisherman's landings have restrooms, but Springstead is the only one with drinking water and a public payphone. Anglers may catch northern pike, musky, large- and smallmouth bass, walleye, panfish, and even sturgeon.

Paddle Summary

This may be the closest thing Wisconsin has to the Boundary Waters, and yet with US 51 just a few miles away, it is easily accessible. Be sure to get a map and have an idea of where you're going. Even a shore-hugging circumnavigation of just the outside border of the voluntary quiet zone would be over 20 miles of paddling. Putting in at Springstead and paddling to Murray's for a takeout would be at least 8 miles.

Wildlife is abundant, and deer frequent the shores for water. Eagles nest through here and can be seen circling for food. Kingfishers and herons lurk in the narrow passages. Woodpeckers are abundant, loons call out at night, and mergansers and various other waterfowl seem to be everywhere. Turtles come ashore to lay eggs. You may even see river otters or a black bear. The number of mosquitoes and blackflies can change with seasons, rainfall, or wind. It's best to prepare for them in droves—and be pleasantly surprised if they are moderate in number.

There are some safety matters to consider. As you can see from the map, some areas of open water are rather large. Especially in the southwestern corner, a windy day can push up sizable waves in areas like this. Be aware of how far you are from your takeout point, both for deteriorating weather conditions and to be sure you can get off the water before nightfall. Take your map or a GPS device, and know how to use it. Everything looks pretty much the same at water level, and it is easy to get turned around—not something you want to have happen at dusk. A compass or GPS can prevent you from getting turned around among the many islands and channels.

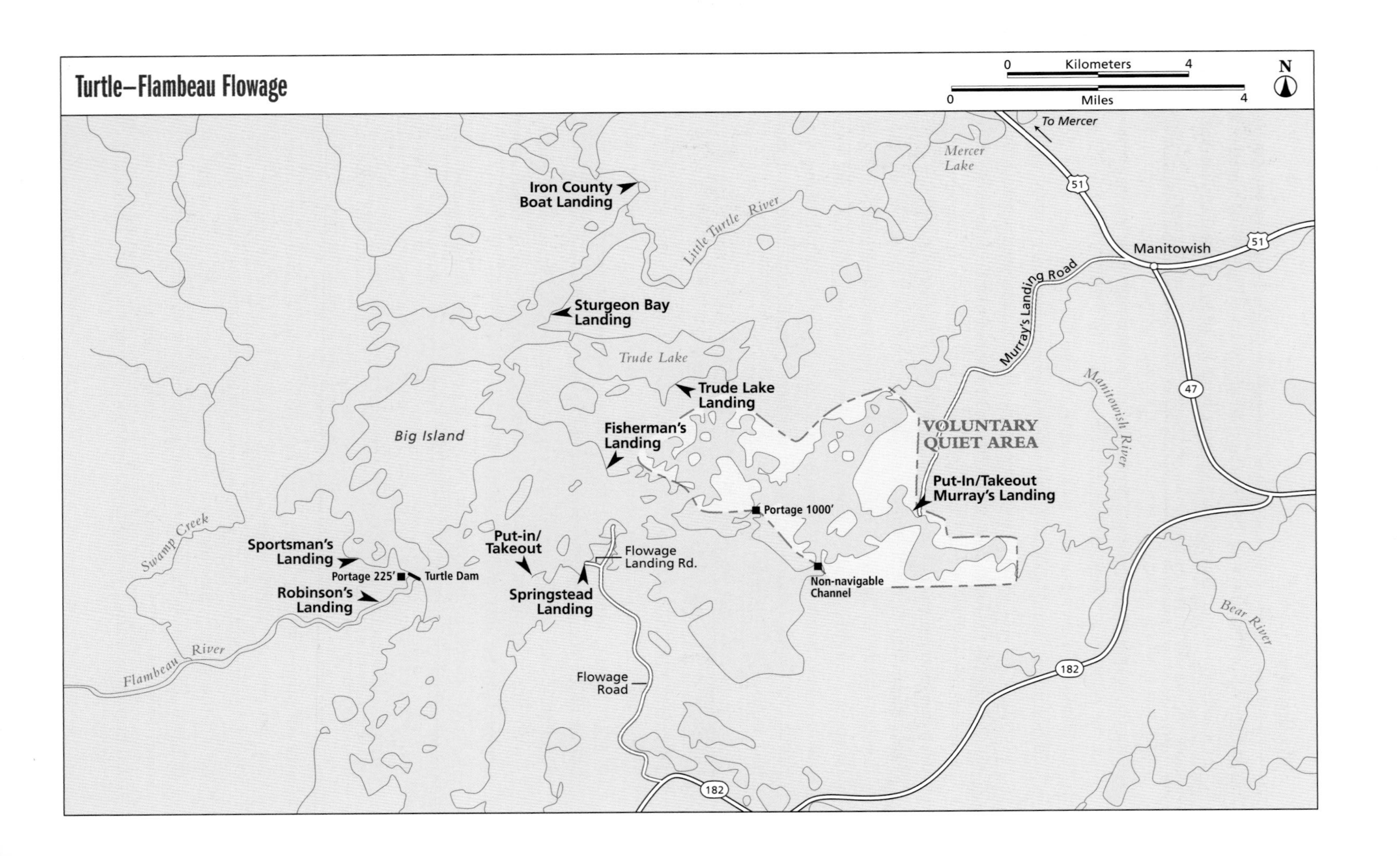
Turtle–Flambeau Flowage
0
Kilometers
4
0
Miles
4
N
To Mercer
Mercer Lake
51
Manitowish
51
47
Iron County Boat Landing
Little Turtle River
Murray's Landing Road
Sturgeon Bay Landing
Trude Lake
Trude Lake Landing
Manitowish River
VOLUNTARY QUIET AREA
Big Island
Fisherman's Landing
Put-In/Takeout Murray's Landing
Portage 1000'
Swamp Creek
Sportsman's Landing
Portage 225'
Turtle Dam
Robinson's Landing
Put-in/ Takeout
Springstead Landing
Flowage Landing Rd.
Non-navigable Channel
Bear River
Flambeau River
Flowage Road
182
182

Sunset and dramatic skies over the Turtle-Flambeau Flowage

A GPS-coordinate map on the DNR's website lists the coordinates for all campsites and landings. Cell phone reception can be hit or miss and, if you're calling for an emergency, GPS data is helpful. Bring a radio to listen for National Weather Service warnings. Tell someone ashore your plan and how long you'll be gone.

Campers have sixty-six sites to choose from, all of them accessible only from the water. Six of these are group sites requiring a fee and reservations, but the rest are fee-free on a first-come, first-served basis. Each site has a fire ring and an open-air pit toilet a short distance away in the woods. Seventeen of these sites, those with an "F" before their number, also include a picnic table. The rest are marked with an "R." The sites accommodate up to six persons, or one family with two guests. Be sure to pack out what you pack in. If you want to buy firewood, make sure you do so within 10 miles of the flowage. But deadfall within the forest is fair game and typically abundant; bring something to cut it with. Campers need to hang their provisions from a bear-proof tree, especially in early summer, when the 2-year-olds are set loose by their mothers. Have a backup plan if you are coming during a busy time. If you can't find a site on the flowage, there is an abundance of nearby "mainland" camping, including Lake of the Woods County Park and sites in Chequamegon-Nicolet National Forest.

42 Willow Flowage Scenic Waters Area

Formed by a dam on the Tomahawk River, this 4,217-acre reservoir somehow flies under the radar. With 73 miles of shoreline (95 percent of which is undeveloped), 106 islands, and seven boat landings, Willow Flowage is ideal for short out-and-back paddles, circles around several bays, or multiday exploration with overnight wilderness camping. Eagles, ospreys, waterfowl, and herons are abundant, and bigger critters include deer and even the occasional wolf or bear. The DNR-managed portion of the property, including the flowage, encompasses more than 30,000 acres, and the nearest major highway is at least 10 miles away, so other than the occasional fishing craft, you'll hear nothing but wind in the trees, water across your paddle, and the call of the loon.

County: Oneida
Start/End: Sandy Landing, N45 42.951' / W89 50.767'
Alternative Landings:
Willow Dam Landing, N45 42.780' / W89 50.730'
McCord Landing, N45 42.200' / W89 56.050'
Talbot's Bay Landing, N45 42.280' / W89 57.440'
Sportsman's Landing, N45 42.810' / W89 56.130'
Jerry's Landing, N45 43.300' / W89 56.020'
Cedar Falls (WVIC) Landing, N45 45.400' / W89 50.870'
Length: Varies
Float time: 2 hours to multiple days
Difficulty rating: Moderate due to distance, navigation, potential wind
Rapids: None
River type: Lake
Current: None
Season: Spring through fall
Land status: Public landings, Wisconsin DNR, and some private
Fees and permits: No fees or permits required, not even for camping; launch/parking fees at Cedar Falls Landing only
Nearest city/town: Hazelhurst
Maps: USGS Burrows Lake, Pier Lake, Lac du Flambeau SW, Mercer Lake; *DeLorme: Wisconsin Atlas & Gazetteer*: Page 88 C1
Boats used: Canoes, kayaks, johnboats, motorized craft
Contacts: Willow Flowage Scenic Waters Area, 8770 Cty. Hwy. J, Woodruff 54568; (715) 356-5211, ext. 248; dnr.wi.gov/topic/lands/willowflow
Outfitters: Chequamegon Adventure Company, 8576 Hwy. 51, Minocqua 54548; (715) 356-1618; chequamegonadventurecompany.com
Camping: Willow Flowage Scenic Waters Area, Wisconsin DNR, offers 30 family campsites and 7 group sites, all with picnic tables, fire rings with grills, and box latrine. No fees or reservations.

Cedar Falls Campground, 6051 Cedar Falls Rd., Hazelhurst, 54531; (715) 848-2976; wvic.com/cedarfalls. Offers 42 sites (30 electric); first-come, first-served with a 10-day limit. Camping fee includes boat launch fee. Showers, laundry, dump station, and fish-cleaning facility are available.

Note: A GPS device is recommended for navigation on long paddles. The DNR website provides GPS coordinates for all campsites and landings. Using deadfall as firewood is allowed, but driftwood is legally protected. Firewood from farther than 10 miles from the flowage is not allowed.

Put-in/Takeout Information

To put-in/takeout: From Hazelhurst head about 9 miles south on US 51 and turn right (west) onto Rocky Run Road. Drive 5.1 miles then turn left (west) onto CR Y. After 1.5 miles, continue straight on Willow Dam Road for 2.5 miles and turn right (west) at the entry to Sandy Landing, where there is a concrete ramp and a sandy beach. Alternatively, Willow Dam Landing is 0.2 mile farther south on Willow Dam Road with a concrete ramp and small pier 100 feet above the dam, and a parking lot across the road, but no facilities. Expect more boats here, however. The road goes over the dam, and paddlers can use wooden staircases on either side to portage the dam and continue down the Tomahawk River.

Lake Overview

Much like Turtle-Flambeau Flowage, its cousin to the north, Willow Flowage is a paddler's playground that seems a lot more remote than it is. A half hour northeast lies Minocqua, and Tomahawk is the same distance south. The Willow River from the west and the Tomahawk River from the north, along with several small creeks, flow into this reservoir formed by a dam at the flowage's easternmost point. Nearly all of

Most of Willow Flowage's 73 miles of shoreline are undeveloped.

the surrounding land is state-managed as Willow Flowage Scenic Waters Area, and as such shows very little development, and that almost exclusively at the southeastern shore. The forest, heavy with red and white pine, comes right up to the water's edge, though narrow, sandy beaches emerge when the water is lower. Surrounding the state land are more marshes, bogs, creeks, and lakes, which add another level of buffer from human construction.

From Sandy and Willow Dam Landings the flowage shows its widest expanse of open water, but farther west channels and bays are smaller and offer more islands. Anglers can expect musky, panfish, largemouth and smallmouth bass, northern pike, and walleye. Free, first-come, first-served rustic campsites are numbered and GPS-marked by the DNR; Campsites 6–10, 17, and 23 are centrally located so you can paddle into the northern and western sections and return to a camp that is about 1 to 1.5 hours paddling from Sandy Landing. Willow Dam, Sandy, Sportsman's and Cedar Falls Landings all offer a concrete boat ramp, Willow Dam being the most frequently used by boaters. As a flowage, water levels are fairly reliable, but during drought conditions they do go down. The result is Talbot's Bay and Jerry's Landings may be inaccessible, and you may have an occasional sandbar to paddle around in shallow areas. A simple sandy canoe entry at McCord Landing starts you off deep into the flowage, but the serpentine roads to get to this and other western landings are crushed rock and can get pretty rough or muddy. ATVs frequent those roads as well, so watch for them at trail and road junctures.

Paddle Summary

Willow Flowage gives you as much or as little paddling as you want. Any of the bays near Sandy Landing could offer a couple hours of exploration. However, a circle around the main body of the reservoir—that larger expanse near the dam, including South, Stump, Hilbert, and North Bays, but not going west of Indian Point—would give you just over 10 miles of paddling, a fairly full day, especially if the wind picks up. On a more-or-less direct route west from Sandy Landing, rounding Indian Point and along the north side of Indian Bay to get to McCord Landing is just over 6 miles one-way. At a leisurely pace without much wind, I often tracked about 2 miles per hour.

The circle route described here (and indicated on the map) is 24 miles, just to give you an idea of distances. It starts from Sandy Landing heading south-southwest 1.7 miles to the opening to Hilbert Bay. Turn to the north and follow the shore, and at 2.7 miles you come around Indian Point. Keep the shore to your left as you come around and paddle south, with Deer Island on your right at 3.2 miles. This takes you into Indian Bay. Bear west across the bay's northern end, with the shoreline closest on your right. At 4.3 miles the channel narrows and you can pass the next island on either side, continuing west until 5.3 miles where you enter a narrow pass with large stones piled on either side. This is Swamsauger Bay, and if you follow the shoreline on the left, you arrive at McCord Landing at 6.4 miles, which looks like just a beach. Beyond here you can reach the Willow River if water levels allow. Otherwise, at

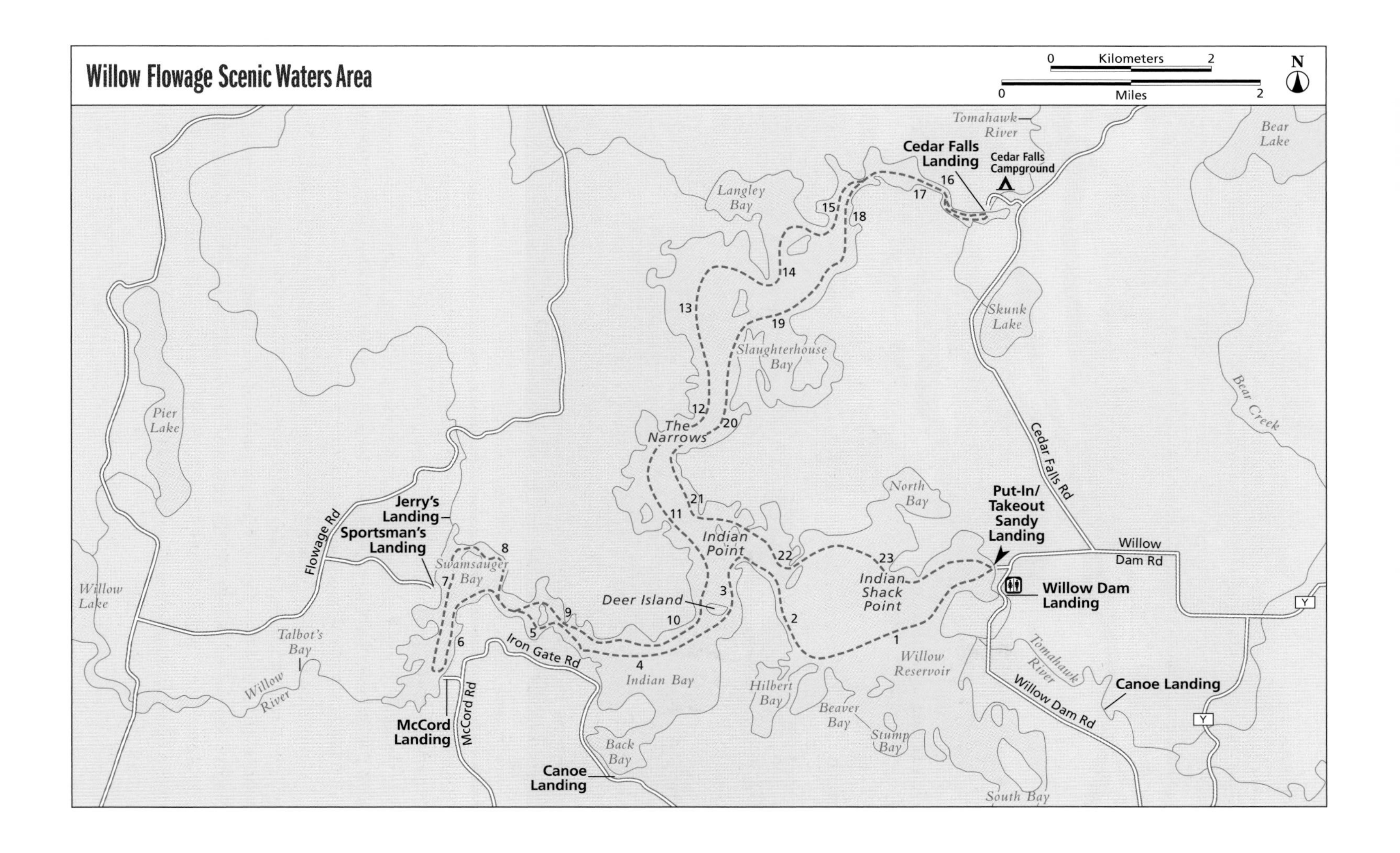
Willow Flowage Scenic Waters Area
0
Kilometers
2
0
Miles
2
N
Tomahawk River
Bear Lake
Cedar Falls Landing
Cedar Falls Campground
Langley Bay
Skunk Lake
Slaughterhouse Bay
Bear Creek
Pier Lake
The Narrows
Cedar Falls Rd
North Bay
Put-In/ Takeout Sandy Landing
Jerry's Landing
Sportsman's Landing
Flowage Rd
Indian Point
Willow Dam Rd
Swamsauger Bay
Deer Island
Indian Shack Point
Willow Dam Landing
Willow Lake
Talbot's Bay
Iron Gate Rd
Willow Reservoir
Tomahawk River
Willow River
Indian Bay
Hilbert Bay
Beaver Bay
Willow Dam Rd
Canoe Landing
McCord Landing
McCord Rd
Back Bay
Stump Bay
Canoe Landing
South Bay
Y
Y

Two eagles overlooking a put-in on Willow Flowage

McCord, cross north to the opposite shore, passing Sportsman's Landing at 7.1 miles. Continue following that shoreline and pass an island on your right at 7.7 miles, then exit through the rocky narrows again at 8.4 miles. Paddling back the way you came, with the shore on the left, you come to Indian Point again at 10.6 miles. (You are 2 miles from your put-in heading due east.)

Continuing north the channel bends east at The Narrows at 11.8 miles. Pass a wide bay on your left, and Langley Bay beyond that, then at 14.8 miles the shorelines come together and the channel continues its bend toward the east. At 16.5 miles you reach Cedar Falls Landing. At the end here is a small, impassable waterfall on the Tomahawk River. Backtrack to Indian Point (21.4 miles) and return east across the lake to Sandy Landing. Aim to go just right (south) of Indian Shack Point unless you want to explore North Bay.

43 Wisconsin River Headwaters

This is the mighty Wisconsin River at its most humble. Several miles below Lac Vieux Desert, the spring-fed source of the river, the Wisconsin is narrow and tea-colored, weaving through lowlands and forest like a small country stream. Development around it is limited, and the takeout is at the second bridge you come to.

County: Vilas
Start: Rohr's Wilderness Tours Camp, N46 6.041' / W89 14.810'
End: CR K bridge, N46 2.858' / W89 15.928'
Length: 7.7 miles one-way
Float time: About 3 hours
Difficulty rating: Easy to moderate for boat control/navigation
Rapids: None
River type: Narrow, winding wooded pastoral
Current: Gentle
River gradient: 1.7 feet per mile
River gauge: USGS 05390100 Lac Vieux Desert near Land o' Lakes; dam-controlled and primarily spring-fed, so always runnable
Season: Spring through fall
Land status: Private, with public landing at takeout
Fees and permits: Put-in/parking fee at campground
Nearest city/town: Eagle River
Maps: USGS Pioneer Lake, Stormy Lake; *DeLorme: Wisconsin Atlas & Gazetteer*: Page 98 D2
Boats used: Canoes, kayaks
Contacts: Upper Wisconsin Basin, Wisconsin Department of Natural Resources; dnr.wi.gov/water/basin/upwis
Outfitters: Rohr's Wilderness Tours Camp, 5230 Razorback Rd., Conover 54519; (715) 547-3639; rwtcanoe.com
Local information: Callie Rohr Memorial Canoe & Kayak Race. Watch for "The Callie," a 26-mile, 2-day paddle marathon in mid-June each year to benefit pediatric brain tumor research (rwtcanoe.com/canoerace.htm).

Put-in/Takeout Information

To shuttle point/takeout: From Eagle River head north on US 45/WI 32 for 9.6 miles to Conover. Turn left onto CR K and go 0.3 mile. Take a soft right just before the bridge and follow the gravel road down to the riverside. The unimproved takeout is on river left upstream of the bridge and offers no facilities.

To put-in from takeout: From the takeout, backtrack 0.3 mile east on CR K; take US 45/WI 32 left (north) 3.1 miles. Turn left onto Rummels Road, and after 1.2 miles turn right onto Razorback Road. Go 1.1 miles; the entrance to Rohr's Wilderness Camp is on the right. Drive in 0.3 mile to the office. The put-in is a simple step down to the water. Parking and put-in require a nominal fee; there are facilities here.

The Wisconsin Department of Natural Resources gives a count of 15,057 lakes in Wisconsin; 5,098 of those are located in the Headwaters Basin, and more than 3,000 of them are small enough not to have names.

A sandy bank along the upper reaches of the Wisconsin River

River Overview

From its origins at Lac Vieux Desert, the Wisconsin runs out the southwest corner through a dam. The river is narrow and winding, with rich forestland and shallow, tea-colored waters. A few rustic campsites are spread out along this upper portion. This is nothing like the wide, powerful workhorse the river becomes by the time it reaches central Wisconsin and fills with sandbars. But those first miles from the dam to this put-in point are not always maintained for deadfall. Starting here, you skip a lot of such blockages and potential beaver dams that may require your feet to leave the craft.

Paddle Summary

The put-in is at mile 12 on the river; you can see the sign for it. The river is 40 feet across here, and the current is moderate. Within a few hundred feet the river comes to a house straight ahead and takes a 90-degree turn to the right, passing what looks to be an old rock dam. Once you leave the signs of development behind, this paddle is reminiscent of the White River trout stream. Tall pines rise to either side, and brush comes up to the banks. At 1.6 miles you pass under the Rummels Road bridge and, just beyond that, an ATV trail bridge smelling of creosote.

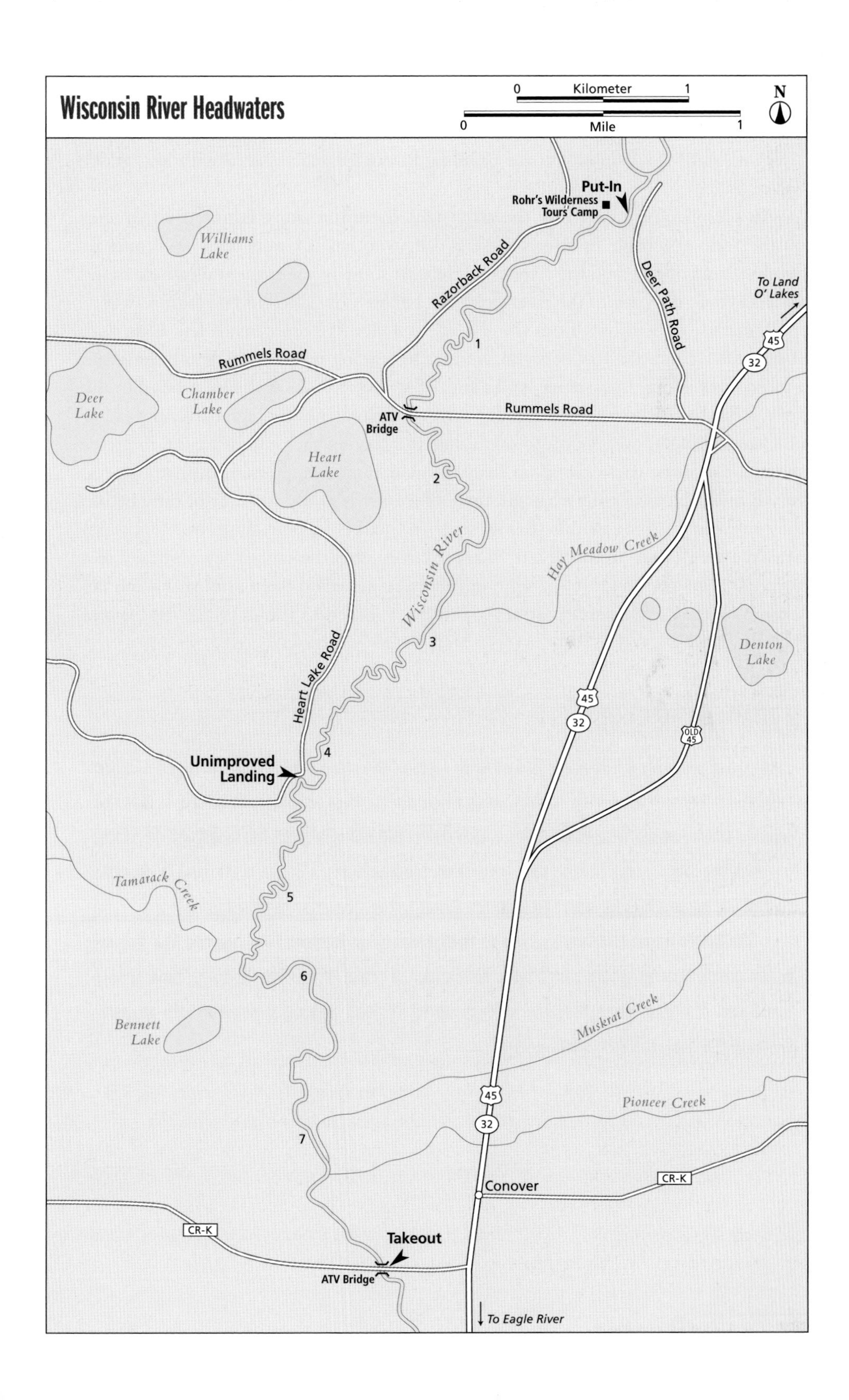

Wisconsin River Headwaters
0 Kilometer 1
0 Mile 1
N
Put-In
Rohr's Wilderness Tours Camp
Williams Lake
Razorback Road
Deer Path Road
To Land O' Lakes
45
32
1
Rummels Road
Deer Lake
Chamber Lake
ATV Bridge
Rummels Road
Heart Lake
2
Wisconsin River
Hay Meadow Creek
3
Denton Lake
Heart Lake Road
45
32
OLD 45
4
Unimproved Landing
Tamarack Creek
5
6
Bennett Lake
Muskrat Creek
45
Pioneer Creek
32
7
Conover
CR-K
CR-K
Takeout
ATV Bridge
To Eagle River

At 1.8 miles there's a little loop to the right; a large, eroding sandy bank lies straight ahead under a stand of pine. At 2.9 miles Hay Meadow Creek flows in from river left, and by 3.1 miles you are paddling through a marshy area with low, grassy banks.

At 4.3 miles, or mile 15 on the river signs, there is a sandy, unimproved landing on the right, reachable on Heart Lake Road. Another 0.1 mile later you come to another stand of pine and the river bends left. At some of the turns you can see backwaters, where the path of the river once ran but are now silted in and fading away.

Tamarack Creek joins from the left at 5.5 miles; the river bends left again and, at 5.7 miles, reaches a low, pine-covered ridge, forcing it left again. You'll see some exposed sand along the steeper banks and a few larger rocks at the next bend in the river. After the rocks, paddle through a series of turns, with the high banks and larger pine trees rising above. As you move along, the current picks up just a bit; the river shows a few more rocks rising up than before and a grassy bottom in many places. At 6.8 miles the river runs a hairpin turn—for now. It's only a matter of time before the river washes through this narrow strip and makes its own shortcut. At 7 miles Muskrat Creek joins from the left; Pioneer Creek does the same a few hundred feet later. From here you start to see signs of residences here and there until you reach the takeout on river left, upstream from the bridge. Another ATV trail bridge lies beyond that one as well.

LAC VIEUX DESERT

This lake of just over 4,000 acres lies on both sides of the state border with Michigan's Upper Peninsula. It is surrounded by marshy areas where the springs bubble up to feed it. This is the humble source of the Wisconsin River, which flows 300 miles, almost the length of the state, to reach the Mississippi. In fact, this watershed, the Headwaters Basin, is unusual in that the rest of the waters this far north flow to the Great Lakes–Superior or Michigan.

The lake's name is French, given to it by French fur traders. They learned the Anishinaabe name, Gete-gitigaani-zaaga'igan, which means "Lake of the Old Clearing," and simply translated it. A dam gives the lake a depth up to 40 feet, making it popular with anglers. Beneath the dam, the Wisconsin begins.

44 Pine River

Deep in the heart of the Nicolet National Forest, this final stretch of the Pine River passes through pristine forest on its way to the Menominee River. The first 3 miles offer the only riffles or rapids on the route, curling around The Oxbow to a takeout for those who wish to repeat the run. Beyond this point the river is gentle, rolling slow and wide past wooded banks and offering good wildlife viewing. The paddle trip ends within a mile of the Menominee.

County: Florence
Start: CR N bridge, N45 50.231' / W88 13.481'
End: WEBCO landing #5, N45 50.376' / W88 8.445'
Length: 9.4 miles one-way
Float time: About 3 hours
Difficulty rating: Easy
Rapids: Three short riffle spots listed as Class I
River type: Wide wooded pastoral
Current: Gentle to moderate
River gradient: 2.1 feet per mile
River gauge: USGS 04064000 Pine River near Florence. Under 2.25 feet, kayaks will scrape in The Oxbow; past The Oxbow landing, the river is consistently runnable.
Season: Spring through fall
Land status: Varied, with public landings
Fees and permits: No fees or permits required
Nearest city/town: Florence
Maps: USGS Iron Mountain SW; *DeLorme: Wisconsin Atlas & Gazetteer*: Page 91 B7
Boats used: Canoes, kayaks, johnboats
Organizations: Chequamegon-Nicolet National Forest; www.fs.usda.gov/cnnf
Contacts: Chequamegon-Nicolet National Forest; www.fs.usda.gov/cnnf

Wild River Interpretive Center, 5628 Forestry Dr., Florence 54121; (715) 528-5377; exploreflorencecounty.com

Outfitters: Wild Rivers Adventure Co., 1000 Central Ave., Florence 54121; (715) 528-5266 or (715) 902-1608 (cell); wildrivers rentals.com.

Put-in/Takeout Information

To shuttle point/takeout: From CR N in Florence, go east on US 2/141 for 7.2 miles and turn right (south) onto Lake Ellwood Road. Go 2.4 miles; turn left onto Menominee River Road and go 0.2 mile to where the road takes a right-angle turn to the left. Stay straight and take the dirt road ahead, Town Road DD, and drive 0.5 mile. Here you will find a gravel lot with no facilities and a simple sloping gravel landing.

To put-in from takeout: From the takeout, backtrack on Town Road DD to Menominee River Road and then take Lake Ellwood Road back to the highway. Go left (west) on US 2/141; continue 6 miles and turn left onto CR NN. Drive 0.2 mile and take the first left to stay on CR NN. Go another 0.8 mile, turn left onto CR N, and continue 4.8 miles to the put-in on the left side of the road, right before the bridge over the Pine River. There are no facilities but plenty of parking in the lot. The landing is a series of steps into the water on river left, just downriver of the bridge.

River Overview

The Pine is listed as one of Wisconsin's Wild Rivers. The upper stretches are narrow and busy, showing frequent Class I and II—and sometimes III—rapids, with the occasional expert or best-portaged spots; the 22-foot drop of LaSalle Falls is one of the latter. Water levels can affect your plans in these areas. However, the lower portion of the Pine, below the dam, is consistently runnable, with wide and gentle waters, and suitable for all levels of ability. The tea-colored waters are home to panfish, bass, northern pike, and walleye. A popular short trip, especially for tubers, is The Oxbow. From the put-in to The Oxbow takeout is 3.5 miles, but the walk back to the put-in is a 10-minute walk. While the forest shows abundant white and jack pine, the aspen and silver and red maple make some fine colors in fall. This trip ends 1 mile from where the Pine River empties into the Menominee River—the watery border with Michigan.

Pristine waters of the Pine River

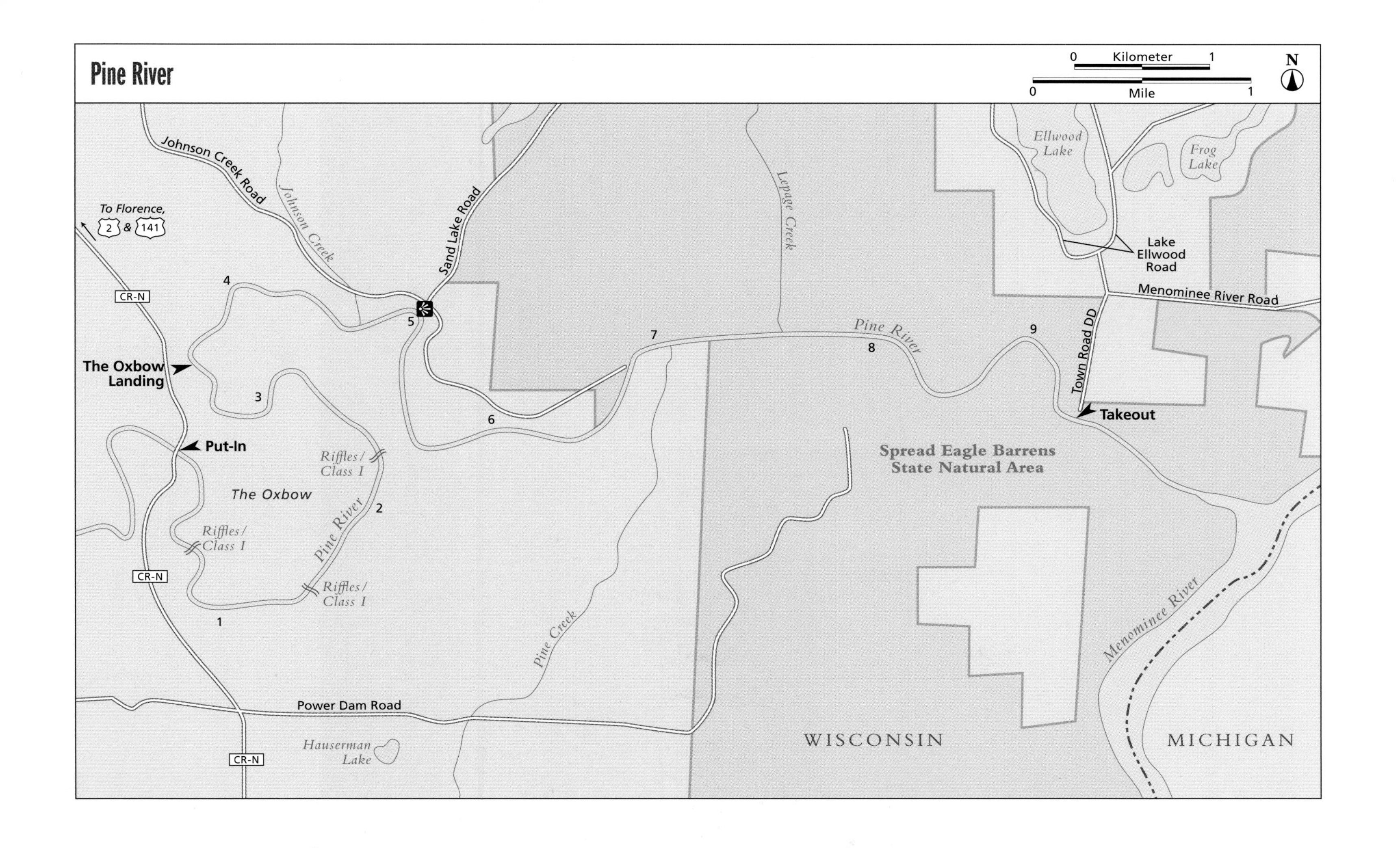

Pine River
0 Kilometer 1
0 Mile 1
N
Johnson Creek Road
Johnson Creek
To Florence, 2 & 141
Sand Lake Road
Lepage Creek
Ellwood Lake
Frog Lake
Lake Ellwood Road
Menominee River Road
Town Road DD
Takeout
CR-N
4
5
The Oxbow Landing
3
6
7
Pine River
8
9
Put-In
Riffles / Class I
The Oxbow
2
Riffles / Class I
Pine River
Riffles / Class I
1
Pine Creek
Spread Eagle Barrens State Natural Area
Menominee River
Power Dam Road
Hauserman Lake
WISCONSIN
MICHIGAN

A dead tree along the Pine River

Paddle Summary

Set off from the put-in; the river is 80 feet wide here. The current is strong coming under the bridge, but the put-in is sheltered from the flow a bit. At 0.6 mile you may encounter some riffles. On some maps they are listed as Class I rapids, but even

CHEAP CAMPING, NO RESERVATIONS

The Chequamegon-Nicolet National Forest has an abundance of rustic campgrounds spread throughout its 1.5 million acres (about 661,400 acres of that is Nicolet). Campsites are self-pay and typically only offer sites with tent pads, a picnic table, and a fire ring, plus a central pit toilet and water pump. These campgrounds tend to feel very remote—and sometimes truly are far off the nearest asphalt road—and are almost never fully occupied, even on busy holiday weekends. Pack your tent and sleeping bag, and give one a try. The national forest website has information about most of them, but I've found a few that aren't even listed there—notably Perch Lake and Lauterman Lake just off WI 70, about 13 miles west of Florence. Chipmunk Rapids Campground is a six-site campground overlooking the Pine River at a more turbulent spot down FR 2450, also off WI 70 but 17 miles west of Florence. Contact the ranger office in Florence or Rhinelander for more information (National Forest Headquarters, 500 Hanson Lake Rd., Rhinelander 54501; 715-362-1300; www.fs.usda.gov/cnnf).

in higher water this section is unobstructed and hardly more than riffles. The river bottom is rock and sand, with big boulders here and there. Thick forest lines the medium-high banks. At 1.5 miles you pass another set of riffles, similarly declared Class I. A third riffle point appears at 2.2 miles. In fact, the riffles appear in lower water. At 3.5 miles you'll come upon a cedar-chip trail up the left bank. This optional takeout is the end of the large oxbow. From here it is about a 10-minute walk back to the put-in. This is popular with tubers, but when the river is at its fastest, some paddlers may prefer to run this again, too. A sign on river right warns that the takeout is on the left, but it is hard to miss.

The Pine River is aptly named—the wind through the pines is an awesome sound. The seclusion of the river is notable, and after The Oxbow you may not see anyone but a random angler. At 4.6 miles Johnson Creek comes in from river left. At 5 miles a scenic overlook for landlubbers is high on the ridge; visitors come to watch the river below. At 6 miles there is a private access from Johnson Creek Road on river left. A sign says that Ellwood Lake is 3 miles from here and the Menominee River is 4. Pine Creek joins the Pine River from the right at 7 miles. At 7.5 miles diminutive Lepage Creek flows in from river left. For the last 0.25 mile, the banks are low to the water and show ferns, cedar trees, and a number of little streams trickling into the river. The takeout is river left, at a gravel parking lot with a wide, unimproved mud-and-gravel area gently sloping to the water.

45 Apostle Islands National Lakeshore—Sea Caves

One of the most significant natural destinations in Wisconsin, the Apostle Islands of Lake Superior are a must on any paddler's list. This trip doesn't wander far from shore as it launches from the beautiful sands of Meyers Beach and hugs the coast, heading east along the high rocky cliffs. Paddlers can enter some of the larger lake-carved caves and even paddle through some tunnels and crevices.

County: Bayfield
Start/End: Meyers Beach, N46 53.027' / W91 2.917'
Length: Roughly 4–6 miles out and back
Float time: About 3 hours minimum
Difficulty rating: Moderate due to rapidly changing lake conditions
Rapids: Rapidly changing wave heights, rebounding waves
River type: Lake
Current: Waves depend on wind strength and direction
Wave gauge: Check SeaCavesWatch.org for wave reports; check local weather forecasts as well. The National Park Service operates a real-time wave monitor at Meyers Beach parking lot. Wave height of less than 1 foot is recommended for beginners, 1–2 feet for intermediate paddlers; anything over 2 feet is for advanced paddlers only or simply not recommended.
Season: Spring through fall
Land status: Public
Fees and permits: National park day-use vehicle fee at Meyers Beach
Nearest city/town: Bayfield
Maps: USGS Squaw Bay; *DeLorme: Wisconsin Atlas & Gazetteer*: Page 102 B4
Boats used: Sea kayaks, motorized craft; canoes are risky
Contacts: Apostle Islands National Lakeshore; nps.gov/apis

Little Sand Bay Visitor Center, 32660 Little Sand Bay Rd., Bayfield 54814; (715) 779-7007 (mid-June through September)

Bayfield Visitor Center, 415 Washington Ave., Bayfield 54814; (715) 779-3397

Outfitters: Living Adventure Inc., 88260 Hwy. 13, Bayfield 54814; (866) 779-9503; livingadventure.com

Lost Creek Adventures, 22475 Hwy. 13, Cornucopia 54827; (715) 953-2223; lostcreekadventures.org

Caution: A 16-foot sea kayak with a skirt and wet suit are recommended. Canoes should be avoided unless conditions are perfectly still—even then, they can change while you are out there.

Put-in/Takeout Information

To put-in/takeout: From Bayfield follow WI 13 north 16.8 miles to Meyers Road, on the right. Drive 0.4 mile to the parking lot and pay the self-pay vehicle day-use fee. Toilets and a couple of picnic tables are on-site. You will launch from the beach at the bottom of some wide wooden steps, down which you must carry your craft. Meyers Road is just over 4 miles east of Cornucopia on WI 13 South.

Lake Overview

Superior is less a lake than a minor sea. Shipwrecks, brutal storms, quickly changing conditions—this lake is not to be trifled with. It shouldn't be missed either. The Apostle Islands are twenty-two isles off the northernmost tip of Wisconsin, the Bayfield Peninsula. Excluding Madeline Island, the remaining twenty-one islands, plus 12 miles of mainland lakeshore, are part of the Apostle Islands National Lakeshore. Paddlers may venture across open water to some of the islands—the sea caves at Sand Island are an option about 4 miles from Little Sand Bay—but most visitors will choose to see the easily accessible and awe-inspiring sea caves to the east of Mawikwe Bay's Meyers Beach. While paddling on Lake Superior can be enjoyed by paddlers of all experience levels, planning, awareness, safety, and patience should always be part of any water activity here. The beauty of this place is the combination of green forest above, reds and earthy colors of the carved sandstone, and deep blue or sometimes turquoise of the lake. There's a good chance you'll see an eagle out here as well.

A dramatic tunnel paddle at the Sea Caves along the Apostle Islands National Lakeshore

Paddle Summary

This is a fairly simple trajectory: Start from Meyers Beach and paddle east along the shore and enjoy the scenery. Turn around and paddle back when you reach the rock column—or sooner if time or weather conditions compel you.

Don't let the simplicity of this paddle route fool you: The lake is the boss and must be respected at all times. The recommended recreational limit is 2-foot waves. Some outfitters will still take you out in waves up to 3 feet, but only with experienced guides with rescue training. While some paddlers might think the waves manageable when they're in the beach area, rebound waves must be considered. Even at 1 foot, the waves rebounding off the uneven rocky cliffs and out of crevices and caves can make you feel as though you are paddling in a washing machine with an agitator; at 2 feet it's no longer even fun. I've seen people get seasick. This makes getting close

CREATION OF THE SEA CAVES

The history of the rock of the Apostle Islands, and the lakeshore they once were part of, goes back over 600 million years ago to the late Precambrian era. At that time, braided rivers flowing through the region deposited the sediments that over time became the thick rock we have today. Glaciers came and went more often than people generally think when they use the term "ice age," but the most recent advance of ice took place about 12,000 years ago. The grinding and depositing of drift had its impact on the land, but the sea caves are another story.

The top and bottom layers of the red-tinted sandstone came from the rivers, while the middle portion, known as the Devils Island Formation–for Devils Island, where the best caves are–was made when those deposits became sand flats, which often lay under shallow waters and were characterized by ripples. The resulting rock layers are thin, soft, and porous. Water gets inside and expands when it freezes.

Take a look northward from Meyers Beach and you have anywhere from 60 to 80 miles of open water between the national lakeshore and the north shore of Lake Superior. When winds come down from Canada across that stretch of water, big waves are the result.

Rising and falling lake levels, expanding ice in cracks and fractures, and that constant erosion of wind and water resulted in the various caves, tunnels, and overhangs you see today on the north side of Devils Island, at Swallow Point on Sand Island, and along the mainland. The waves undercut the cliffs, carving what are called reentrants; over time, some of these reentrants become deep enough and wide enough to connect to others, thus creating a tunnel or cave behind parts of the cliff face that haven't worn away as yet.

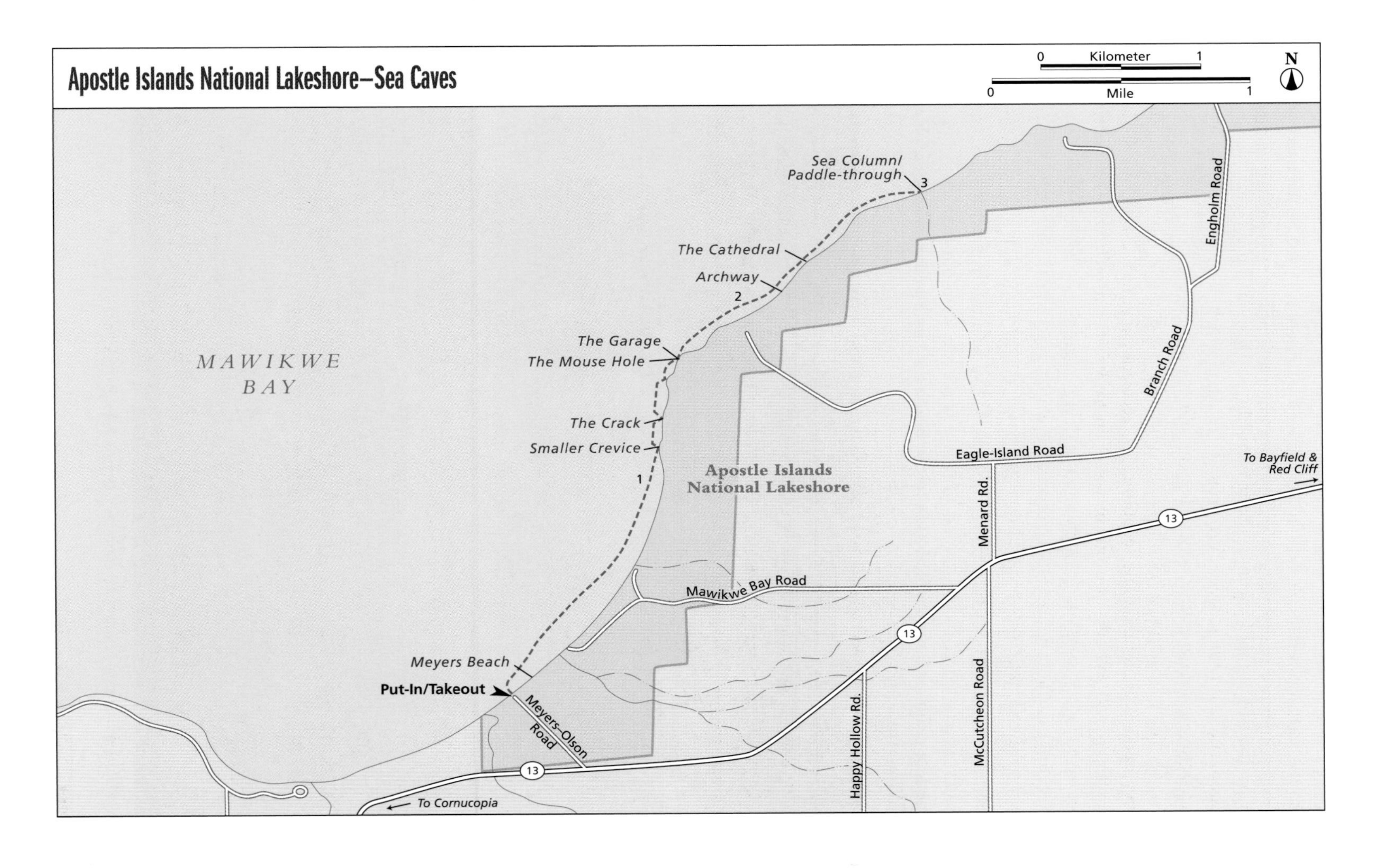
Apostle Islands National Lakeshore–Sea Caves
0 Kilometer 1
0 Mile 1
N
MAWIKWE BAY
Sea Column/ Paddle-through
3
The Cathedral
Archway
2
The Garage
The Mouse Hole
The Crack
Smaller Crevice
1
Meyers Beach
Put-In/Takeout
Meyers–Olson Road
Apostle Islands National Lakeshore
Engholm Road
Branch Road
Eagle-Island Road
Menard Rd.
Mawikwe Bay Road
McCutcheon Road
Happy Hollow Rd.
To Bayfield & Red Cliff
To Cornucopia
13

to the formations difficult and, in fact, dangerous. There is a sobering story posted back at the parking lot of a fit athlete getting battered to death when he fell out of his kayak. The biggest risk is not necessarily drowning—though that's one too—but hypothermia. Even in July water can be 55°F, and people have perished after capsizing in the Great Lakes. Take it seriously. Wet suits are recommended—a spray skirt is indispensable.

A 1.8-mile trail from the parking lot takes visitors through the woods to view the sea caves from above. The caves are also reachable over the ice in winter.

Think of the time it took to wear away the sandstone here. It is a lesson in patience, which is what you need to bring on this trip. If conditions are not right, do not force it. If you are halfway through and the conditions change, head back. I've been on trips where the conditions were good at the beginning, got ugly while we were out there, and became perfect again after we paddled back to the beach for lunch and to wait for a change in the wind.

Paddling into a cleft in the cliffs along the Apostle Islands National Lakeshore

Watch the weather. Check the wave forecasts and the real-time data. Wind from the north and northwest will mean waves coming right into the caves. Have an alternative plan or wait for another day if conditions are not good. (Outfitters often use Bark River Slough or Romans Point to the west of Cornucopia when the sea caves are unreachable; consider paddling inland waters at the White River or the Bois Brule featured in this book.) If you get south or southwest winds, the water can be like glass.

Put in near the steps on Meyers Beach and paddle to the exposed rock to the right (east). When you reach that area just over a mile later, give yourself a little distance first to assess the wave patterns and determine whether it is safe to approach the cliffs. At 1.2 miles you will find a massive crack in the shoreline, known as The Crack. Go deep into that cleft, as far as you can until you eventually have to back out. When the water is choppy, it feels like a rushing river, but there's no current. The sheer rock face rises up 30 to 40 feet and closes in over you a bit; the colors and patterns are beautiful when seen up close. You can see pine and birch up top. On either side of the wide opening of this cleft you can find low, short archways, which you can sometimes paddle through, depending on wave height.

At 1.7 miles you'll reach The Garage, a rather large cave; a nearby tiny archway, the Mouse Hole, is a 50-foot-long tight squeeze, but a paddle through. Notice the bright yellow of sunburst lichen along the rocks, a sign of clean air and water. There's another archway, a 20-footer, at 2.2 miles. At 2.3 miles you come to the largest of the caves: The Cathedral, which features another paddle-through archway, more spacious than previous ones. At 2.9 miles you come to a column of rock that has been separated from shore. Paddle around it and head back to Meyers Beach.

Paddle Index

Sunset over the Turtle-Flambeau Flowage

About the Author

Kevin Revolinski was born and raised in Marshfield, Wisconsin, and as a child was fascinated by the Northwoods and Lake Superior whenever he visited his grandparents along the Big Lake's shores in Ashland. He has written for Rough Guides guidebooks, and is the author of numerous regional outdoors and brewery guides as well as a travel memoir about the year he lived in Turkey. His articles and photography have appeared in a variety of publications, including the *New York Times, Chicago Tribune, Wisconsin State Journal,* and *Wisconsin Trails*. He has lived abroad in several places, including Italy, Guatemala, Panama, and Thailand, but currently keeps base camp back in the homeland in Madison, Wisconsin. He maintains a travel website at TheMadTraveler.com.

Other Books by Kevin Revolinski

Camping Michigan
Best Easy Day Hikes Grand Rapids Michigan
Best Easy Day Hikes Milwaukee
Best Hikes Near Milwaukee
Best Rail Trails Wisconsin
Hiking Wisconsin
Insiders' Guide® to Madison, WI
The Yogurt Man Cometh: Tales of an American Teacher in Turkey
Michigan's Best Beer Guide
Minnesota's Best Beer Guide
Wisconsin's Best Beer Guide
Backroads and Byways of Wisconsin

Visit the author's website at www.TheMadTraveler.com.